abraham geiger
and liberal judaism

THE CHALLENGE OF THE

NINETEENTH CENTURY

Hebrew Union College Press
Cincinnati, 1981 · Reprinted 1996

Distributed by Behrman House, Inc.
235 Watchung Avenue
West Orange, New Jersey 07052

abraham geiger and liberal judaism

THE CHALLENGE OF THE NINETEENTH CENTURY

compiled with a biographical introduction by

MAX WIENER

translation from the German by

ERNST J. SCHLOCHAUER

Library of Congress Cataloging in Publication Data

Geiger, Abraham, 1810-1874.
  Abraham Geiger and liberal Judaism.

  Reprint. Originally published: Philadelphia: Jewish
Publication Society of America, 1962.
  1. Reform Judaism—Addresses, essays, lectures.
2. Judaism—History—Addresses, essays, lectures.
3. Geiger, Abraham, 1810-1874—Addresses, essays, lec-
trues. 4. Rabbis—Germany—Biography—Addresses, essays,
lectures. I. Wiener, Max, 1882-1950. II. Title.
[BM197.G38213 1981] 296.8'346   81-4524
ISBN 0-87820-800-3 (pbk.)   AACR2

manufactured in the United States of America

designed by SOL CALVIN COHEN

foreword to the new printing

Although most of today's American Jewry traces its ancestry to Eastern Europe, the religious ideas and forms that characterize it more closely approximate those that were developed west of the Russian Pale. The endeavor to participate in modern society and culture while resisting the forces driving toward complete assimilation, the development of new types of Jewish identity, the religious positions represented today by Reform, Conservative, and modern Orthodox Judaism—all of these were pioneered by German Jewry in the century before Hitler.

Among the leading figures of German Jewry, Abraham Geiger is one of the most interesting and significant. As scholar, pulpit rabbi, theoretical and practical reformer, he left an indelible mark upon the Jewry of his own time and on succeeding generations. His path was tortuous; he was beset by doubts, bedeviled by angry disputes, sometimes at odds with himself. But he fought his way through to a new conception of the Jewish religion. Especially for Reform Jewry, he became one of the founding fathers.

Nearly twenty years have passed since Max Wiener's biography of Geiger together with his selections from Geiger's writings appeared under the aegis of the Jewish Publication Society of America. For much of that time, the volume has been out of print, unavailable to a new generation of interested readers. Yet attention to Geiger's legacy has not flagged. In 1974, on the occasion of the hundredth anniversary of his death, the Hebrew Union College-Jewish Institute of Religion in Cincinnati sponsored a symposium on various aspects of Geiger's creativity. Shortly thereafter, the four lectures, together with a bibliography of secondary literature, appeared in print as *New Perspectives on Abraham Geiger*, edited by Jakob J. Petuchowski (Cincinnati: H.U.C. Press, 1975). More recently, HUC-JIR joined the Hebrew University and the Zalman Shazar Center in issuing a selection of Geiger's writings on religious reform in Hebrew translation (Jerusalem: Shazar Center, 1979). With permission kindly granted by the Jewish Publication Society, the Hebrew Union College Press now makes the present volume once again available, this time in a paperback edition photographed from the original text. The legacy of Abraham Geiger may thus continue to address the Jewish consciousness of our time.

MICHAEL A. MEYER

Cincinnati, Ohio
Tevet 5741

publisher's preface

THE PUBLICATION OF BOOKS ON THE MOLDERS OF CONTEMPO-
RARY JEWISH LIFE AND THOUGHT HAS ALWAYS BEEN PART OF
THE JPS PROGRAM. TO THOSE WHICH HAVE ALREADY APPEARED
WE ARE HAPPY TO ADD THIS VOLUME ON ABRAHAM GEIGER, WHOSE
INFLUENCE ON CONTEMPORARY JUDAISM HAS BEEN SO POWERFUL.
❧ THE LATE DR. MAX WIENER UNDERTOOK THE TASK AS EARLY
AS 1948. IT SEEMED PROPER, IN THE CASE OF SO CONTROVERSIAL A
FIGURE AS ABRAHAM GEIGER, TO HAVE HIM EXPRESS HIMSELF IN
HIS OWN WORDS. CONSEQUENTLY, DR. WIENER PREPARED A BIO-
GRAPHICAL SKETCH AND THEN PICKED STRIKING EXAMPLES FROM
GEIGER'S ADDRESSES AND WRITINGS TO ILLUSTRATE HIS APPROACH
TO JUDAISM AS WELL AS THE VIGOR OF HIS CHALLENGE. DR.
WIENER CONCLUDED HIS TASK IN 1949. ❧ TWO CIRCUMSTANCES
DELAYED THE PUBLICATION OF THE BOOK. ONE WAS DR. WIENER'S
DEATH SOON THEREAFTER. THE OTHER WAS THE DIFFICULTY IN-
HERENT IN GEIGER'S STYLE. THE TRANSLATION OF THE BOOK WAS
EVENTUALLY UNDERTAKEN BY DR. ERNST J. SCHLOCHAUER, WHO
COMPLETED THE FIRST DRAFT OF IT SEVERAL YEARS AGO. TRAGI-
CALLY, HE TOO DIED—A VICTIM OF HIS EXPERIENCES UNDER THE
NAZIS. ❧ DR. THEODORE WIENER, OF THE HEBREW UNION COL-
LEGE IN CINCINNATI, WAS GOOD ENOUGH TO GO OVER THE TRANS-
LATION OF HIS FATHER'S WORK. FINALLY, IT WAS ENTRUSTED TO
MISS GERTRUDE HIRSCHLER WHO REVIEWED THE ENGLISH STYLE
OF THE MANUSCRIPT AND MADE MANY VERY HELPFUL SUGGES-
TIONS. ❧ ABRAHAM GEIGER SPEAKS TO US IN THESE PAGES IN
THE BOLD AND PROVOCATIVE TONE WHICH SO IMPRESSED THE PEO-
PLE OF HIS DAY AND INFLUENCED LATER GENERATIONS.

table of contents

1. BIOGRAPHY OF ABRAHAM GEIGER 3

2. LETTERS

    to Joseph Naftali Dernburg 83

    to Various Correspondents 97

    to Leopold Zunz: Reminiscences of Days Gone By 138

3. EXCERPTS FROM GEIGER'S WORKS

    A General Introduction to the Science of Judaism 149

    Reports of the Jewish Institute of Religious Instruction 170

    Judaism and its History 177

    The Original Text and Translations of the Bible 216

4. SERMONS AND LEAD ARTICLES

    Sermons 247

    Lead Articles 265

    An Open Letter: On Renouncing Judaism 283

NOTES 295

1

---

biography

OF

ABRAHAM GEIGER

The sun of a more promising day seemed to be rising for the Jews of the Free City of Frankfort when Abraham Geiger was born there on May 24, 1810. Two years before, the old *Judenstaettigkeit* (Jew Ordinance) of 1616, which had somehow managed to survive through the Era of Enlightenment and had kept the Jews in medieval bondage, had been replaced by more humane legislation. In 1811, the proclamation of full equality encouraged a feeling among the Jews that, at long last, they had attained the status of full citizenship. But these advances, wrested from the legislators of Frankfort by the triumphs of Napoleon, were short-lived. Only two years later, after Bonaparte's crushing defeat on the field of battle, all this receded into pre-Revolutionary darkness. As a matter of fact, these same magistrates of the city of Frankfort were proud to use their "freedom" regained to deprive their Jewish subjects of all rights. Now the laborious struggle for equal rights, dogged by reverses, proceeded step by step through the half-century that followed. It had barely been ended when the Free City of Frankfort-on-the-Main was incorporated into the state of Prussia.

Here, as in all the other German lands, the spiritual and cultural development of the Jews had outdistanced their political and social progress. Since 1804 the Philanthropin School had been the center for enlightened Jewish and secular education. It was intended to open, for the young generation, the road to modern culture. The educators who taught at this institution—men like Joseph Johlson (1777-1851) and Michael Creizenach (1789-1842)

—were typical representatives of moderate Jewish enlightenment; they differed essentially from radicals like Herz Homberg (1749-1841) and Lazarus Bendavid (1762-1832). Yet, moderate or militant, the very existence of the feeling that something basically new had appeared upon the horizon was bound to bring about a rift between those who dwelt in the world of yesterday and those who lived in the world of today, or even of tomorrow.

Abraham Geiger's family was not spared this conflict. His half-brother, Salomon (1792-1878), remained of strictly Orthodox orientation throughout his life. A sound scholar in the field of rabbinic literature, Salomon was his younger brother's teacher, faithfully concerning himself with the task of rearing the boy after the death in 1823 of their father, Michael Lazarus Geiger. A strong bond of affection united the two brothers who were eighteen years apart in age. In fact, Salomon even though Orthodox was so far removed from fanaticism that he always looked with pride upon Abraham even after he rose to fame by striking out in quite another direction. Abraham's mother, too, was deeply rooted in traditional Judaism. All the letters which Abraham ever wrote to her, until the time of her death, were written in Hebrew characters. It is clear, then, that Abraham Geiger did not seek to bring reforms to his father's house, even as the latter hardly would have impelled him in the direction of change.

What, then, made Geiger into the personality that has come to be of historical interest? He was not permitted to attend the Philanthropin School, for that institution was considered suspect regarding adherence to traditional Judaism. He did not receive a systematic, modern education, at least not in his earlier years. He was that true Jewish child prodigy, who was taught to read the Bible at the age of three, progressed to the Mishna at four, and was initiated into the Talmud by his father at six. Acquisition of secular knowledge was left to chance, or rather to the consuming zeal for study, so typical of the young people who were then emerging from the ghetto, expecting to find paradise beyond its pale. Mathematics to him was a world of wonderment. But he was also attracted by German language and literature, and by the classics.

The traditional Jewish studies were his daily bread. But beyond that, there lay much that made life rich and deep and beautiful, and Geiger's talents were great enough to covet both the world of Judaism and that which awaited without. He did not look back with any degree of fondness to the Judeo-German *derashah*, the learned address he had had to deliver as the culminating point of his Bar Mitzvah feast. And who can tell to what fields Geiger, ever hungering after knowledge, would in time have applied his intellectual powers and ambitions, had not his brother Salomon gently but effectively guided him, preserving and intensifying his interest in Jewish lore.

Soon he knew enough of the writings of classical antiquity to compare the achievements of that era with the Jewish values that had been handed down to him through the generations, and his Orthodox believer's conviction of the unquestioned superiority of his own heritage began to weaken. All the greater then was the zeal with which he imbedded himself into the soil of Judaism. In this respect he differed from many of his Jewish contemporaries of similar family background and emotional development. The bent for skeptical evaluation of traditionalism, which he developed so early and which remained with him all through his life, may at time appear to have led him to complete rejection of the old, but it never really undermined his Jewish loyalties. His desire was always to reform, never to destroy.

This may be all the more readily assumed since his scholarly aptitude, which became quite evident even in early youth, might certainly have drawn him, as it did many of his contemporaries, to some profession other than the rabbinate. However, it was the ideal of the learned theologian who might kindle the flame of a modern Judaism that remained his guiding light at all times. He prevailed upon his family—though not without a struggle—to permit him to attend the university, a step which the traditional Jews of Geiger's day viewed as a dangerous experiment, one that might easily lead to estrangement from their time-honored way of life, or indeed to worse.

Geiger was barely nineteen when he moved to Heidelberg. The romantic appeal of this famous seat of the muses, immortalized by song and story, seems to have been lost on him. Neither was he particularly impressed by the academic program offered in those subjects that were closest to him, such as philosophy and Oriental languages. It may be that the precocious young scholar, whose grounding in the Hebrew disciplines had been thorough, and who had long since passed far beyond the fundamentals of theology and problems of general philosophy, had expected a little too much. It seems that he derived greater benefit from the lectures on cultural history and Greek philology, subjects with which he had not yet become too familiar. For Rabbinics, he had to rely upon independent study and on work with other Jewish students who, like himself, were contemplating a rabbinical career.

It was in those days that Geiger began to form friendships which were to have a far-reaching influence on his life. There was Randegger, a native of the Italian sector of Austria. He first drew Geiger's attention to Samuel David Luzzatto whose star was just rising. Here, too, Geiger first met Berthold Auerbach who at the time intended to become a rabbi himself, but in the end discovered that, by both talent and inclination, he was drawn toward poetry and narrative art.

After a brief summer semester, Geiger left Heidelberg for Bonn. In those days study at a university was by no means the usual thing, especially for Jews, and those young men who were enrolled at such institutions of higher learning represented an intellectual elite.

In Bonn, Geiger met a number of young men who were to grow famous in years to come. Among them was Sam-

son Raphael Hirsch (see below, p. 15), the restorer of
Orthodox Judaism who, despite the convictions to which
he remained unswervingly true in both thought and practice, made a profound impression on Geiger. Another
friend who remained faithful to tradition was S. Frensdorff (1805-1888) ; he was to become famous for his works
on the Masorah. But at that time all three were still
young and flexible and had not yet fallen prey to party-
bound rigidity, so that each of the trio benefited greatly
from this association. They even undertook to form an
oratorical society, perhaps as a substitute for a seminar
in homiletics; apparently they did not fear that the ideological contrasts, which would be bound to come to the
fore in this manner, might have a disruptive effect on
their friendship. For, in their actual field of study, these
rabbinical students were completely dependent upon their
own initiative.

This was all the more reason why the university should
have been to them a *universitas literarum,* a place where
true freedom of learning reigned supreme. It was up to
the student to make sure that he did not overextend his
scope. Geiger's interests were not confined to Oriental
languages. He was drawn also to philosophy and classical
philology, and to astronomy and zoology. His was an infinite thirst for knowledge; of course, the acquisition of
this knowledge took the form of study in and through
books. Whatever excursions he made into natural sciences
hardly impelled the young student to enter into a more
intimate relationship with nature itself. Apparently he
was not too deeply moved by such beautiful scenery as
he might have beheld on the trips he occasionally took.
What impressed him was not beauty which the eye could
see, but solely that which came to him through the medium
of the mind, through literature. Ideas were always closer
to him than anything that might be found in nature.

The fact that Geiger the boy had delighted in the works
of Lessing and Herder and that Geiger the youth had
been an avid reader of Goethe and Schiller is indicative

of the times in which he lived, rather than of some particular personality trait.

His deepest interest, however, lay in the field of Judaism, in the proper practice of his faith based on sound theory. To the young man in his early twenties there was no question but that there would have to be a parting of the ways between the Old and the New.

To him, the function of knowledge in this process of clarification and purification was to provide the historical attitude toward the whole of Jewish living, and therefore the viewpoint from which the way for this separation was to be prepared. This firm faith in the knowledge of history as the true remedy for what ailed Judaism remained with Geiger as long as he lived. He was convinced that once the correct theory—or, better, the *historically* correct theory—could be found, there would be no need to worry about the development of a wholesome practical application of the faith. In his optimistic, rational faith, Geiger was confident that this was bound to come to pass. He was confident that the scholars, Joseph Dernburg[1] and Leopold Zunz, with their studies in philology, would create the foundations for a new Judaism. In one letter to Zunz, dated April 22, 1831, he unburdens his heart on this subject. With the caution characteristic of him, he requests that the letter be kept in strictest confidence since, in the nature of things, freedom of expression is not usually granted a fledgling theologian. True, what he requests in this letter does not sound especially radical: he merely pleads for freedom of thought and expression. He suggests that Zunz become the head of a scholarly journal, in which representatives of every existing trend would be given an opportunity to present their viewpoints. Such an enterprise, he felt, would certainly have a most salutary effect and bear rich fruit. He hails Zunz as the man who, from within Judaism itself, would know how to create a new and revitalized Jewishness.

Geiger already felt himself ripe for literary work. Georg B. F. Freytag, Geiger's professor in Oriental studies, in obvious deference to his student, had posed a prize-essay theme entitled "What did Mohammed take from Judaism?" Geiger's thesis, submitted in Latin, was awarded the prize and published the following year (1833). This marked the conclusion of his university studies and was the first work to reveal him as a scholarly researcher.

With the end of the Bonn period, his actual years of preparation had come to a close. He was then only twenty-three years old, but the basic course which his life was to take henceforth was already charted. At that time he was also contemplating marriage, having conceived a deep affection for Emilie Oppenheim, the daughter of a Bonn merchant. Another seven years were to pass, however, before he actually could make her his bride.

He now had to find a rabbinical post from which he would be able to dedicate himself to his ideals: to the study of Judaism as it was and to the organization of a new Judaism, one which would meet the demands of the present and of the future. In his native Frankfort, the young preacher's sermons had been received with such enthusiasm that the Jewish congregation of the neighboring town of Wiesbaden invited him to be guest speaker, and soon thereafter elected him rabbi. This small congregation, which formed the nucleus of a rural district with a widely scattered Jewish population, could not offer him much financially. His annual compensation amounted to 400 florins (less than $200), in addition to a furnished apartment and some modest extra income. This certainly was even less than the limited financial resources of the local Jewish community might have been able to expend. On the other hand, the prospect of independence in his work, which would afford him ample time for private study, appealed to him, and he accepted.

He had left Bonn without taking his academic degree, and had yet to earn his rabbinical diploma. He achieved both without difficulty. The Faculty of Philosophy at Marburg thought his prize essay of sufficient worth to be accepted by them in lieu of a doctoral dissertation. Some of the professors there, such as Hermann Hupfeld,[2] the theologian, had heard of the essay and read it even before Geiger became a candidate for the doctor's degree. Their authority obtained a unanimous faculty vote in favor of granting him the doctorate. The rabbinical diploma was awarded him by Gosen, the rabbi of Marburg, in accordance with the practice then prevailing, when rabbinical seminaries as we have them today were still unknown. With his clear intellect, supported by an innate gift of oratory and a rapidly increasing store of knowledge, Geiger had no difficulty in discharging his pulpit chores. Save for exceptional cases, he did not find it necessary to write his sermons down, yet he gave them infinite thought and arranged every detail with the utmost care. As a matter of fact, he required more preparation for what he was *not* going to say than for what he was actually going to expound from the pulpit, for his fiery temperament, if not sharply curbed, might have done more harm than good among his audience, who, for the most part, were simple country people of little education. This was not the place where he could truly unburden himself of his innermost thoughts and strivings. For this he had to write to like-minded friends and intimates. With these he could discuss the great need he felt for extensive transformation and change in the rituals and expressions of Judaism as it was practiced in those days. His letters to Joseph Dernburg, in particular, show how frequently he was brought to the edge of despair by the dull-mindedness, the dearth of ideas and the shallowness of feeling that confronted him in his congregation.

It may be that the young man did not as yet have sufficient psychological insight to understand that, even if they could have grasped the true meaning of these demands, the good people who were under his pastoral care considered a great many other things much more urgent than the need for reforms in their religion. With the state authorities of the little principality of Nassau, who knew of everything that went on among their Jewish subjects, the youthful rabbi stood in good repute. The authorities fully approved of the "modern" type of Jew. In the official records of the day there is the following notation, which, on the whole, is expressive of none too friendly an attitude toward Jews in general: "Geiger performs the duties of a teacher of religion with zeal and willingness; he frowns upon those principles that make the Jew untrustworthy in his relations with the Christians and, in his sphere of activity, generally conducts himself to our satisfaction."

To many of his own congregants, of course, the young rabbi, who preached in flawless German and did not worship routine as hallowed ritual, appeared highly suspect. Some of the backward rural congregations petitioned the government of Nassau for permission to sever their connections with the *Rabbinatsverband*, the official federation of rabbis, which was recognized by the authorities. The authorities rejected these petitions; on the other hand, they were unwilling to bestow upon Geiger the title of a *Landrabbiner* which would have given him broader powers.

Let us see what it was that made these people view Geiger as a dangerous innovator. Actually, his "reforms" at that time were extremely limited in scope; they hardly went beyond the demands of decorum and dignity in worship. Abridgements in services were limited to the omission of a few *piyyutim*, liturgical poetry, whose contents no longer had meaning and which had owed their preservation merely to habit, an outgrowth of that religious feeling to which all that is old is automatically sacred. His efforts to enhance the beauty and dignity of the service through choral singing, for which purpose he had founded a society, were universally condemned. But those who were free of narrow prejudice were most favorably impressed with the rabbi's honest zeal. They backed his efforts to obtain the title of *Landrabbiner;* they stressed his excellent sermons as arguments in his favor, praised the impressiveness of the Confirmation exercises he had instituted, the solemnity of the wedding ceremonies he conducted and his success in revitalizing religious instruction in his congregation. However, their efforts in his behalf were of no avail. Disappointed, Geiger resigned from his position in 1838. Not only the state authorities, but even most of his congregants, were sorry to see him go. It was characteristic of his optimism that he folded his tent without knowing where he might set it up again. There were offers from Gotenburg, Sweden, and Karlsruhe, Baden, but these negotiations came to naught. In the meantime, Geiger had become well known as a spiritual leader in German Jewry. But this was not due to his practical work as the rabbi of a small-town congregation; his official duties there could neither have filled his time nor utilized his vital energies to the full. However, he had gone about with tenacity laying the foundations for his ideal—religious reorganization through spiritual and historical insight. Serving as his instrument for this purpose was the *Wissenschaftliche Zeitschrift fuer juedische Theologie* (Scientific Journal for Jewish Theology) in which he sought to combine historical research with practical recommendations for a reformation of Jewish religious faith. This journal was founded in 1835. The fact that Geiger, who was then only twenty-five, succeeded in raising the funds needed for publication—in all likelihood he hardly gave a thought to the payment of author's fees—without the support of wealthy sponsors is testimony to his ingenuity. Moreover, the fact that members of the Jewish scholarly elite such as Joseph Dernburg, Marcus Jost, Leopold Zunz, Salomon Munk and L. Rapoport[3] were willing to become his collaborators indicates the great confidence which his ideal inspired. The basic idea of course was not new; even as early as 1819, the conviction had been expressed over and over in Zunz's *Kulturverein* that it was only through a thorough scientific examination of its history and literature that Judaism could have a new birth.

Let us dwell for a moment on this phenomenon which is so typical of the spiritual development of Geiger and his followers. The *Wissenschaft,* or scientific knowledge, of which the Jews of that day made such a cult, was confined exclusively to history. They were convinced that, given the historical facts, it would be possible to draw the correct practical conclusions with regard to the means by which their religion could best be served and elevated to the level of contemporary culture. Strangely enough, it occurred neither to Geiger nor to any other like-minded scholar that the science of nature, which was making mighty strides forward at the time, was presenting an even more dangerous threat to the religion which they were intent on saving. The consequence of tradition misunderstood or misconceived was, at worst, a distortion of religious expression. The new natural science, however, frequently struck at the very roots of that spirit from which every belief in God, including that of the Jews, had sprung. Apart from a few to whom no one paid any attention, why did it never occur to these clever men, those leaders who were so well acquainted with the scientific trends of their times, that here, nurtured by contemporary natural science, a philosophy was being born in which there would hardly be room for even the most enlightened form of religion in the traditional sense of the word? Even if, aided by philological sifting and an aesthetic sense, it should be possible to produce an "up-to-date" prayer book, what good would that be to the many (including large numbers of Jews) whose faith, in a traditional sense, seemed irretrievably lost?

The answer is quite simple. It lies in the fact that, for all their critical and even skeptical attitude, the intellectualists and modernists of Geiger's stamp were still deeply rooted in the religious tradition of Judaism. Their entire beings were anchored in it. To tear themselves loose from this soil would have meant for them utter homelessness in a vast universe. Thus the validity of Judaism, and of the Jewish view of the world, remained the rock in which their personalities were still deeply imbedded. If we keep this in mind, we will be able to understand Geiger's mentality, and we will be convinced that he really believed he would be able to cure the ills of contemporary Judaism by a penetrating analysis of the sources of its spirit and of its evolution. More than any other proponent of the

"Science of Judaism," Geiger was impelled by practical zeal and a driving desire to effect reforms. He listened to the voices of the ancient authorities because he was genuinely convinced that the heritage from the past should and could bear fruit in the present day. He believed in the genius of his people and in its vocation to lead Jewish men and women through all time. It was for this reason that he conceived of the "Science of Judaism" as not just an end in itself but as a guide to the construction of a living present and future.

The spirit of Judaism, as Geiger conceived of it, has a *priori* human and universal significance. Consequently, the "science" which seeks to serve the understanding of this spirit and of its development through the centuries should not serve merely as an end in itself. Much rather, it should be fully exposed to the bright light of broad, general knowledge. Only in this fashion, Geiger felt, could Judaism assume the place in world culture that was its just due. Thus, one of his first demands was for the establishment of a Faculty of Jewish Theology that might be made part of one of the German universities; in all probability he thought of Heidelberg or Marburg. The way in which this idea was carried out, through Jewish institutions such as the Rabbinical Seminary of Breslau and the Berliner Hochschule fuer die Wissenschaft des Judentums (the Berlin Academy for the Science of Judaism), probably seemed to him only a makeshift solution. Ludwig Philippson[4] had long been active in behalf of a similar plan. But the motives that impelled Geiger in his appeal could hardly have found a more zealous heir than Hermann Cohen.[5] Both of these men viewed this idea as the culminating point in the emacipation of the Jews. If emancipation was to be something more than the attainment of civic equality by the Jews, then the *idea* of Judaism as such had to be given recognition by the world. But according to German concepts this could not come about without the approval of the state. Thus, since Geiger conceived of this idea primarily in its religious form, he demanded the establishment of a Faculty of Jewish Theology under the aegis of the state. Only on such a level could the fight be waged diligently and effectively against the intolerance of the churches, which was founded at least as much on plain ignorance of Judaism as on malice. Geiger always took a lively interest in what went on within the Christian camp, and he was an avid reader of Christian theological periodicals.

His own periodical, particularly in those articles which he contributed himself, reflected a happy combination of timely problems and learned treatises. From the very beginning it comprised a wide range of divergent fields. Thus, for instance, Geiger wrote, with exemplary thoroughness, on the order of synagogue services arranged by Maimonides, on problems of the Mishna and on modern Hebrew poetry. These were all subjects that lay beyond the anxiously guarded sphere of the Bible, and even conservative scholars did not regard objective, historical treatment of such topics as outright violations of religious statute. However, his intellectual honesty could not be confined within arbitrary boundaries. He felt that no historical data, not even the Bible itself, should be immune to factual analysis. Thus he soon became the outspoken pioneer advocate of a movement which traditionalists of all shades were bound to oppose.

No one was more acutely aware of this than Samson Raphael Hirsch,[6] Geiger's one-time fellow-student from the Bonn days, who, in the meantime, had drawn up a platform for a "Neo-Orthodoxy" in his *Nineteen Letters*. The romantic sentimentality that pervaded this book was more than Geiger's rational mind could bear and he made no attempt to disguise his distaste for such a program for the restoration of the old form of Judaism. At that time those of the Orthodox school found in most of the German governments, particularly those of Prussia and Austria, powerful allies in their struggle for self-assertion. They could be certain that, in any disputes involving synagogue worship and ritual, the authorities would always take their side. The Prussian Cabinet Decree of 1823, which prohibited any innovations in Jewish religious practice was used for decades as an effective weapon by the protagonists of Orthodoxy.

It was difficult to achieve sufficient unity for effective action even among those who sided with Geiger in principle. This became very obvious at the conference of rabbis which the young spiritual leader called at Wiesbaden in 1837. In theory, the fourteen colleagues who accepted the invitation were very close to one another. But as soon as attempts were made to set up a point-by-point program of what was to be done in the various congregations, deliberations were stalled. Geiger realized that nothing could be gained merely by shared tendencies, inclinations or disinclinations, if a strong will and a clear-cut program were lacking. His practical sense was fortified by his knowledge of and insight into the processes of history. He sensed that the course to follow would have to be one of care and caution, of minor reforms only. He realized that it was one thing for an author-scholar, guided by the scholar's conscience only, to assume an obligation to teach ideas, but quite a different matter for a rabbi, preaching and teaching in a congregation, to put his ideas into practice. The thinker, the searcher for truth, was duty-bound to resist compromise. But the practical teacher, without thereby being guilty of either hypocrisy or of seeking to make life easier for himself, must keep in mind at all times that truth could not prevail overnight. Thus the device he adopted as his own was to go on working and hoping.

The *Zeitschrift* served as a banner. There were, in the 1830s, a sufficient number of educated Jews in Germany who admired its editor and were convinced that this man had the temperament and that combination of will power and intellectual ability which would succeed in awakening Judaism to a new life. The split between right and left, which threatened to undermine the very existence of many a congregation, posed an even greater threat to the survival of religious Judaism than the losses suffered through apostasy. On the other hand, the intense concern for the future of religious Judaism was by no means

limited to the rabbis. Enlightenment, which was only then
beginning to reach large numbers of people, together with
the rapid spread of modern education, gave birth to a
spirit of liberalism that aimed to build rather than to
destroy. At least, such was the honest ambition of many
of the men who occupied positions of leadership in their
religious communities. The forms that these struggles
were to assume and the issues that were behind them
were all shown most clearly and forcefully in Geiger's
fight for the soul of the Jewish community of Breslau, a
mission that was soon to come to him and occupy the best
years of his life.

The Jewish community of Breslau, which had been
organized less than a century before, had grown to considerable dimensions. Despite a large influx of immigrants
from the Polish territories of Prussia, the spirit of modern
thought was no less in evidence here than in the central
and western regions of Germany. The Wilhelms-Schule
had become famous as a training ground for general education, and the Gesellschaft der Brueder (Society of
Brethren), which had been founded in 1779, was a bulwark
of the champions of Enlightenment. In those days the
head of the adherents of Reform was Wilhelm Freund
(1806-1894), a classical philologist of note, who gave voice
to this movement in his monthly *Zur Judenfrage in
Deutschland* (On the Jewish Problem in Germany). However, the official community continued to run along the
well-worn tracks of the old, first under scholarly Gedaliah
Tiktin, who served as Chief Rabbi of the Community of
Silesia until 1820, and then under his son Salomon A.
Tiktin, who was Orthodox, but was not nearly his father's
equal in stature.

The liberal adherents of Freund believed that the time
had come for a man of broad secular education to assume
the spiritual leadership of their community. In 1838,
the community's board of directors announced that they
were seeking a *Gottesgelehrten*, a scholar in sacred theology, who would combine "comprehensive biblical and

talmudic scholarship with both sound secular education
and strict piety, and who would be qualified not only to
take over the official functions of a *dayyan* (assistant
rabbi), but to deliver edifying and instructive sermons at
the synagogue in proper German." Geiger was invited
to be guest preacher and delivered a sermon at the
synagogue on July 21, 1838. This had been done over the
protests of Tiktin. The local state authorities, who had
to approve any such invitation by a synagogue, overruled
the protest. Tiktin appealed to the Ministry of Berlin
which then handed down a decree prohibiting the community from taking such action, but the decree did not
reach Breslau until after the service. Geiger was elected
almost unanimously and everything appeared to be in
perfect harmony.

Actually, this proved to be the beginning of open warfare. Tiktin declared that Geiger was not deserving of
his position, since he had attacked religion in his journal.
Besides, Tiktin pointed out, Geiger was not even fit to
hold rabbinical office, since he had been graduated from a
university. Rumor had it that he had been obliged to leave
Wiesbaden after he had been seen violating the Sabbath
in public. And of course there was the Prussian Cabinet
Decree of 1823 which prohibited all innovations in synagogue services. The fact that Geiger, gowned in official
clerical robes, had delivered a sermon in pure German,
was construed as a violation of this decree. Accusations
of a different sort, and a good deal more dangerous, were
also leveled against Geiger; in these, he was linked with
suspect political circles and tendencies, and the Prussian
authorities were always prompt and thorough in ferreting
out the truth behind such charges. The representative
from Berlin in the Bundestag[7] in Frankfort was charged
with the task of conducting a thorough investigation,
and this gentleman went to the trouble of wading through
all the volumes of Geiger's *Zeitschrift*. In the end, he
had to admit that these revealed not a trace of political
radicalism. An investigation was made also concerning
Geiger's activities in Wiesbaden and, again, the officials of

the dukedom of Nassau could report only favorably on Geiger's personality and his conduct in office. The reason for all this caution on the part of the Prussian authorities was that the candidate elected to the rabbinical position in Breslau had to acquire Prussian citizenship before he could assume office, and political radicals, particularly if they were Jews to boot, were not considered desirable. All these events occurred while Geiger was in Berlin, where he hoped to win over the central authorities. He succeeded in obtaining a personal interview with Altenstein, an influential Cabinet Minister. The Minister convinced himself that the Jew from Frankfort was indeed politically harmless, but he was in no hurry to give his consent to his naturalization as a citizen of Prussia. Thus the matter dragged on for months, to the great discomfiture of Geiger, who found it difficult to finance his protracted sojourn in the capital. He grew increasingly nervous. He also found out then that even men of high intellect and of undeniable scholarly achievement, such as S. L. Rapoport, not only failed to plead his cause but were actually known to have made some highly critical comments concerning the views he manifested in his practical rabbinical endeavors. Only then did Geiger realize that there were also other types of Orthodoxy than the extremely narrow form of the Tiktin variety. On the other hand, he could take comfort in the approbation of Gabriel Riesser, the eminent lawyer and pioneer in the fight for the emancipation of the Jews.

Here historical fairness necessitates a few comments to make it easier to understand the bitter struggle between the old and the new, and the personalities who participated in it. Religion is a sacred cause. Yet the records of history regarding wars and hatreds carried on in the name of religion plainly show that those who fought one another in the cause of the "true" faith frequently employed weapons which were something less than sacred. The honesty of Tiktin is no more subject to doubt than that of Geiger. But once religion had become the object of a struggle for power, those involved persuaded themselves that the end justified the means. It was no more than natural that Orthodoxy should be alarmed at the attack, from the radicals, which sought to undermine its position; and it was only human that its advocates should make an attempt to defend it. Orthodoxy was no less convinced of its monopoly on the truth than was Geiger of the validity of his own approach. It was natural, then, that Orthodoxy should regard the mere existence of a "rabbi" of Geiger's type as a thorn in its flesh. But could Geiger have given in to it without becoming untrue to his innermost nature as it had developed from the days of his earliest youth? Geiger was a man who was not satisfied merely to possess for himself what he believed to be the truth; his was the nature of a reformer, a revolutionary, driven by an innate urge to make his influence felt in the world. He was a man of fiery, active temperament and of boundless vitality. Thus, of necessity, things had to come to pass in the fashion in which they then occurred, although the followers of Tiktin were not medieval fanatics by any means. They were simply men to whom the idea of a religious structure differing from Judaism as it had come down to them from their ancestors seemed absurd. Naturally, men of that sort remained quite unimpressed by theories of historical evolution; but this does not mean that their Orthodoxy was any less genuine than Geiger's belief in Reform.

Naturally, those who opposed Geiger tried everything in their power to keep him from taking office in Breslau. They even appealed to the king of Prussia. The king, however, left the decision up to his Ministry, and these officials, of course, were not so concerned about Geiger's anti-talmudism as were the partisans of Tiktin. The opposition now claimed that Geiger's election had not been valid to begin with. To bring about his defeat, they proceeded to mobilize whatever opposition he had engendered in the course of his previous activities.

But then Geiger, too, had friends who used their influence in his behalf. It may well have been some private remark made by Alexander von Humboldt to Minister

Altenstein that tipped the balance in Geiger's favor. At any rate, in the end his Prussian citizenship was officially confirmed. Geiger's fifteen months' wait in Berlin had not been in vain.

It should be pointed out, though, that Geiger did not spend all that time waiting in ministerial antechambers and drawing up petitions. He found time, too, for work that was much more pleasant and congenial to him. It was during this period that his anthology entitled *Melo Hofnayim* came into being.[8] This anthology contains Hebrew texts with German translations, including the letter of Joseph Solomon ben Elijah del Medigo of Candia to Zerah ben Nathan the Karaite of Troki, and other material dealing with Maimonides, Judah Halevi and Profiat Duran. Nor was the *Zeitschrift* discontinued. In it he took issue with Samson Raphael Hirsch's *Horeb*, a collection of "Essays on Israel's Duties in the Diaspora." The gulf between the views of the two men who had once been friends had become too wide to be bridged.

However, it was not books, written or as yet unwritten, but human beings, that claimed Geiger's attention during those tense and anxious years. He had always been interested in people, and sought out personalities of intellect both within and without the Jewish fold. True, he was somewhat disillusioned by the reception which the men in authority at the University of Berlin accorded him. "They received me like a student," he once said. We do not know to what scholars in particular this complaint refers. But then the men on whom he called, such as Vatke and George, the theologians, Ritter the geographer, and Trendelenburg the philosopher could hardly have been expected to share the interests of the youthful Jewish theologian. At that time, too, he met Bettina von Arnim,[9] who had once basked in the sunshine of the great Goethe.

More rewarding intellectually and more heart-warming to Geiger was his relationship with Leopold Zunz, sixteen years his senior, to whom he looked up with reverence and affection. The two men were very different in temperament. While Geiger's striving, until the very end, was directed toward the goal of reform which he had set for himself, Zunz's fiery passion for a revitalization of Judaism had been sudden but short-lived, followed by a gradual withdrawal into purely scholarly endeavors. In fact, as time went on, any radicalism, perhaps any desire whatsoever to effect reforms, came to grate on Zunz's nerves. With all his scholarship and critical approach, combined with broad secular knowledge, Zunz, apart from the endeavors of his youth, never attempted to determine what a new Jewish way of life should really be like. His skepticism did not allow him to look to the future with cheerful optimism, and thus, to him, as to many a lesser mind, the "Science of Judaism" came to be simply a personal religion, a way of life that embraced every fiber of his being. And yet there was no one whom Geiger respected more highly. For although his practical nature made him view the value of knowledge in terms of the action to which it led, Geiger still regarded scholarly research as the most distinguished and worthy of endeavors; he looked down with a measure of contempt on those who were drowned in daily routine.

Actually, he himself was to be engulfed in just such routine when he first began his work in Breslau. He took office in 1840. Under the terms of his contract he was obligated to deliver a sermon on every Sabbath and holiday and to supervise all religious instruction. He was not required to pass decisions on questions of religious Law. This may have been a concession to the supporters of Tiktin; at any rate, it eliminated one factor that would inevitably have precipitated a head-on collision between the two parties. The fact that this limitation made him the rabbi of the Liberal element only rather than the spiritual leader of the congregation as a whole did not trouble him. The limited nature of his position in Breslau was demonstrated also by the circumstance that only half his salary (800 thalers, or around $600 per annum) was paid out by the treasury of the religious community. The rest was contributed by certain individual wealthy members who were particularly interested in his cause.

By that time a synagogue sermon in German was no longer a novelty, but it had not as yet become general practice. In any event, a sermon of this type provided not just religious education but also instruction in cultured speech for a good many people who had never had such instruction before. The Jewish population of Breslau in the early 1840s was only slightly smaller than that of the capital. There were among the people quite a number who were well-bred and who proved receptive to academic instruction given in a popular style. An adept teacher such as Geiger had no difficulty in gaining their interest for history and literature, or for glimpses into the Mishna and the Talmud. A program of this sort was relatively novel in those days, but it was of vital importance in effectively combatting the contempt in which the Jews themselves held their own spiritual heritage. Only a few of Geiger's sermons appeared in print. Interestingly enough, those that were published dealt particularly with the relations of the Jews to the state; there is one address paying tribute to the Prussian Edict of Emancipation of 1812, and another welcoming the accession of Frederick William IV. In the latter, Geiger voiced his own accord with the hopeful enthusiasm with which the new king was acclaimed by Jews even more than by Christians. The Jewish community felt most elated and flattered by the impression which Geiger's addresses made on non-Jewish audiences.

Breslau truly became his home when, at last, after seven long years of waiting, he could marry Emilie Oppenheim. The wedding took place in the summer of 1840 in his native Frankfort, and Geiger gladly took the opportunity to preach an inspiring sermon to his old friends and countrymen. The home which the newlyweds proceeded to establish in Breslau did much to help win the hearts of the congregants for their young rabbi. To Geiger himself it remained a constant source of strength. Emilie did not live to grow old; she died in 1860. But during those stormy decades in Breslau her presence gave him that courage which stood him in good stead in his endeavors. They had four children, two sons and two daughters. One of the sons, Ludwig, became his father's biographer and the executor of his literary legacy. In his capacity of Professor of Literature at the University of Berlin, Ludwig was well qualified for this task.

The Breslau period was by no means an idyllic one for Geiger. The battle still raged. Though the authorities had rejected the claim that his election had been invalid, new articles (in volume V of the *Zeitschrift*) gave his opponents cause for further indignation and hostile agitation. One such essay, entitled "The Task of the Present," argued that the present generation had the right to make changes in the order of prayers and in synagogue music, to employ the sermon as a means for education toward intellectual progress, and to put special stress on the ethical requirements of religion during religious instruction. Geiger cited in his support the sages of the Talmud who had expounded the Scriptures in the light of their own understanding of religious truth; and he claimed the same prerogative for himself. But in the opinion of the Orthodox this view did violence not only to sacred tradition but —and this was much more dangerous to Geiger—also to the Cabinet Decree of 1823. Once again the government was requested to intervene. However, the authorities decided that the royal statute was applicable solely to the actual practice of divine worship. Theoretical discussions in learned essays, even if they advocated reforms in the synagogue service, were therefore not to be construed as violations of the law. The theologians in the government noted that, while the *Zeitschrift* clearly revealed a tendency to Reform, it did not by any means advocate mere deism as Geiger's opponents had claimed. It was felt that Geiger had done no damage to the historic faith; nor did he seek to establish a new sect. All he wanted to do was effect a cleansing of the "Jewish Church," guided by the pattern of its historical development.

In the early years of the reign of Frederick William IV the Prussian policy toward the Jews was not clearly defined. At one time it was felt—this was a pet idea of the romantic monarch himself—that the Jewish group, if one took any positive notice of it at all, should be preserved in its ancient form as a kind of special entity. At another time, in accordance with a more liberal trend in the spirit of Emancipation, it was preferred that the Jews should be regarded as individuals linked together only by the bond of religious denomination. It appeared that the novel concept of a "cleansing of the Jewish Church" would render useful service in the assimilation of the Jews. In the following year the king visited Breslau in order to receive the homage of the province. On this occasion Geiger served as the spokesman of the Jewish deputation and, on behalf of the 200,000 subjects of the state of Prussia who professed the Jewish faith, he asked for a gradual (*sic*) extension of equal civic rights to them. The Jews, who until then, had been merely tolerated but actually did not differ from the king's other subjects in anything else but their professed faith, confidently looked to His Majesty's Grace for the rights of full citizenship in their country. The king's reply was both gracious and noncommittal; he promised that the right of Jews to hold public office would be expanded and also mentioned that changes in their ecclesiastical affairs were imminent. Unlike the opposition party in the Jewish camp, the king expressed his gratification at the fact that the sermons at the Breslau synagogue were being delivered in German, and delighted the Jewish delegation by his public recognition of the famous men who were numbered among his Jewish subjects.

Geiger's good relations with the government authorities were not without significance, especially since his adversaries within the Jewish fold remained implacable. It may be that Tiktin was only a tool of the opposition rather than a powerful adversary on his own initiative. He ran the gamut from petty squabbling to downright scandalous conduct. For instance, Tiktin refused to officiate at a wedding at which Geiger was to deliver an address in German. He refused to attend the dinner of the Burial

Society because he did not want to meet his "reformed" colleague, although the latter had been present at the cemetery just before when Tiktin had delivered an address. He made his *derashah* on the Sabbath preceding Passover the occasion for violent attacks from the pulpit against innovations and innovators. When, at the funeral of a prominent member of the congregation, Geiger was about to begin to speak, Tiktin simply cut him off with a volley of angry invective against both his colleague and the organizations within the religious community. This incident aroused such furor that it came to the notice of the chief of police. Once again the government was drawn into the private war within the Rabbinate of Breslau, and even the king learned of it. At that time the Ministry of the Interior was headed by Von Raumer, a man who, at the extreme right in religious as well as political views, had little liking for the movement led by Geiger.

The Jewish community of Breslau was in a state of high agitation which culminated in the suspension of Tiktin by the board of the congregation. It was suggested that the seemingly irreconcilable dispute be resolved by the establishment of two separate religious entities under one common overall administration. Tiktin, however, refused to be part of any congregational organization that would include Liberals. In order to remove Tiktin as gracefully as possible, the board of directors announced that the Orthodox leader had voluntarily resigned his office. When this somewhat transparent device failed, a formal list of complaints against Tiktin was drawn up. Among the charges were that, in his two annual *derashot,* he had made no attempt to give moral instruction to the congregation, that he had neglected the religious instruction of the young, and that he had failed to visit the sick under his pastoral care.

The defendant refuted these charges, and, supported by endorsements from rabbis of Posen and Silesia, he opened a counterattack. For one thing, he declared, a man who, like Geiger, did not observe the 613 commandments of the Torah could not be considered a Jew, let alone a member of the rabbinate. Some time previously, in a published "Address to My Congregation," Geiger had defended himself against the strange accusation that he, Geiger, was a follower of the Sadducee or Karaite movement. He pointed out that the Talmud itself had abolished some of the commandments of the Bible. He denied ever having insulted either the Talmud or talmudic scholars.

In the fall of 1842 and again in the spring of 1843 the board of directors of the congregation published *Rabbinical Opinions concerning the Compatibility of Free Research and the Rabbinical Office*. In this work, seventeen liberal rabbis, some of them quite well-known, such as Samuel Holdheim and David Einhorn, upheld Geiger. Others, although convinced of the justice of Geiger's cause, did not want to have their opinions made public. Zacharias Frankel and S. L. Rapoport made no attempt to conceal their outright opposition to Geiger.

Strangely enough, neither party could realize that, in such a dispute, neither side could possibly be one hundred per cent in the right. It seems strange, too, that it took so long to effect the final solution, namely, the peaceful separation of the two groups under the aegis of one overall Jewish community. Nor was it considered undignified to appeal to the state authorities for intervention. Such was the bitterness that had been generated in this dispute. It goes without saying that no petty political stratagem, in the worst sense of the word, was left untried. In the meantime things appeared to have changed in the high places and it seemed as if the Tiktin wing had cause for hopes that the Cabinet Decree of 1823 would now be invoked in their support. They repeated all their old charges. The struggle involved issues which would seem a downright waste of the combatants' energies to anyone but those in the midst of the actual battle; it entailed such things as the delivery of sermons and the intoning of certain prayers in the German language, choral singing at services, whether or not it was permissible for the rabbi to wear clerical robes, to make changes in traditional synagogue melodies, or to call worshipers to the Torah by their German rather than their Hebrew names. These charges called for a reply by Geiger. He sent to the Cabinet Minister his "Address to My Congregation" with an accompanying letter, in which he attempted to reduce the basis of the real difference between the two movements to ignorance and hostility to culture on the one side as opposed to genuine and sensitive religious feeling on the other. He gave thanks to God that, after a long and tragic history, Judaism was at long last seeking to attain a higher morality and genuine piety. Geiger claimed that rigid adherence to outworn forms did not ennoble but only led to increased indifference to religion. The board of directors of the Breslau community denied that Geiger had advocated any such revolutionary innovations as might have justified the action of the complainants, and they pointed out, in their defense, Tiktin's lack of modern secular education.

Thus two Prussian Ministries, the Ministry of the Interior and the Ministry of Public Worship, were besieged in the interests of a case in which even with the best of intentions they could not possibly have rendered an impartial decision. The government had sufficient good sense, however, not to enter into the substance of the dispute, but to view the argument merely in its purely formal legalistic aspects. The government pointed out that whether or not Tiktin had properly discharged the duties of his office would have to be decided by a regular court of law rather than by a Ministry. The question that still remained to be settled, however, was whether or not the reforms introduced by Geiger could be construed as changes in worship such as were prohibited by the Cabinet Decree of 1823. The king himself was petitioned to decide whether the rabbinical gown represented an unjustifiable imitation of Christian custom. The sovereign, however, had no desire to become involved in the religious disputes among his Jewish subjects, and merely suggested that, in the future, the Jews could establish separate synagogues for congregations representing different movements. He pointed out, though, that imitations of Christian church customs in a Jewish house of worship would not be tolerated.

With this the inhibiting effect of the royal Cabinet Decree appeared to have been annulled, at least for all practical purposes, although the problem of the rabbinical gown still remained unsolved. This question had now become a shibboleth for both sides, with even the Christians participating in the dispute. As regarded eagerness to influence the high and mighty in behalf of their cause, there was very little difference between the Orthodox and the Liberals. Geiger took advantage of a visit by Eichhorn, a Cabinet Minister, to Breslau, to expound to him his conception of Judaism. He also sent him his essays which, he firmly believed, would be bound to convince all but the prejudiced or the outright malicious of the reasonable nature of his endeavors. It has always been typical of "enlightened" religion to consider its viewpoint so obviously clear that only obscurantists or those blinded by prejudice could fail to accept it. This attitude may not always have been voiced publicly, but it existed in the thoughts of many.

Orthodoxy did not by any means think that its cause was lost. The religious school became the next battleground. It was Geiger's aim to have it made compulsory for all Jewish children in the community to attend the classes he had organized. When the opposition party complained of this to the authorities, it was decided that, since the religious school was a strictly private institution, attendance there could not be made obligatory by law. It was also decided that no general tax could be levied by law on members of the community to defray the expenses of the school, nor could delinquent tuition payments be recovered through public lawsuit. This decision represented a material setback in an important area of communal activity. Nor was the situation improved for Geiger by an Orthodox victory in a relatively minor matter which, however, in its very pettiness, is a good example of the issues that then—and perhaps not only then—gave rise to the most passionate exchanges. The question was whether or not it was permissible for the rabbi to wear special robes of office. The Orthodox, both Jewish and Christian, replied in the negative. The Breslau authorities had been instructed by the Ministry to report whether this request on the part of Geiger constituted a departure from the time-honored Jewish custom. They replied that, even though the robes Geiger was wearing were not those worn by the Christian clergy, they had directed the Hebrew preacher to remain true to Jewish tradition and dispense with the gown. Geiger had been cautious enough to ask Catholic and Protestant clergymen to certify that the official robes he wore were not identical with those worn by them and their colleagues during church services.

Now it was Geiger's turn to file a complaint with the Ministry. Neither religious precept nor sacred custom, he declared, prescribed a special garb for synagogue functionaries. This was rather a matter of personal taste and of individual views on propriety. Since the government did not recognize the rabbi as a state official, it had no more right to prescribe what he should wear than to pass on what constituted proper clothing for any other private citizen. After all, the rabbi did not presume to don military or civil service uniforms, nor did he wear robes identical with those of the privileged Christian clergy. The authorities agreed that, indeed, the rabbi was not a state official. Nevertheless, they insisted that any costume, even one of the rabbi's own devising, could not be worn if it met with the disapproval of a large segment of Breslau Jewry.

There was another incident which, though in itself insignificant, was symptomatic of the gradual change for the worse in the attitude of the authorities toward the Liberals. It occurred on the occasion of the official welcome tendered to the new mayor of Breslau. The officials of the Jewish community and the rabbi had been invited to attend the festivities. At the last moment, however, their invitation to the church ceremony was withdrawn. The authorities of Breslau considered this incident of sufficient importance to report to the Ministry of State. According to them, the appearance of a rabbi in church would have offended the sensibilities of the Christian worshipers. But more than that, Geiger would have given offense to members of the opposition party in his own community by appearing at the Christian service in his rabbinical gown. It seems, then, that Geiger was courageous enough to be willing to defy the state authorities in a matter which he felt was none of their concern.

All these events transpired while the "old" rabbi, Salomon A. Tiktin, was still alive. His death on March 20, 1843, marked the beginning of a new phase in the struggle. Geiger, wanting to avoid the possibility of undignified public scenes, did not participate in the funeral procession. In his sermon on the following Sabbath, however, he spoke kindly and warmheartedly of the deceased talmudic scholar. The Orthodox faction proceeded to elect Gedaliah Tiktin, Salomon's son, as his successor. But the government was in no hurry to confirm him in office. Some of the more level-headed elements in the congregation utilized this period of truce for attempts to achieve a solution of the conflict by peaceful means. When, however, Wilhelm Freund's proposal for a legal separation of the Orthodox and the Liberal worshipers failed of acceptance and the confirmation of Tiktin was subjected to further delay, the Orthodox members actually agreed to a continuation of the old arrangement whereby the two rabbis held the office jointly. But Tiktin's election was invalidated by the government on the grounds that only one segment of the congregation had participated in it, and for a time it looked as if the rabbinic appointment would go not to a member of the Tiktin dynasty but to Hirsch B. Fassel, a man of moderate, conservative views.[10] After protracted negotiations back and forth the Breslau authorities finally decided in 1846 that Gedaliah Tiktin might be confirmed in office, though not as *Gemeinderabbiner* (rabbi of the Jewish community as a whole), but only as the spiritual leader of that particular group which had elected him. Thus the Orthodox party once again had gained the upper hand in their dealings with the authorities. True, the legal advisors of the Prussian administration might not have been especially concerned with the subtle distinctions between degrees of radicalism in the Jewish fold, but neither State nor Church had any liking for liberalism. Hence Gedaliah Tiktin stood in the good graces of both the Evangelical General Superintendent of Silesia and the Catholic Archbishop of Breslau, and both these prelates commended him highly to the Cabinet and even to the king.

Thus Tiktin, whom the government originally did not wish to recognize as the rabbi of the Jewish community of Breslau, was soon in a position to expect appointment to even higher office, that of *Landrabbiner* over all of Silesia. The king himself fulfilled Tiktin's ambitious request and significantly made the following notation on the pertinent recommendation: "It is true that Tiktin has no right to claim the title. I am, however, inclined to confer said title upon him so that the movement which he represents may receive support, which would be a desirable thing for political reasons."

The Minister of the Interior did not quite share His Majesty's enthusiasm. On the basis of information obtained from Breslau, the Minister had come to the conclusion that, although the Orthodox movement was worthy of preferred status, neither Tiktin's secular learning nor his other qualifications were such as to suit him for the position of *Landrabbiner*, let alone *Oberlandesrabbiner*. Moreover, since he had been elected by a limited group only, he could not even, strictly speaking, be regarded as the spiritual head of the entire Jewish community of Breslau. It should not be forgotten, of course, that, in those days, the majority of the Jews of Breslau still sided with Orthodoxy. Statistically, 945 members had come out for Tiktin, but only 648 had voted for Geiger.

The final result of the constant fights that dragged out over a period of several years was that, in 1853, the three Prussian Ministers concerned with the case, the Secretaries of the Interior, Justice and Public Worship, finally agreed in the name of grace and mercy no longer to oppose the conferment of the title on Tiktin, with the recommendation, however, not to let him advance beyond the office of *Landrabbiner*. Early in 1854 this decision was put into effect by Royal Cabinet Decree, much to the displeasure of the organizations constituting the Breslau Jewish community. The Jews in the provinces, too, had no wish to have the new *Landrabbiner* presume to exercise any jurisdiction over them. At any rate, the outcome of the long struggle was far more fortunate for the Tiktin party than for Geiger and his followers.

This period of trial and error, of ups and downs, should be of interest to us even today, because it reflects much of the history of European Jewish communities in the early days of Emancipation and because it revolves around a fighter of the stature of Abraham Geiger. Through it all, Geiger did not for a moment lose sight of greater and broader aspects of life. He did not, however, withdraw into an ivory tower; he remembered at all times that lofty goals could be attained only by those who had sufficient patience, courage and self-denial to approach them step by step. The fight for what he deemed to be right broke down into countless petty skirmishes, but he never evaded these. Viewed in itself, the problem of the cut of the rabbinical gown was a detail of ludicrous pettiness, but this problem, too, had to be tackled with as much energy as were weighty questions of philosophy or serious scholarly studies. His courage never failed him. It never occurred to him to evade the annoyances of such insignificant trifles by withdrawing to the privacy of his study to indulge in labors that yielded him personal gratification.

His happy family life, and his communion with likeminded friends, offered relaxation, but struggle and contention were his very life. Occasional journeys to Silesian spas, to Vienna (in 1841) and to Munich (in 1849) broke up his workaday routine; but then Geiger was never in a rut. Complete release from work and the enjoyment of nature gave him less satisfaction than continued contacts, in varying environments, with other men of intellect with whom he could share his own thoughts. He needed other people. He was sincerely grateful for the opportunity to meet men like Mannheimer, the eloquent preacher,[11] and Leopold Dukes, the scholar, who introduced him to Jewish society in Vienna. When he was in Munich, Geiger was not only attracted by the manuscripts in the Staatsbibliothek there, but found pleasure also in accepting the invitation to deliver a sermon in the synagogue. His name had become a battle cry, and it may well be that Rabbi Aub,[12] who was rather inclined to be cautious, was not particularly delighted to have the troublemaker preach in his synagogue. By then, however, Geiger had influential followers everywhere, and his fame had spread beyond the confines of the Jewish fold. A banquet given in his honor received coverage in political journals like an event of major importance.

His *Zeitschrift* continued to be the platform from which he campaigned in behalf of his interpretation of Judaism and attempted to explain how he based his aims on historical developments. He selected such writings as seemed to him of timeless significance. When he examined the *History of the Controversy over the Study of Philosophy from 1232-1306*,[13] he felt as if he were breathing the air of his own century. In his studies on biblical exegesis and Hebrew poetry of the Arabic Jews of the 10th, 11th and 12th centuries, he delved into the depths of medieval Jewish culture.[14] When Bruno Bauer, the philosopher and critic of religion, attacked talmudic Judaism and at the same time criticized modern Judaism for breaking with the traditions of the past, Geiger replied that the controversy within the synagogue was a sign not of decay but of rebirth. He declared that an end must be put to the dichotomy between the Law and actual life; he blamed this dichotomy for the present state of stagnation, and for the Jews' lagging behind the scientific *Zeitgeist*.[15] Today, more than a century later, such phrases may strike us as commonplace. But the formulation of thoughts that become self-evident to future generations is in itself a notable achievement.

Of special significance among the original works of that period were *Ein Lehrbuch zur Sprache der Mischnah* (A Compendium of the Language of the Mishna), published in 1845, and *Lesestuecke aus der Mischnah* (Readings from the Mishna), published later that year. These studies found grateful reception even among Christian readers. Among the *Beitraege zur juedischen Literaturgeschichte* (Contributions to the History of Jewish Literature), which were published in 1847, the first section, entitled "Die nordfranzoesische Exegetenschule im 12. Jahrhundert" (The Northern French School of Exegesis in the 12th Century), gained particular importance.[16]

Geiger was forever striving beyond the fixed horizon; in scholarship as in daily life he found a ghetto intolerable. He sought to explore new and distant realms and thus did not seek to resist influences from the outside. His numerous essays and discussions show that his sources were by no means confined to Jewish publications. Christian theologians, including orthodox ones such as Hengstenberg[17] and Tholuk, were given due recognition. Within Judaism, multifarious and deeply split as it was, he saw in scholarship a bond that was to knit together all genuinely intellectual endeavors. This explains his interest in the Hebrew journal *Kerem Hemed*, and also his sincere respect for Samuel David Luzzatto, a personality diametrically opposed to Geiger's own, who from the very bottom of his heart condemned the zest for innovations shared by the German Liberals under the leadership of Geiger, a sentiment which Luzzatto never attempted to disguise.

Geiger was in a very real sense the teacher of his concongregation, of both the young and the old. He organized educational groups or worked through existing organizations in order to provide some knowledge of Jewish subjects for those to whom pertinent literature was inaccessible, if, indeed, such literature was at all available in those days. His *Einleitung in das Studium der juedischen Theologie* ("An introduction to the Study of Jewish Theology," 1849) was intended for a very limited audience only.

But his lectures on Jewish history extending to his own day satisfied a very real need of many of the members of his congregation. It became evident that the widely-touted indifference to things Jewish could indeed be overcome if only the teacher and educator could find a way to expose the buried seeds of intellectual curiosity and to stimulate their renewed growth. Judaism was, after all, not just an old faith, but a new, a very timely personal concern. The presentation of the works of personalities such as David Friedlaender, Ludwig Boerne, Heinrich Heine, Berthold Auerbach and Gabriel Riesser[18] and debates on the new trend made the listeners feel that this was their very own cause which was unfolding before them. Geiger knew how to paint his pictures in the most vivid colors. The role of the Jews in general intellectual developments, their relationship to the world around them, and the opinion that the world had of the Jews—all these he evaluated with great precision and critical judgment. Notes from the memoirs of Henriette Herz, characteristic lines of the career of Adolphe Crémieux and passages from letters of Wilhelm von Humboldt[19] were used and integrated in order to create as faithful and vivid a picture as possible. Geiger became the reporter of contemporary history, as it were, thus following a procedure which was then, even as it is today, a good method for awakening interest in things Jewish; for it comes close to the sphere of politics, and there are few who are not interested in politics or who do not think themselves capable of forming authoritative opinions of their own in this field.

Even as the question of antisemitism is in the foreground of Jewish consciousness today, so the progress or stagnation of Emancipation policies dominated Jewish thinking in the middle of the last century. There were then hardly any organized movements for the attainment or defense of civil rights. Like hardly any other rabbi, Geiger was endowed with the skill and energy to be a leader in this fight. When the Faculty of Philosophy at the University of Breslau sought to keep Jews from attaining the doctorate, he promptly lodged a protest with the state government (1842). When the Breslau Citizens' Hospital refused to admit Jewish patients, he defended the rights of the latter by pointing out convincingly that the institution was being maintained not by church money but by public funds. He raised his voice in protest, too, concerning the discrimination against Jews in the formulation of the court oath. On the other hand, he saw to it that his coreligionists made full use of whatever civil rights they already possessed, that they participated in the election of city officials, to cite just one example. Through public lectures before non-Jewish audiences he attempted to spread enlightenment and understanding. And in those days functions such as these were by no means universally accepted as pertinent to the general duties and tasks of a rabbi.

The development of the relationship between religion and politics was in full swing in the 1840s. The state-legislated reorganization of synagogue affairs of 1847 was preceded by lengthy debate. Geiger had earlier sent a petition to the Minister of Public Worship which was typical of his conception of the relationship of the religious community to the State and of the position of the rabbi within that community. For the religious community he demanded complete freedom of growth and development, unhampered by any interference from secular authorities. He desired to see the function of the Jewish school limited to religious instruction, since he felt it important to have Jewish children attend public school together with their Christian contemporaries. The rabbi, he felt, should not be a member of the congregational board of directors. Only candidates whose qualifications had been approved by the State should be permitted to hold the office of rabbi. These basic ideas advanced by Geiger later were incorporated into the religio-political program of the Liberal Jewish movement in Germany. The Jewish problem occupied an important place in the deliberations of the Diet of 1847, which functioned as a kind of people's representative body prior to the Revolution of 1848. The Jewish community of Breslau sent Geiger, by then a man of considerable experience in politics, to Berlin to influence important politicians in behalf of Jewish interests and aspirations. This was extraordinary proof of confidence given a rabbi, the like of which is hardly found elsewhere in the annals of the history of Jewish congregations in Germany during the 19th and 20th centuries. The fact was that Geiger did not need to insist on being a member of the board of his congregation, for he could easily exert his influence on that body by virtue of the power of his personality alone. It was only natural that he should be made chairman of the commission which submitted to the government recommendations concerning community by-laws, the election and authority of rabbis, and other matters basic to the existence of a religious community. With the ratification of the Prussian Constitution of 1850, the reorganization of Jewish affairs as far as state legislation was concerned was brought to a tentative conclusion.

The political and religious stirrings within Judaism in that decade culminated in rabbinical conferences. The purpose of these conferences was to create a unified plan for effecting those changes which by then were generally acknowledged to be necessary. Orthodoxy gradually began to recover from that paralysis which through many years had rendered it practically inarticulate.

Conservatives like Zacharias Frankel (in Dresden and then in Breslau) and Michael Sachs (first in Prague and then in Berlin)[20] were too much the followers of romantic sentimentality, too deeply rooted in the aura of traditionalism to be amenable to a boldly outlined program of change and innovation. Thus it was the belief of the Liberals, under Geiger's leadership, that no efforts should be spared to invest the living manifestations of Judaism with a clear-cut, sharply-defined form, before widespread indolence and indifference could cause irreparable damage. It will be recalled that Geiger had already inaugurated a convocation of rabbis in Wiesbaden in 1837. Now a series of conferences were planned which would bear a more official character and which, Geiger hoped, would lead to decisions that could be considered binding on all those participating. These conferences (the first in Brunswick in 1844, another in Frankfort-on-the-Main in 1845 and finally one in Breslau in 1846; others did not materialize) made it clear, however, that it was easier by far to agree on general principles than to find a common basis for unity with regard to concrete details. This had become apparent even at Wiesbaden. The basic program, of course, had long been firmly formulated in Geiger's own mind. Judaism was to be constituted as nothing more and nothing less than a religious community. Judaism, to the greatest extent possible, was to be accepted and acknowledged as a universal faith, stripped of every vestige of tribal rite and custom. It was to be, or to become, the religion of the "modern" Jew who, it then seemed, was shortly to be admitted as a full citizen to a state which would hold a position of neutrality in matters of religion. If the binding force of the Talmud was incompatible with these aims, then its unqualified validity would have to be officially countermanded, and if the traditional order of prayers no longer reflected contemporary thought and emotion, then that would have to be changed.

But was it actually possible to draw a clear dividing line between "nationalistic" and "purely religious" content? The debate on the subject of circumcision, and Geiger's polemics against the prayers relating to the ancient sacrificial cult, clearly showed up the difficulty. For instance, was the Hebrew element of the divine service to be viewed as "nationalistic" or as part of the purely religious aspect of Judaism? Geiger sought to retain it "in its essentials," but he pointed out that the retention of Hebrew in prayer, while serving a useful purpose, was not commanded by religious precept. It was obvious that the strictly Orthodox, and even conservative minds, such as Frankel and Michael Sachs rerpresented, would not feel at ease in this atmosphere. The right wing did not participate in the second conference, which was held in Frankfort, and Frankel pointedly walked out in the middle of deliberations. The conference that was then held at Breslau and which Sachs, despite a personal invitation from Geiger, failed to attend, was no more than a rump assembly. Details do not concern us here. But it is essential to point out the psychological error of which Geiger, the positive Liberal, was guilty then, and which he probably continued to commit throughout the rest of his life. In his opinion, religious reform had to grow out of *Wissenschaft*, a term which he equated with the concept of the understanding of historical evolution. He probably thought that, once men became aware of the relativity and the fluidity of all the phenomena of history, they would find it an easy thing to renounce rigid tradition and to accept new forms. The fact of the matter, however, is that Jewish ritual, which was the primary object for this reform, is rooted in the same spiritual soil as the faith in mysterious dogma. Neither philosophy nor the natural sciences have succeeded in tearing irrational or even antirational tenets of faith from the hearts of those to whom the mystery of the divine forms the basis for their very existence. Nor is it possible to reduce the practical Jewish way of life *ad absurdum* among those who feel compelled by sentiment and by their own free will to embrace it. It is never education or erudite knowledge that undermines Orthodoxy or the faithful observance of the Law. First the attitude of loyaly to tradition must have been shaken or must have collapsed entirely; it is only thereafter that science or learning is called upon to legitimize defection. To be sure, the old type of Orthodoxy of the Tiktin variety, which gave Geiger so much trouble, did indeed appear to be an archaic remnant of the long-buried past. But Samson Raphael Hirsch, Michael Sachs, Zacharias Frankel, Isaac Bernays,[21] Samuel David Luzzatto, L. Rapoport and other worthy men within the ranks of the neo-Orthodox and the middle-of-the-road parties saw no conflict whatsoever between modern secular education and Jewish scholarship, on one hand, and strict adherence to religious precept, on the other. We do not intend here to minimize the significance of the efforts that were made to simplify the overly complex nature of Jewish ritual. The abolition of the observance of the second days of the festivals was left to the discretion of individual rabbis or congregations, and such mourning practices as had originated in ancient national or tribal custom only were declared to be meaningless for the present day. The question of the observance of the dietary laws was broached but no radical solutions were advanced. It was suggested that *mohelim* be required to undergo some medical training before being permitted to perform circumcisions. Proposals for reforms in marriage law were also discussed but not so seriously as to be set forth even in the form of resolutions. It turned out, however, that the Orthodox were not the only group to refuse to make any concessions; the Reformers themselves were split into radical and moderate camps.

The Reform congregation founded in Berlin under the leadership of Samuel Holdheim[22] and ideologically related groups were much too radical in practice for Geiger's liking. Reform bodies such as these had little use for a "gradual development" which entailed nothing more radical than a three-year cycle of Torah readings, the permission to use non-Passover sugar, butter and dried fruits during Passover, and to eat *hametz* foods on the last day of that festival. They might well have turned against Geiger the very reproach which he himself had directed at his right-wing neighbors, to the effect that nothing would be accomplished by mere patchwork efforts and that the time had come for decisive change. He may have differed from them in opinion as regarded the speed with which reforms were to be put into practice; that was all. But what criterion could serve to determine what speed was compatible with the course of natural evolution, and what, on the other hand, would be tantamount to a total, unnatural break with tradition? Geiger consistently pointed out that the right to effect reforms in the present day was derived from the fact, scientifically confirmed, that even the past had seen constant change. However, he overlooked the fact that change through the course of time, so gradual as to be almost unnoticed by contemporaries, was by no means the same as deliberate reformation, openly proclaimed as such.

Geiger's basic principle was clear and consistent in itself. To him Judaism in its ideal form was religion *per se*, nothing but an expression of religious consciousness. Its outer shell was subject to change from one generation to the next. Hence the Talmud, too, was to be regarded as time-bound. Since Judaism was destined to be a universal religion, he felt that it had to divest itself of all nationalistic elements. It never occurred to the adherents of this view that they might ever wish to form a political entity such as Judaism had been prior to the fall of the Second Commonwealth. To them, the nation whose citizens they were, or desired to become, was their sole Fatherland.

The Frankfort "Friends of Reform," to whom Geiger expounded his thesis, were able to accept it word for word as the expression of their own conviction. But they might well have queried in their turn why the dietary laws, too, could not be declared no longer binding, and why so many other ordinances which the pioneer of Liberalism had not dared touch could not be abrogated in the process. From the purely logical point of view, the position of extremism is always more easily defensible than that of moderation. Geiger's ultimate goal, however, was so obvious that whatever traditional ritual he permitted to endure was clearly a mere concession. This was the reason why the Reform Congregation of Berlin, the only radically Liberal one of its kind in Germany, felt that he might consent to become their rabbi. The evasive reply which he made to this offer was followed by a lecture in Breslau in which he voiced general approval of the Reform program. With this he incurred great displeasure among his adherents in Breslau. An unpleasant controversy ensued, and an anonymous pamphlet called for his resignation. In all likelihood it was Dr. Freund, Geiger's erstwhile devoted follower, who now sparked that opposition which felt that Geiger's most recent pronouncement on organized Reform had gone too far. The real reason for Geiger's eventual rejection of the Berlin offer was clearly his feeling that any rift in the organization of the Jewish community could only do grave damage. True, he wanted his reforms, which he held to be historically justified, to go to the utmost limits of what he deemed possible. But he had no wish to burst asunder the inherited, firmly knit and for many reasons highly useful bond of a unified religious community. The subsequent development of German Jewry proved him to have been right. Wherever groups of divergent ideologies joined under the protective shelter of a unified communal administration, each could preserve its ideological integrity, and the strength of the *kehillah,* the organized religious community, was preserved by its unity in all matters save ritual and worship. Thus we see that Geiger was not merely a theologian and religious reformer, but also an intelligent politician when it came to communal affairs.

His position, however, had become difficult. Just how difficult, is best shown in the history of the founding of the Jewish Theological Seminary of Breslau. In his will, *Kommerzienrat* Jonas Fraenkel, who was well disposed toward Geiger, had set aside a sum of money to be used for the establishment of an institution for the training of rabbis and teachers. Fraenkel died in 1846. The institution which he had contemplated was to be realized in 1850. The drawing up of statutes was left to the discretion of the board of trustees of the foundation. Geiger, widely recognized scholar and respected rabbi that he was, had every right to expect to be consulted in these deliberations, all the more so since he had quite early and very forcefully insisted on the necessity for a Jewish institution of higher theological studies. However, it was not Geiger, but Wilhelm Freund, the classical philologist, whose advice was asked. Yet, although Freund's relations with Geiger had grown somewhat cool, Freund was sufficiently objective to suggest the name of the *Gemeinderabbiner* of Breslau among those authorities who he felt were qualified as experts to state their opinion in this matter. In a letter written in February, 1851, Freund once again expressed the hope that Geiger would be assigned an appropriate function at the proposed institution. Freund too, like Geiger, wanted the seminary to be an academic institution independent of party affiliation. For years the entire affair seemed at a standstill, until a practical-minded member of the board, Joseph Lehmann, at that time railroad director at Glogau, took matters into his own hands. It is certain that he had an active interest in Jewish affairs; in his youth he had been a member of Zunz's *Kulturverein*. He was a middle-of-the-roader in his religious views. But he could not be considered an expert on questions of Jewish academic training. Strangely, Zunz, the greatest Jewish scholar of the century, was extremely sparing in his advice; he merely cautioned against having the students of the institution lead a quasi-monastic existence, and declared himself opposed to the conferment of academic titles. Just before the board of directors proceeded with the election of the first dean of the seminary, Freund once again brought Geiger's name to their attention; but his efforts were in vain. The dean they chose was Zacharias Frankel, a man who, though undoubtedly eminently suited as regards personal qualifications, was far to the right of the Liberal leader in his views. Furthermore, the statutes of the institution required the instructors to adhere to historical and positive Judaism. Thus Geiger and all of his followers were actually excluded from the seminary by statute, as it were.

To Geiger this was a bitter blow, perhaps the worst defeat of his entire career. To him academic teaching had always appeared a great vocation, perhaps the greatest of his life. It had been he who at an early date had called for the creation of an academy of higher Jewish learning; and now he had to taste the bitterness of defeat. It was a twofold disappointment: he felt deeply hurt personally, and at the same time it seemed an indication to him that his concept of "the Science of Judaism" had still hardly taken root. Any expansion of the scope of his activities, he thought, was now thwarted. In the position of professor at a rabbinical seminary, the only one existing in Germany at the time, he could have made his influence far more greatly felt than was possible in the practical work in his rabbinical office, which itself had become the center for violent dispute. To be sure, no one could keep him from writing books, and his greatest literary achievements were yet to come. But the immediate approach to the goal of large-scale creative achievement was barred. And Geiger was a man to whom life meant not merely work but active and creative achievement.

His friends attempted to have him appointed head of the Philanthropin School[23] in Frankfort; but to Geiger that was poor compensation. His energy, however, and his implicit faith in himself turned even this bitter experience into a release for an unprecedented drive to work. Now Geiger devoted himself with redoubled zeal to the religious instruction of the young. The erudite scholar was also a born educator. He possessed a sufficient measure of that self-denial which, often entirely absent in men of high intellect, enabled him to adapt his thinking to the minds and the needs of the young. He did not consider himself above the task of taking personal charge of the intermediate grades in his school. At the same time, he attempted to secure capable instructors who would contribute to the growth of his religious school into a living organism, an endeavor which was by no means common in those days when Jewish education suffered from gross neglect. It was only after he had secured competent helpers that Geiger limited his own actual teaching activities to the upper grades and the Confirmation Class. As far as his students were concerned, Geiger certainly did not act the impetuous reformer. Hebrew occupied a prominent place in his curriculum. He saw to it, too, that the religious instruction of his school would not drive a wedge between his students and their parents. At the same time, he knew how to orient them toward his own ideals. He had an excellent associate in M. A. Levy (1817-

1872) who was an expert also in epigraphy, numismatics and Phoenician antiquities. Levy's talents as an educator are clearly evident in the sound textbooks of which he was the author.

Breslau Jewry had long respected intellect and scholarship, so that the well-educated merchants of that golden age of German culture had the proper appreciation for a man of Geiger's stature. The Cassierer and Wollheim families, who were prominent not only in business but also in intellectual life; Lina Morgenstern, the pioneer in the movement for women's rights; and Ferdinand Cohn, the botanist who was to grow famous in later years, were all members of Geiger's social circle. Scholars like David Chwolsohn,[24] who later became the leader of Russian Orientalists, and Robert Schroeter, the Protestant theologian, also sought Geiger's company.

Geiger had a happy disposition. True, he was not a stoic who could remain unaffected by reverses. But his vitality kept him in that state of productive restlessness which forever spurred him on to new effort. A combination of devotion to his practical work in the rabbinate and zeal for scholarly research created a pattern which made for real harmony in his personality. Experience, often painfully acquired, had taught him that practical work should not prematurely reap the fruit of the tree of theoretical knowledge. But he remained certain that everything truly worth studying and knowing must, in the end, yield benefits for day-to-day living. During the 1850s he was engaged in studying those literary productions of past centuries that could make clear to his own contemporaries the broad scope and many-faceted character of the Jewish spirit. In that decade appeared studies on the great medieval Jewish poets, dealing with Judah Halevi, Abraham and Moses ibn Ezra, Judah ben Shelomo Alharizi, and Kalonymos ben Kalonymos.[25] He wrote a brief biography of Judah Halevi, and produced several essays in which he tried his hand at imitating the style of the older poets. The fact that Geiger should have been fascinated by the figure of Leon da Modena (1571-1648),[26] the Venetian rabbi and representative of the borderline epoch between the Middle Ages and the modern era, is not in itself particularly surprising. He was impressed by the independent critical attitude which Rabbi da Modena had displayed toward both Jewish tradition and Christian religion, and he wished that Lessing, that critic of classical mold, could have known this Jewish controversialist. Such thoughts engendered threads that tied in with the figure of Isaac Troki,[27] another religious critic who had refuted the assertion of the Church that the Holy Scriptures of the Hebrews contained allusions to Christ.

Two essays, written in 1858, were of more timely significance. In these, Geiger dealt with the problem of apostasy from the religious, moral and civic points of view. An actual case offered him the opportunity to take to task all those who, not content silently to evade their obligations as Jews for opportunistic reasons, insisted on flaunting their personal lack of integrity by public declaration. Rarely had Geiger spoken out in so sharply critical terms as in these polemical writings, and what he said here could hardly have been better or more forcefully expressed elsewhere.

An immediately constructive task in behalf of his religious ideal was the preparation of a new prayer book. This work stemmed from a demand which Geiger had made some time before, during the Hamburg Temple controversy of 1842. After the publication in 1849 of his *Grundzuege und Plan zu einem neuen Gebetbuch* (Outline and Plan for a New Prayer Book), Geiger continued to work on the project for several years, until it was finally completed in 1854. This prayer book consistently reflected that religious philosophy and theological conviction which had long become firmly consolidated in Geiger's mind. To Geiger, Israel continued to be a people, but one united solely by a common historic faith, renouncing once and for all whatever political or nationalistic aspirations it might have had in the past. As a consequence, all reminiscences of that sort, including recollections of medieval martyrdom, were to him no longer meaningful. Even

Haman and Amalek were to be forgotten. Enlightened theologian that he was, Geiger removed from his prayer book all references to angels and to a physical resurrection of the dead. His aesthetic sense demanded the elimination of the *piyyutim* and a limitation of the many repetitions in the original *siddur*. However, despite all these innovations, which must have seemed highly suspect to the traditionalists, Geiger's prayer book in its essentials retained the traditional form. It differed from radical Reform particularly in that most of it still was in Hebrew. It is "Liberal" in the German sense of the word only, and has more in common with American-type "Conservative" worship than with the Union Prayer Book. Geiger's recommendation of the use of German in home worship is not an innovation in itself, and in public worship the use of German was restricted to a few prayers to be read by the rabbi which did not affect the pre-eminent place of Hebrew in the synagogue service. Nor had traditional features been blurred, at least not with regard to the Sabbath and the festivals. Of course, no provision was made for days of fasting and penitence or for the observance of the New Moon. The recommendation to omit the additional days of Passover and Sukkot was not carried out. The Sabbath was preserved, though Geiger did not reject the idea of occasional services on Sunday morning in addition to the regular Saturday worship.

Geiger was not the first to make a German adaptation of the *siddur*. Beginning with the German translation made by Isaac Euchel in 1787,[28] there had been many renditions of the Jewish prayer book into that language. The novelty of Geiger's undertaking lay in the fact that, whereas former attempts at the reorganization of divine services had been confined to smaller, private groups, Geiger's project was intended for an entire community. Of course, his translation, partly in elevated prose, partly in poetry, clearly shows that even the vernacular, used in a house of worship, must undergo revision from time to time if it is not to become archaic. The concept of "holiness" or immutability can be associated by the living only with a linguistic pattern that has taken shape outside the sphere of everyday usage. It may therefore be said that sermons as well as prayer in the non-Hebrew idiom, regardless of their content, represent the flexible factor, while the sacred tongue constitutes the fixed pole in the welter of phenomena.

Geiger did not wish to become the founder of a new dogmatism, nor was his authority great enough to assure the distribution of his prayer book to other influential congregations. It was not even to maintain itself for any length of time in Breslau. His successor, Manuel Joel, in his own readaptation of the liturgy, was already demonstrating an approach closer to the middle-of-the-road position. To Geiger the reinstitution in Joel's work of the prayers relating to sacrifices seemed particularly retrogressive. In his thoroughly logical presentation, a short essay entitled "Etwas ueber Glauben und Beten zu Schutz und Trutz" (On Faith and Prayer as Shield and Armor), Geiger overlooked those imponderable factors that are particularly manifest in the worshiper and defy all logic. At any rate, the congregation of Breslau preferred Joel's moderate innovations to the more radical reforms of Geiger.

No matter how much time, strength and mental strain they entailed, these practical chores were essentially relaxing. This was of particular significance during those years when Geiger labored over that work which he considered the crowning glory of decades of thought and research. His magnum opus *Urschrift und Uebersetzungen der Bibel in ihrer Abhaengigkeit von der inneren Entwicklung des Judentums* (The Original Text and Translations of the Bible in their Relation to the Inner Development of Judaism) was published in 1857. This work, of course, shares the fate of every bold historical theory in that it becomes itself a part of historical thinking and thus is incapable of revealing any final or definitive truth. The question of what is still valid today, a full century later, and what is now out-of-date is not as important here as the basic tendency of the work.

It is obvious that Geiger was motivated, both in theory and in practice, by the idea of evolution, and it was his intention to develop this principle as the historic *leitmotif* in a most important era of the Jewish past. Judaism was rooted in the Bible and in the Talmud. Were these two documents, particularly the biblical writings, the expressions of a static, unchanging intellectual viewpoint? Must the ideological content of canonical literature, which had been set down once and for all, be viewed as the only valid source from which the teachings of the rabbis and consequently all of Jewish religion in the future could derive nourishment? Or was there such a thing as an evolution peculiar to the genius of Judaism that lay imbedded in the biblical text, which was by no means rigid or lifeless, and which would therefore serve to make the Bible a reflection of the gradually unfolding ideas of the Jewish people?

Geiger believed that the latter assumption was the correct one. There was such a thing as a history of the text, from the study of which the history of the faith might be derived. It had long been known and proven that the ancient translations (*targumim*) and punctators had made alterations in passages of the original text which they thought might appear objectionable to the simple reader for some reason or other. Geiger meant to present this basic thesis in its full significance. A critical study of the text indicated to Geiger that in the days of the Second Temple the position of leadership was occupied by the Zadokites, a priestly dynasty who managed to weave their own religious-nationalistic consciousness into the textual structure of the Holy Scriptures.

Geiger's research yielded a new picture of the Sadducees and the Pharisees. The former were the spiritual heirs of the Zadokites of the Bible, the strict guardians of traditional institutions, while the latter spoke out in behalf of progress in both religion and politics. After the destruction of the Second Temple and the abortive revolt of Bar Kokhba, the Pharisees asserted themselves decisively. Though the views of the Sadducees became apparent at times in aggadic literature, and could be deduced from the teachings of the Samaritans and Karaites, it was the Pharisees who dominated the Mishna and the Talmud. A study of the Greek and Aramaic versions of the Scriptures revealed that viewpoints were subject to change in the course of time. The *Targum Onkelos*, the Aramaic rendering of the Pentateuch, for instance, was shaped on the pattern of the Halakhah valid at that particular time. The adoption of the final text and its final vocalization did not take place until centuries after the completion of the Talmud; hence there had been time enough for the advocates of a variety of viewpoints, not yet restricted by a canonized text, to inject their particular convictions into their version of the Holy Scriptures.

What Geiger sought to prove by this demonstration is quite obvious. It was not the Bible that created and molded the religious spirit of Judaism; instead, it was the spirit of Judaism that left the stamp of its own form and expression upon the Bible—Life, and its needs and strivings, change from age to age.

From this theory practical conclusions might be drawn for religious endeavors in both present and future. But Geiger's book, scholarly work that it was, was entitled to evaluation quite independently of such tendencies. Distinguished Jewish scholars, such as Moritz Steinschneider and Leopold Loew, as well as Christian savants such as Theodor Noeldecke[29] and Julius Wellhausen, were generous in their praise and recognition of Geiger's work. Heinrich Graetz, on the other hand, rejected it. The author himself always looked upon the *Urschrift* with a good deal of gratification, for he viewed it as the culmination of his scholarly achievements. He was pleased with every word of praise bestowed upon this work, in particular, and would give expression to his disappointment when it was ignored where in his opinion it should have been given due mention. He scarcely derived financial benefits from the book; even its printing had been made possible only by the generosity of well-to-do sponsors.

It might be said that the work was a gift which Geiger

had made to himself and to the world on the occasion of his twenty-fifth anniversary (1832-1857) in the rabbinical office. The celebration of this occasion was a great event in the Breslau community, and Geiger, who was by no means immune to public approbation, was particularly gratified at the impression his contribution to scholarship had made. Jewish students presented him with a formal address that paid respectful tribute to his literary achievements. This was praise after his own heart, and in his response he pledged eternal allegiance to the ideals of scholarship. It was a happy day for Geiger, for this was an occasion when he, who indeed had a goodly number of opponents, could see a host of friends pass in review before him—admirers from his own congregation, and colleagues and scholars from far and wide who had come to pay him tribute. There was an elaborate testimonial banquet at which he himself proposed a toast to the German Fatherland. It was indeed a great day for Geiger, all the more so since his wife, who was then still in the best of health, was there to share it with him.

Geiger now stood at the zenith of his life, or, more precisely, his personality had attained that depth and range which was to distinguish him to the end of his days. Basically, he was an intellectual. His interests outside of his official and scholarly endeavors did not mark him as a friend of the muses. If he sought relaxation in general literature, he would turn especially to books of philosophical content. His work, dedicated to the dissemination and acceptance of his religious ideal, had come to be a kind of personal faith. The attitudes and spirit of traditional Judaism no longer affected his spirit to any great extent. A letter which he wrote to his wife from Karlsruhe in 1855 is revealing. On his way to Paris, Geiger stopped at the home of a married sister who resided in the capital of Baden, and spent Tisha b'Av there. He wrote that the entire family had fasted, but that he had found himself unable to share the gloomy mood of mourning. In the end he succeeded in persuading the women of the family and a young boy to break their fast at noon. He himself did not fast, but he ate dairy food only, and even this he did behind closed doors and windows so that no coreligionist might see him and take offense. He spoke of food also in a letter written on a trip to Strassburg. Here he wrote that he had enjoyed quite a decent dinner at the kosher restaurant, but that the meal had not been inexpensive by any means.

In Paris, Rabbi Aaron became his mentor and showed him the sights of the city. Above all, however, he rejoiced in his reunion there with Joseph Dernburg, the companion of his youth. The change of environment and, more important still, the opportunity to meet other great personalities invigorated him. In Strassburg, for instance, he called on Edouard Reuss, the noted theologian, and in Paris he had the chance to fulfill his long-cherished wish to make the acquaintance of Ernest Renan. He did not go to the theater because of the language difficulty. However, he was greatly attracted by the monuments to art and science that Paris had to offer. His "expert" evaluation of Paris Jewry is of interest. He found Isidore, the *Grand Rabbin*, not exactly a like-minded partisan, but nevertheless a fairly liberal man who merely lacked the requisite zeal and energy. Consequently the divine service at his synagogue, though not actually in a state of neglect, was not really well balanced. It represented a strange conglomeration of the old and the new. On Friday night the organ was played only until the Sabbath had officially begun, but it lent the service dignity and edification. As for the ritual of the Sephardi synagogue, he found its dignity and propriety praiseworthy, though reminiscent of long-departed Spanish *grandezza*. There the organ was played even on the Sabbath. Geiger was given a most distinguished reception in both synagogues, which apparently filled him with great pride.

Generally speaking, Geiger seemed more interested in the French aspects of Paris than in the Jewish life of that city. Typical of this is his comparison of the Pantheon of Paris with the hall of fame which King Ludwig of

Bavaria had erected in his Valhalla in Regensburg. He was greatly impressed with the idea of consecrating a common shrine to all great men of genius. Of course, he felt that the process of selection of candidates might be difficult and degenerate into a Tribunal of the Dead. It seemed ridiculous to him that relatively unknown senators of the First French Empire should have been given places next to Voltaire and Rousseau. But then it was equally unjust not to have placed a bust of Martin Luther, the great reformer, into the German Valhalla. This attitude on the part of Geiger, in our opinion, reflects a high degree of objectivity. The rabbi, who well knew Luther's hostility toward Judaism, was concerned over the unfair treatment given a great German, whereas the German Catholic king had made no attempt to conceal his instinctive antipathy to the man who had been the enemy of his Church.

When, in 1858, the University of Jena celebrated its tercentenary, Geiger sent there, as his anniversary gift, all of his major works which had then been published. They were accepted with thanks after the representative of the Department of Oriental Studies had declared them to be of scholarly value. In his congratulatory message Geiger praised the liberal German spirit which the University had nurtured. No doubt this epistle was sincere, for Geiger loved the German spirit, even if some of its most prominent representatives remained hard and inaccessible to even the most justified Jewish claims for equal civic rights. He had often expressed his bitterness against individuals, but, with a quasi-messianic optimism, he clung to the belief that German thought and German scholarship represented the supreme expression of all human intellectual achievement. With this attitude, Geiger, the learned rabbi, was only typical of the large number of others who manifested this, the emancipated Jew's unrequited love for his German Fatherland.

In the meantime, clouds had begun to gather on the horizon of Geiger's personal life. His wife, who had been ailing for some years, failed to improve. For months she lay in a hospital in Berlin, far away from home. At the end of 1860 she died. This was a crushing blow for the man who, helped by her devotion, had found a home in alien eastern Germany. Yet Geiger remained unbroken; now, perhaps more than ever before, he cherished his work as the very essence of his existence.

In the following year he drew up plans for a new journal. He, more than anyone else, was in need of such a personal medium of communication that would bear the highly individual imprint of his own research and practical ideals. The *Juedische Zeitschrift fuer Wissenschaft und Leben* (Jewish Journal of Life and Letters), which first appeared in 1862 and survived until Geiger's death, served no other person or cause than the convictions of its publisher. This was the forum where he could defend the principles on which his prayer book was based and elaborate on the ideas he had set forth in his *Ur-Text,* as, for instance, in his essay entitled "The Sadducees and the Pharisees." His increasing interest in the Bible is reflected throughout the new periodical. The literary announcements and book reviews listed the works of Jewish and Christian authors alike. The fact that Jewish achievements had been consistently ignored outside Jewish circles had always been a source of chagrin to Geiger, for this attitude of neglect ran counter not only to his Jewish pride but also to his personal concept of the open-minded universal nature of scholarship.

There was much to be said about timely political and partisan Jewish religious affairs. Full equal rights for Jewish citizens were still not completely achieved. In an article marking the fiftieth anniversary of the Prussian Edict of Emancipation of March 11, 1812, Geiger pointed out these shortcomings and called upon the Jews to take strong measures in their own defense. He advocated the creation of an organization which would follow up all cases of abuse and, by voice and pen, would further the cause of complete emancipation. The course of study at the Breslau Seminary was a bitter disappointment to him. It certainly did not mirror the type of progress which he had expected this academic institution to advocate. The historically oriented or "middle-of-the-road" clique, who had quickly turned the seminary into their private haven, he found thoroughly repellent. To him the romanticism to which they appeared to be dedicated was nothing but a new reactionary trend. Of what avail was slavish devotion to the past, if it could not establish a constructive and intelligent relationship with the needs and demands of the present day?

Thus the balance sheet that Geiger drew up on his work, especially his activities in Breslau, did not yield a picture that could satisfy him. He could not forget that the very community in which he had labored had never provided for him a position of academic teaching, nor could he overlook the fact that the struggle within his congregation, which he had waged with such zeal, had altogether failed to bring triumph to his cause. He even began to feel that he would do well not to over-estimate the enthusiasm of his liberal friends. In addition, with the passing of his life's companion, he felt desperately lonely in an alien world. Now, whenever he thought of his native Frankfort, of the friends of his youth, of whom many still resided there, or of his relatives, he longed to return. Besides, Frankfort was close to the center of German cultural life; Breslau merely straddled its periphery.

The time seemed right for such a step. Leopold Stein, the rabbi of Frankfort, had quarreled with various organizations in his congregation. He had refused to submit to censorship from his board of directors regarding sermons or official business in which he served as the representative of the community before the public authorities. Since a settlement of the dispute seemed impossible, his appointment was considered terminated, and at the end of 1862 Geiger was unanimously elected rabbi of the congregation. Out of consideration for Stein, Geiger was reluctant to accept the call, for Stein had been hopeful that the Frankfort board would yield if all of his colleagues rejected their offer. However, once Geiger had become firmly convinced that a reconciliation between the rabbi and his board was impossible, he agreed to serve, even though the Breslau board immediately indicated its willingness to adjust his salary to that which he had been promised in Frankfort. He gave his final consent on February 7, 1863. He still remained a controversial figure in his former congregation, as was shown by an anonymous lampoon entitled "Dr. Geiger and His Departure from Here for Frankfort-on-the-Main." But the voice of hatred was drowned out by that of respect and affection, and there were many who greatly regretted the departure of this extraordinary man. The congregation he left vied with the one he was about to enter in expressions of sincere admiration and esteem. His salary was to be 4,000 florins (approximately $17-18,000), a sum which, after ten years in office, he would be entitled to receive also as a permanent pension. He was also assured of generous compensation for the expenses involved in making the move from Breslau to Frankfort. Geiger and his children left Breslau early in July and, after several weeks' vacation at the Baltic Sea resort of Kolberg, he assumed his new post in August.

Almost a whole generation had come and gone since Geiger, then a student, had left his native city. The city of his childhood and youth was no longer the same. True, those of his friends and relatives who were still alive were glad to welcome him back. But the festive mood engendered by an occasional visit is one thing, while the everyday routine that soon engulfs the returning native son is quite another. After all, most of his old acquaintances were average people, occupied less with high spiritual interests than with the sober demands of their daily work. True, Frankfort was a cultural center of long standing, but whether the spirit of Judaism as Geiger conceived of it was especially imbedded there could not easily be ascertained. His idea of a Jewish Theological Faculty was still part of him. Yet this dream could not be realized; for the University of Marburg, the one institution which might have incorporated such an institute of Jewish learning into its organization, was never going to move to Frankfort.

Of those closest to him, Salomon, the brother whom he loved and esteemed, was still alive, firmly ensconced in the world of Orthodox tradition. Salomon's son Lazar was an odd phenomenon, by no means rare among Jews; in his personality he harmoniously combined a radicalism of thought that might have led him to the edge of atheism, with the strictest adherence to religious precept. Lazar had great respect for his learned uncle and was in a better position than most to appreciate his achievements. But he would not touch even a morsel of food from the table of the Liberal rabbi. He was a peculiar personality who later was to become widely known for his research into the relationship between language and reason.

When Abraham Geiger returned to Frankfort, he was fifty-three years old. He had reached a stage in life when new friendships are no longer likely to be formed and when, indeed, it is frequently difficult to secure anew even those older relationships that have worn thin after decades of separation. Thus there were only a few of his former associates left to whom he still felt close. He was grateful for the opportunity to move among high-minded and intelligent friends such as Raphael Kirchheim,[30] distinguished for his great Jewish learning; Jacob Auerbach, the head of the Philanthropin School; his old friend Sigismund Stern, and Heinrich Schwarzschild, the erudite physician.

Here there was no militant camp of adversaries to incite his fervor for spirited controversy. By and by, his children left home, either to marry or to attend out-of-town universities. They still maintained close contact with their father, but it was no longer the same as when they had shared his home. His son Ludwig left an account of a letter in which Abraham gave his reaction to his son's decision to abandon the study of Jewish theology, the field he had originally chosen. The father made no attempt to persuade the son to reconsider; he merely tried to understand and was anxious to help his son overcome this spiritual crisis. The religion which the father set forth in this letter was little more than humanism and devotion to things spiritual. It was the father's hope that Ludwig would always remain true to this idealism.

In Frankfort modern congregational organization was well-established. Thus the learned scholar did not have to expend his energies on tasks for which other gifted teachers were available. The advantageous geographic location of the city was fully exploited. Frankfort was a railroad hub, a fact that greatly facilitated contact with friends in transit. This made for an intellectual climate in which Geiger could feel a home. Visitors from Frankfort had never turned up in Breslau, but old friends from eastern Germany would stop in Frankfort on occasion. Jules Oppert, the Orientalist,[31] would often stop over on his way from Paris. M. A. Stern, the mathematician from Goettingen, frequently came, as did the ever faithful Joseph Dernburg.

The agitation of the past decades gradually wore off. Year after year Geiger could now publish consecutive volumes of his journal, with regularity and at a leisurely pace. His interests embraced all the phenomena of Judaism, past and present, viewed, of course, from his personal vantage-point of rational liberalism. This was the criterion which he applied when he found fault with a study of the medieval era for bestowing unjust praise on this "period of darkness," and when, in an essay entitled "The Schools in the Orient," he warned of false romantic enthusiasm for the Holy Land. He gave careful and sympathetic study to the fate of the Jews the world over. He addressed an appeal to the governments of Europe to put an end to the shame of the Rumanian pogroms. Championing the honor of the idea of Judaism, Geiger reprimanded Rudolf Virchow, the great physician and liberal politician, for having declared in the Prussian Parliament that modern Judaism had been influenced by the spirit of Christianity and that the principle of universal brotherly love was basically of Christian origin.

The wealth of tributes published in the pages of Geiger's journal in the 1860s reflect the large number of great Jewish personalities of the time. The honor roll of the deceased lists such names as Simcha Pinsker,[32] N. Mannheimer, Samuel David Luzzatto, Eduard Kley,[33] Salomon Munk, L. Rapoport and Michael Sachs. The living also received their just due. It was truly a "journal of life and letters," through which a scholar, very much alive and alert, sought to exert his influence on others.

Since it had been denied Geiger to mold the minds of academic youth by means of the spoken word, he had to find another type of responsive audience. This was the origin of his lectures on *Das Judentum und seine Geschichte* (Judaism and its History). The first two series were delivered in Frankfort; the third and last one in Berlin. The presentation covered Jewish history down to the end of the 16th century. Actually, these were not formal lectures but informal talks that showed spontaneous inspiration and allowed for direct audience participation in the creative endeavor of the speaker. They were popular and at the same time profound. To Geiger, Jewish history was the development of a spiritual culture in whose genesis creative individuals might have had some share, large or small, but which, in the final analysis, must be viewed as the product of a whole community. It is that idea of religion that at all times has vested Judaism with the right to existence and to a place of importance in the world; it is the same idea which to this very day stands its ground against the claims of Christianity. Precisely because he was a Liberal, Geiger could not acknowledge any rapprochement of his own concept of religion with that of a "broad" Christianity. To him, Judaism was the typical, and indeed the supreme manifestation of religious consciousness. However, he felt that Judaism must renounce for all time the cult of nationalism; it must realize that the whole world is its sphere of action, and it must not wilfully isolate itself from other cultures. It was a misfortune of major proportions that the Judaism of the past, and East-European Jewry even in Geiger's own day, had not appreciated this danger and had been overburdened with rigorous precepts ensuring its isolation from the rest of the world.

The above expresses the typical concept of Jewish Liberalism, especially of the German variety, before the rise of the nationalist movement. Even Graetz, whose romantic nationalism surely was far removed from Geiger's viewpoint, indicated by his derogatory comments on the Yiddish language that he, too, was taking a dim view of the inbred life of the Jewish masses. Geiger, on the other hand, a more sober temperament, succeeded in molding the temper of his liberal contemporaries into a program which is still accepted today by a considerable number of Jews.

Once Judaism is accepted primarily or even exclusively as a religious faith, its relationship to Christianity assumes particular significance. This is what prompted Geiger, when he published his *Jewish History*, to append a number of addenda continuing the discussions between the two faiths. At that time the "problem of Jesus" had been turned into a burning issue by the works of Ernest Renan and David Friedrich Strauss.[34] Both were taken to task by Geiger because they had attempted to tell the story of Jesus without actual knowledge of the Palestinian Judaism of the time; had they had this knowledge, Geiger declared, they would not have condemned that Judaism as the source of all rigidity and intolerance. In an open letter address to Professor H. I. Holzmann of Strassburg, accompanying the second volume of the *Lectures*, Geiger criticized Christian theologians in general for their ignorance of rabbinical sources and for their deliberate slighting of the achievements of modern Jewish scholarship. Holzmann had reviewed the first part of Geiger's *History* in great detail, had condemned it and practically equated Geiger's religious attitude with that of Hegel and Schleiermacher. An ideological indebtedness of that kind would have been less painful to the Christian scholar, who was much more deeply hurt by the rabbi's undisguised criticism of the Christian theological system. Whether and to what extent the critic was correct in presenting Geiger as a disciple of these two German thinkers in particular remains an open question. It was no more than natural that, in attempting to explain their own inherited ideological values in terms of modern philosophy, the Jews of the time might express themselves in terms of the German intellectual spirit.

In the meantime Geiger had resumed his work on medieval Jewish poetry, and in 1867 he published *Solomon Gabirol and His Poems,* an opus based on earlier studies made by Carmoly and Dukes. Translations of selected excerpts, textual corrections and a biography were added to make the book interesting, not only to the scholarly reader but also to the interested layman.

The ordinary duties of his rabbinical office in Frankfort entailed no undue excitement. The sermons Geiger delivered in those days—only a few of these appeared in print—mirror the political turmoil that eventually led to the unification of the German Reich under the Hohenzollern dynasty. Geiger, who had been born in Frankfort but had become a Prussian by naturalization, came out for the Prussian conqueror, and a strikingly large number of other Jews did likewise. It was his hope that this unification would bring a new freedom to his coreligionists. Outspoken pacifism was then a rare phenomenon and there was no distinctly Jewish or non-Jewish attitude on that issue. Generally, people were impressed by Bismarck, and nearly everyone had had enough of the tiny state governments which, despite occasional displays of patriarchal benevolence toward the Jews, held out little hope for finding a long-range solution of the problem that confronted them especially.

In a sermon on the occasion of the fiftieth anniversary of the Battle of Leipzig (October 18, 1863), Geiger extolled the victory of the spirit over armed force. This surely was a far too tolerant opinion of the Germans, which may be explained by Geiger's own adaptation to the general mood and temper of the time, when the liberation phase of the French Revolution had long since been forgotten and Napoleon was remembered only as a conquering despot. The War of 1866 between Prussia and Austria put an end to the political independence of the city of Frankfort. In a sermon delivered during that conflict, Geiger called on his audience to join in the effort to bring about the unification and freedom of the German people, an appeal which indicates his unconcern about the loss of Frankfort's civic sovereignty. It was Geiger's wish to be a German of the Jewish faith, and he wanted to see the spiritual greatness of Judaism respected as part of the cultural life of the German nation. It was for this reason that, in his eulogy of James de Rothschild, he called upon the Rothschild family to finance his project of an academic institution "so that we (Jews) need not gather crumbs from alien tables."

Geiger's "rational alliance" with Prussianism prevented him from sharing the antipathy of the citizens of Frankfort toward the supremacy of Berlin, but he never became a blind advocate of Prussian brutality. His sense of justice was outraged by the many acts of violence committed by the alien occupation army in the former Free City. When, to top it all, Heinrich von Treitschke,[35] the nationalist historian, publicly accused the citizens of Frankfort of improper conduct toward the Prussians, Geiger replied with a belligerent letter. He defended his fellow-citizens and declared all the accusations leveled against them to be idle slander. It was the duty of a man of honor to retract such libelous statements if, even innocently, he had allowed himself to become a tool for their dissemination. Treitschke's Prussian chauvinism, however, was stronger than his desire to see truth prevail; he made no reply to the rabbi, either directly or through the *Prussian Year Books* in which he had originally published his charge.

For more than two decades now, the idea of rabbinical conferences had lain dormant. Much of what the impetuous advocates of years past had proposed or demanded had been realized, not always in the form of a program universally adopted, but more often as the logical result of an orderly process of congregational stock-taking. Thus the twenty-four Liberal rabbis who met in Cassel in the fall of 1866 were able to look back on a history of gradual achievement. The project of a uniform prayer book had begun to take tangible shape, since developments in individual congregations for some time had tended to a definite uniformity in liturgy. Above all, it seemed that the time had come to lay the foundations for closer collaboration between the rabbis and the laity. A synod for this purpose was convened in Leipzig in 1869.

Moritz Lazarus,[36] the philosopher, who enjoyed high regard both within and beyond the Jewish community, served as president; Geiger was vice-president. The influence of the lay element was one of moderation, evidently much more so than Geiger would have liked.

The main issue on the agenda was to promote the spiritual and religious interests of Judaism within the framework of what appeared to be a rapidly unifying commonwealth of German states. What type of *Kulturpolitik* was to be advocated by the Jews? The relationship of the State to the school and to religious instruction presented an important problem. The synod hailed the strictly non-sectarian school which, it seemed, would be more willing than any other to grant equal status to the Jewish minority. Geiger wanted those schools that were open equally to all faiths to include provision for Jewish religious instruction also. He felt that in those schools where no religious education whatsover was given, special arrangements should be made for such training for Jewish students. In this way the needs of Jewish youth would not be prejudiced. The lessons for Jewish students were to include Bible, post-biblical history, religious studies and Hebrew. The discoveries of science in this area must not be ignored, but at the same time they must not be used for purposes of destructive, negative criticism. Geiger and the synod urged, too, that Jewish teachers' colleges be set up to train instructors in both religious and secular subjects. At the same time, Geiger felt it desirable to have Jewish teachers at state teachers' seminaries too, lest the emissaries of Jewish culture be barred from the more comprehensive scope of universal intellectual life. The culmination of the entire conference, once again, was the proposal to establish a Faculty of Jewish Theology at some great German university. Most of these recommendations did not actually materialize. But they are of interest to us today as an expression of what Liberal Jews, rabbis and laymen alike, under the leadership of Geiger, expected of the *Kulturpolitik* of a state which had adopted a policy of complete emancipation for its Jewish subjects. Thus a unified platform had been achieved at least on the most essential issues, and Geiger frankly acknowledged that much of this success had been due to the adeptness and dignity with which Lazarus had led the synod.

Apparently it had been easier to agree on demands to be made of the State than on ways and means for resolving the difficulties arising from within the Jewish community, as was demonstrated at the synod at Augsburg in 1872. The old issues that had been discussed at the rabbinical conferences were brought up once again. In accordance with Geiger's proposal, weddings were to be permitted during the *sefirah* period, and a widow would be free to remarry even before her youngest child had reached the age of two. The testimony of truthworthy female witnesses was to be admissible with regard to the ritual immersion of female converts to Judaism. A lengthy discussion on modifications in the dietary laws failed to yield concrete results. It was decided that the subject matter had not been adequately prepared and that, therefore, it was to be resubmitted, "after more thorough study" to a later synod, for final clarification and decision. This was to be the last assembly of its kind that Geiger was to attend, and it no more satisfied his expectations than any of the previous meetings had done.

When Geiger came to the Augsburg conference, it was in the capacity of rabbi from Berlin. Germany's largest congregation had long wanted to secure his services and after the untimely death of the incumbent, Michael Sachs, in 1864, several influential personalities sought to have Geiger appointed his successor. It took a number of years, however, before actual headway was made in this matter. When Geiger's old friend, Berthold Auerbach, very discreetly began to sound him out on his availability for the post, he obtained a reply that was noncommittal but favorable in principle. H. Makower, the celebrated jurist, was so deeply impressed by one of Geiger's sermons that he applied whatever influence he possessed with the officers of the congregation to bring about the appointment of the rabbi of Frankfort. Others, too, rallied to Geiger's cause, among them men who took leading parts in congregational politics, such as Philipp Wertheim, the secretary of the congregation; A. Horowitz, the noted educator, and H. Bram, the scholar, adept and successful in communal public relations. Great and unusual effort was indeed required to bring about the election of so controversial a personality. The board of directors had long been ready and willing to elect him, but the two-thirds majority of voting members of the Representatives' Assembly of the community, required by statute for the appointment of a rabbi, was not to be forthcoming for several years. There was strong sentiment in favor of the appointment of Manuel Joel, Geiger's successor in Breslau, as representing the forces of peace and conciliation. The influential Makower, however, stood firmly by his candidate and, when new elections for membership representation resulted in a shift to the left, Geiger's appointment was finally confirmed, in the fall of 1869.

He did not find it too great a wrench to leave Frankfort. He had been disappointed in his native city. The pulsating Jewish life in Berlin, on the other hand, promised a widening of the scope of his activities, particularly if a theological institution, as conceived by him and under his actual direction, could be founded there. He delivered his installation sermon on January 22, 1870, and his friend, Berthold Auerbach, wrote him on the impression it had made: "You may well be content, for you have greatly moved everyone present, and you will achieve great things." At that time two main synagogues existed in Berlin side by side, the "Old" and the "New." Although the Orthodox and the Liberals had not yet formed separate communities, the former considered the "Old" synagogue as their house of worship and wanted to keep the dangerous innovator away. They were unable, however, to impose their will upon the board of directors and, in the end, both the preacher and his Orthodox audience were well content with one another. The congregation listened to the words of the gifted and erudite man with great devotion; and Geiger, for his part, knew that the Jewish content of his sermons would be genuinely appreciated there by an intelligent audience. At any rate, untoward incidents such as had been feared by some over-apprehensive elements did not occur.

Geiger worked in close harmony with Joseph Aub, his colleague, and with the officers of the community. This good relationship continued undisturbed even when Geiger made a number of changes in the German prayers and staunchly insisted upon his right to do so independently, when the board claimed that he should have cleared it with them in advance. From this phase of Geiger's work we know more of the great impact of his sermons than of the sermons themselves. His eulogy of J. R. Kosch, the parliamentarian,[37] was universally admired, as was his sermon delivered on September 10, 1871, on the occasion of the bicentennial celebration of the congregation. His dauntless energy in defending the dignity of his people against attacks from without continued undiminished. Thus, when the Church authorities directed their clergy to invoke Divine mercy and enlightenment in their churches upon any of their parishioners who had embraced the Jewish faith, the Jewish community of Berlin duly protested. Geiger himself attacked this directive in a pamphlet entitled "The Attitude of the Church toward Judaism in the Modern Era." Particularly, his displeasure was aroused by the wording of a prayer recited at all churches, admonishing all the faithful servants of the king-emperor to be ever mindful of their oath of allegiance as Christians, and commending the "Christian authorities" to Divine protection. He pointed out that an article in the new German constitution specifically declared the holding of public office as independent of religious affiliation. There no longer was such a thing as "Christian authorities," for, as Geiger pointed out, there were Jewish judges in Prussia now, and a Jew was then Minister of Finance in the Cabinet of Baden. All the Church would accomplish by such measures, Geiger concluded, would be to withdraw into a medieval world, losing all contact with the world of the present day. It was regrettable, of course, that this open-minded spirit was more strongly manifested by the Jews than by the Gentile majority, particularly within the ruling class.

Occasionally, though, the political liberalism of Jewish leaders went further than Geiger might have wished. One such instance involved a bill which had been submitted by Eduard Lasker,[38] a Jewish member of the Prussian Diet; this bill eventually became law. In Prussia, as in most of the other German states, every Jew was then obligated to be a member of the local synagogue community, unless he expressly declared his wish to secede from the Jewish community. This step involved a specified legal procedure. If a Jew made a declaration to this effect, it was considered not simply a resignation from synagogue membership, but an act of separation from the Jewish religious community as such. Lasker's proposal was to permit Jews to resign from synagogue membership without the automatic inference of secession from Judaism as a whole. This proposal opened the door for the formation of all kinds of splinter groups, and thus for the undermining of the principle of unity in congregational organization which Geiger had always championed as the most constructive and effective way for Jewish communal living. The experiences which Geiger had had in his younger days in the district of Wiesbaden tended only to deepen his concern lest this innovation lead to a serious weakening, or even the disintegration, of many smaller congregations. As a matter of fact, the measure provided a pretext for the establishment of separatist Orthodox communities, a development which Geiger deplored, as did many others who were by no means radicals themselves. He prepared a thesis against Lasker's proposal, but refrained from publishing it on the advice of cautious communal leaders who felt that these polemics against Lasker might be harmful. According to Geiger's son, Ludwig, this controversial treatise was quite acrimonious.

Herein lay the drawback of Geiger's fighting Liberalism. His attitude was occasionally reminiscent of the militant manner in which the Jewish "enlighteners" of the beginning of that century had sought to force their "less progressive" brethren onto the road they felt led to salvation. Throughout his life, Geiger was a partisan fighter, fully convinced that his principles alone had a monopoly on the truth and would win out in the end. He believed that he had succeeded in leading Judaism to the very height of awareness of the contemporary spirit. When Lasker, in one of his speeches, mentioned the "spiritual punitive and disciplinary measures" that were supposedly still in use in Jewish communities, the rabbis of Berlin made a formal declaration that such proscriptions had long been abolished and that the Jewish religion in its present stage of development rejected all means of force or coercion. In order to lend additional weight to this pronouncement, Geiger called on the officers of the congregation to endorse it publicly. But the community leaders did not wish to take a stand against Lasker in this controversy.

Geiger felt that the state should guarantee the equal status of the Jewish faith as such, and not merely the equal civic rights of Jews as individuals. When in 1873 a Prussian ecclesiastical law was passed that set forth the qualifications for office of the Christian clergy but failed to set similar standards for rabbis, Geiger opposed this omission. In letters to Lasker and to a liberal Christian member of the Diet, he protested against the inconsistency of the state which, while it took full advantage of the services of Jewish religious functionaries, had seen fit to ignore them in its new law. At the same time, however, he shared the anticlerical attitude, in the realm of *Kulturpolitik,* of the German liberal element of the time. In his address on the occasion of his installation on the Jewish school board, he emphasized the link between a pure spirit and religious faith, but rejected the concept of a specifically Jewish school. He did not want to inject himself as a rabbi into the regular course of secular education. Those Jewish schools that were already in existence Geiger accepted solely on the premise that they would make every endeavor to bring Jewish studies closer to the enlightened humanities. He obviously wanted no part of that type of ecclesiastical school supervision which was still to be firmly entrenched in Germany for another half-century.

His private life was uneventful, and Geiger had only a few close friends. But Steinschneider and Zunz, whom he revered, both lived in Berlin, and Berthold Auerbach came every winter. His more intimate circle consisted of Philipp Wertheim and Makower, who had prepared his path to Berlin, L. Goldbaum, his physician, and Joseph Aub, his colleague. The Franco-Prussian War of 1871 brought forth a mighty wave of patriotism on the part of Jews and Gentiles alike. Geiger, as a Jew and as a man of liberal and broad humanitarian views, was an advocate of peace; yet, together with nearly all of his coreligionists, he regarded it the duty of every good German to put up a spirited defense against the French attackers. Although his exuberant enthusiasm diminished markedly after the fall of Napoleon III at Sedan, his faith in the righteousness of Germany's cause in this war remained unshaken, and he regarded the immediate outcome of the war, the founding of a new German Reich, as an achievement that had been worth every sacrifice.

At this turning point in European history, personal experiences led Geiger once again to evaluate the relationship between German nationalism and Judaism. Revealing of his views on this subject is some interesting correspondence between him and his old friend Joseph Dernburg. Dernburg, who now had resided in Paris for the span of a generation, had thoroughly assimilated both French thought and feeling; to put it more accurately, he had turned "European." When mail service was resumed after the termination of hostilities he expressed in a letter to Geiger his indignation over the conduct of the German occupation troops in France. He feared that German militarism triumphant would degenerate into chauvinism of the worst order. He felt that this change would result in new outbreaks of antisemitism in Germany itself, and that the Jews of Germany might now have to go through experiences similar to those their fathers suffered in 1813, after the overthrow of the original Napoleon.

Geiger's reply was so acrimonious as to be insulting. In his evaluation of Napoleon III he shared the opinion of the average German who viewed the French emperor simply as an adventurer, out for the spoils of battle. But more than that, he compared the active and vigorous intellectual life of German Jewry with the barrenness of its French counterpart. He did not deny that in his own country traces still remained of a medieval approach to the Jewish problem; but such minor imperfections did not lessen his joy in the total picture as he saw it in his Fatherland. His letter concluded with these words: "Over and above everything else, I am a human being; it is only second to that, or in constant relation to it, that I am a German and then a Jew." All this sounds very cosmopolitan; and, as a matter of fact, the Jews in the German empire, more than those of any other nation, were indeed of a cosmopolitan turn of mind. Dernburg's prediction, on the whole, turned out to be correct. But Geiger had not erred when he extolled German thought as fertile soil for Jewish cultural and intellectual development. This correspondence and then its publication on Geiger's initiative seriously strained the bond between the two old friends, and it took considerable time for their intimate friendship to be re-established.

Geiger's journal remained the fortress from which he

was able to observe the trends in Judaism of his day and to endeavor to influence them. He felt the lethargy that now became manifest in life in general. The rising economic prosperity of the young Reich in which the Jews had a full share was not conducive to spiritual or religious activity. In an article, "Disintegration," in volume IX, Geiger deplored the fact that the age was strong in its ability to criticize, but less vigorous in the sphere of reconstruction and reform. This was true not only of the great and powerful religions of Christianity and Islam, but also of Judaism. For a century now, Judaism had been part of the general process of disintegration, and its soil was still so hardened from the long period of petrification that it was not yet receptive to new seed. These sentiments, however, were merely the outgrowths of temporary moods and could not shake his optimistic conviction that an awareness of history, coupled with vital energy, would eventually lead to regeneration. He remained certain that, once theoretical knowledge of history enabled Jewish scholars to trace the clear line of development that Judaism had followed from the days of the Bible onward, practice would of itself find the proper basis for well-directed leadership.

On occasion, Geiger was carried away by his faith in the power of ideas. It is interesting in this respect to note his criticism of the Alliance Israélite Universelle ("Spirit or Money?"—two articles in volume X). Little was gained, he said here, by appeals to foreign powers and by the raising of funds for the fight against antisemitic movements. According to Geiger, there was only one effective weapon for combatting the barbaric treatment to which Jews were still subjected in some of the nations of the world, and that was the fight against ignorance, religious fanaticism and obscurantism. Much the same thought was expressed in the last of his essays ("Dichotomy of Thought, Struggle for Power") which appeared in volume XI. In this essay Geiger, the progressive, claimed that the state, by its support of ecclesiastical fortresses (meaning, of course, the Churches) was inhibiting freedom and the idealistic tendency in man. If this support were to cease, the striving after higher ideals would be assured of victory, and a genuine religious spiritual life, propelled forward by inner knowledge and perception, would triumph. Actually, the victory of science and learning had already been won, even though thus far its fruits had not as yet been reaped.

Such, too, were the tenor and sentiments of the faith which Germans in general had in progress during the era of liberalism. The battle against Orthodoxy in his own camp gradually came to be fought on the broader front of general political liberalism. The cause of progress had become Geiger's own, not merely because he felt that its victory would bring about full civic and social equality for the Jewish people, but because that spirit, to him, had become the very basis of his personal religion. For to Geiger, religion was truth as sifted from the continuous flow of evolution by an advanced process of science and learning.

Therefore he waged a lifelong fight in behalf of a Jewish Institute of Research, a struggle which now appeared to be crowned with success just a few years before his death. Geiger had left Frankfort only because he had received the assurance that such an institution would be founded in Berlin and that he would be given a function in it that would be commensurate with his abilities. For a number of years distinguished personalities such as Moritz Lazarus, Moritz Veidt and Salomon Neumann[39] had laid the groundwork for the execution of such a project in Berlin. The project was already close to actual realization when a generous donation from City Councillor Meyer removed the financial obstacles as well. The decision to found the institution was made in December 1869. Geiger was not altogether in agreement with the idea that major courses should be taught by men of differing ideologies, but he was wholeheartedly willing and ready to cooperate in this venture. Soon after his arrival in Berlin, he was asked to submit a proposed course of studies. His proposal, following the pattern of the state universities, provided for a division of the academic work into lectures and seminars. For biblical studies he required that attention be given not only to critical research but also to the significance which the Scriptures had acquired for the development of Halakhah and Haggadah. Nor were Talmud and Rabbinics to be neglected. He emphasized that preliminary philological studies should not be limited to the Hebrew language. The study of philosophy and ethics, of the theory of religion and of the abiding values of Judaism he considered important tasks of the institute. It was not to confine itself merely to the theoretical study of philology, history and archeology, but to apply all that knowledge to practical living. He wanted this academy to be known as a Faculty of Jewish Theology, thus conveying both the claim and the commitment that the institute would be on a üniversiy level, promoting the knowledge of Judaism in relation to broader comprehensive science and learning.

The fact that the institution had no other funds but those derived from private donors he viewed as a shortcoming—a makeshift, temporary arrangement. He would have preferred the State to subsidize the school. But since this could not be, he had to content himself with stressing repeatedly the necessity for making adequate provisions to ensure complete academic freedom for professors and students alike. The institution, not beholden to any one party or dogma, dedicated solely to the goal of pure and unbiased insight and to the advancement of learning and scholarship, was to stand surety for the development of a pure religious outlook.

The War of 1870-71 necessitated the postponement of the formal opening of the academy by one year. In the fall of 1871, Geiger was appointed Professor of Jewish History and Literature. At the dedication ceremony, held on May 6, 1872, his address, on the significance of the "Science of Judaism" and on the important place of a college devoted to its pursuit, was the feature of main interest. It was a matter of deep gratification to Geiger—although, unfortunately, a short-lived joy—that he had lived to see his lifelong dream fulfilled at least in part. He himself certainly stood in no need of the express obligation, as provided in Article 21 of the Statutes, that the lectures were to be carried on "with the sole aim of preserving the Science of Judaism, and of fostering its progress and dissemination." After all, it was for this very ideal that he had fought most of his life. With somewhat naive pleasure he liked to compare himself to a university professor. Indeed, he would have been an asset to any famed institution of higher learning. With his freedom from prejudice, and with the keenness, depth and scope of his research, he would have been a glorious example of a dedicated member of a true *universitas literarum*. In his lectures, of course, he could draw on the vast fund of knowledge that he had amassed over decades of study. But what he had to offer now, in his *Allgemeine Einleitung in die Wissenschaft des Judentums* (General Introduction to the Science of Judaism), did not merely represent the best of what he himself had conceived and formulated; it showed, at the same time, the gigantic progress that the Jewish spirit had made during half a century of self-clarification. His introductions to various books of the Bible—a subject which most Jewish scholars had sought to avoid—bears further testimony to the independence of Geiger's own stand from the studies of the Old Testament conducted by Protestant theologians with which he was thoroughly familiar. His commentary to the Ethics of the Fathers was an exploration of territory that had been well-known to him from his earliest youth.

He hardly ever gave more than five or six lecture hours per week. Yet, much time went into their preparation, though he never actually "read" from notes but spoke to his students extemporaneously. Measured in terms of the number of students and faculty members, the "academy" was still a small one. But Geiger counted many a promising scholar among his personal disciples. Personalities such as Felix Adler, the founder of the Society for Ethical Culture, Emil G. Hirsch and Immanuel Loew[40] did not fail their master.

This combination of academic teaching and practical rabbinical activity afforded to Geiger what was possibly the deepest satisfaction of his life. In the best of health, and filled with energy and vitality, he might well have believed himself to be standing on the threshold of a new beginning. Actually, he was to live only another two years and a half, to teach only for another five academic semesters. But he was fortunate enough to enjoy the blessings of full vigor and activity to his very last hour. On the day that was to be his last, he worked without rest until the evening. He was to have resumed his lectures on October 26, 1874, after the summer vacation. He had completed the labors of the High Holy Day sermons. During that year he had already officiated at sixty wedding ceremonies. October 22 was still crowded with activities. On the morning of October 23 he was found dead in his bed. Without warning, a cerebral hemorrhage had struck, and put a quick end to his life.

Geiger was a man of unusual vitality, helped in his work by strict self-discipline and a well-ordered way of life. He would rise at seven o'clock each morning and go to bed at ten each night without fail. At five in the afternoon, after a consultation hour in his office, he would go out for a walk. His work alone made up the world in which he lived. He was no ivory tower scholar, however, but continuously exposed himself to impressions of the most varied aspects of this world, through the medium of literature that was by no means limited to his own field of scholarship. He favored lucid, even sober expressions also in the realm of religion and had no great liking for outbursts of emotion or for groping in the twilight. Like most of the Jewish scholars of his day, he was not inclined by personal temperament to appreciate the element of mysticism in faith, nor would he even make the attempt to understand any form of religion built on mystical contemplation. His lively temper would on occasion prompt him to passionate aggressiveness and would at times cast a shadow on his relations with his friends. Although he knew his own mind and was unwavering in the pursuit of his higher goals, he found it difficult to make quick decisions. His task as a practical reformer frequently compelled him, who had been raised in a completely Orthodox environment, to disregard whatever personal, spontaneously emotional attitude he might have had toward the ancient heritage of tradition in which he had been reared. But his personal sympathies for even those of entirely different persuasion remained strong throughout, as shown particularly by his relationship with his older brother Salomon. Ever vibrant, spirited and witty, he was exceedingly fond of stimulating conversation with younger men and with his students. The sympathetic spiritual advisor who never failed anyone in need of counsel or practical aid was in no way submerged by his intellectual and scholarly personality.

All these personal characteristics, however, still do not make him unique in the more recent history of Judaism. What distinguished him from many another was that he, more than anyone else, succeeded in carrying out a program that had been the vision of many an intellectual leader of the early Emancipation movement, namely, to base Jewish and religious life on the clear, unbiased knowledge and understanding of indigenous history, and thus, through the medium of learning and knowledge, to liberate Jewish life and Judaism for a rejuvenated present and future. Geiger was probably the only one among these leaders who succeeded in achieving so much both in theory and practice, and who had truly attempted to bring about a genuinely close interrelation between these two spheres. He thought of himself as a theologian. Unlike that of Zunz and members of the *Kulturverein*, Geiger's concept of the "Science of Judaism" was confined strictly to the idea of religion and its development. And since, to him, the zenith of religion was a universalistic faith, he was interested in the strictly nationalistic elements of Judaism only insofar as they appeared to him to lead to the broader goal of a purer humanism.

Yet, neither personal inclination nor transitory ideological movements ever obscured Geiger's rational, scientific outlook. Of course his *Urschrift,* his theory on the Pharisees and the Sadducees, which had been viewed as epochmaking in his own day and even long thereafter and which in some respects is of interest even today, is, on the whole, outdated. Many a hypothesis, such as the one suggesting that the Karaites had been the "physical and spiritual descendants" of the Sadducees, must have been untenable from the very beginning. But even in such instances— where later insights, derived from newer discoveries, were no longer in harmony with his theories—his original suggestions had proven fruitful and valuable. He knew how to bring to life the history and literature of times long past, for they were both still very real and vivid in his own mind. When he probes into the controversy over the writings of Maimonides, when he studies Isaac ben Abraham of Troki, the Karaite, and his apologetics, or attempts to trace the "modern" approach of such "spirits of enlightenment" as Joseph Solomon del Medigo and Leon da Modena, his partiality for "kindred" ideas and their protagonists becomes distinctly apparent. Geiger was attracted by the aesthetic appeal of medieval Jewish poetry and by the lucid thought of the exegetic school of northern France. Yet neither affection nor sympathy could lead him to deviate even one hair's breath from the path of sober, conscientious research. The goals and ideas of the reformer never interfered with the balanced judgment of the historian.

Geiger considered the history of the Jewish people as a nation to have come to an end for all time. To Geiger, as to most of the other spokesmen of Western Jewry of his day, the future of Judaism was anchored exclusively in its religious content. The liberal optimism which he shared with many a contemporary made him certain that the messianic ideal of universal justice, which he felt to be the backbone of Jewish religious faith, could most effectively be advanced through the dissemination of truth. For this reason, true scholarship and learning in any field—and certainly neither last nor least the "Science of Judaism"

—represented to him a lofty religious value in itself. Even his cosmopolitan outlook was deeply rooted in the soil of Judaism, more deeply, probably, than he himself knew. He was known frequently to have taken exception to the use of the Hebrew language by modern Jewish scholars. Nevertheless, he enriched scholarship by learned treatises which proved his own mastery and skill in that idiom. To him, Judaism was a religion "only," yet he often praised this religion as being the outgrowth of the native strength of what had been a distinct national entity, revealing an earthy and healthy definiteness, in contrast to Christianity, which seemed to Geiger colorless and vague.

This may be the reason why, despite all his independence and liberalism of mind and intellect, Geiger, the innovator, never really developed into a radical reformer. He held Samuel Holdheim, the leader of the Reform movement of Berlin, in high esteem. Indeed, both Holdheim, with his many practical achievements, and the great American Reform movement could claim to be the heirs of Geiger's attitude toward Judaism. Geiger's direct influence, and even more so his indirect influence, on men like David Einhorn, Kaufmann Kohler and, for that matter, on the entire Reform ideology, especially in America, is unmistakable. We would be inclined to ascribe this, not so much to Geiger's personality as an individual, but rather to the fact that he was the most articulate exponent and leader of an intellectual school which, from the beginning of the 19th century, had sought to bring about a religious renaissance of German Jewry. There can be no doubt that to him, the theologian and thinker, the logical inferences drawn by the radical faction were by no means uncongenial; but as theoretical conclusions only, rather than as part of a program to be put into practice immediately. He lived in German lands with an ancient heritage of tradition which extended not merely to religion as such, but also—and not only on the surface but much more profoundly than it might have appeared—to Jewish life as a whole: to the group, to the religious community and to its basic makeup. It is true that, in youthful fervor, or perhaps despair, he had toyed with the idea of schism. Yet he rejected this solution because he considered himself the educator and pathfinder of the *K'lal Yisrael*, of the Jewish community in its entirety. He found himself unable to sympathize with the historical middle-of-the-road movement that rallied around Zacharias Frankel and Heinrich Graetz; the practical aspirations of these leaders, if they could be clearly defined at all, seemed to him hardly distinguishable from "cultured" Orthodoxy. There was nothing left for him except, within the sphere of Reform, to follow that path of moderation which he had taken. He was a "liberal" in that undogmatic sense that would no more have permitted the rearing of an insurmountable barrier against the left than the Historical Movement of Breslau would have been able to close itself off from the right wing. Geiger was a liberal of the 19th century, with all the greatness but also with all the limitations that characterized this ideology. A mighty searcher, bent only on the discovery of the truth, he lent a new interpretation, determined by his own personality, to the saying that "an ignoramus cannot be pious." Yet, like many thinkers who are also active leaders of men and are compelled to be so by their temperaments, Geiger was easily inclined to underestimate the pyschological difficulties involved in the attainment of his goals. Herein lies the shadow that accompanies the clear and penetrating rays of Liberalism. Yet even this limitation cannot alter the judgment of history that all of Judaism became the brighter for the light which shone from the personality of Abraham Geiger.

2

letters

TO

JOSEPH NAFTALI DERNBURG
from Allgemeine Zeitung des Judentums

VARIOUS CORRESPONDENTS
from Nachgelassene Schriften

LEOPOLD ZUNZ
Reminiscences of Days Gone By
from Nachgelassene Schriften

letters to joseph naftali bernburg

Wiesbaden, September 30, 1833

I believe that Judaism at present is in the same diseased state as that which befalls any group that has long been secluded and inaccessible to the influence of general progress. This is especially true in the case of Judaism if we consider that what the Jewish ecclesiastical establishment has sought to preserve throughout was a totally alien religious system, imported entirely from foreign lands. . . . Even thinking Jews, who seek to derive meaning for their lives by delving into the religious element of Judaism cannot point to any idea that would permeate it and give it life. Thus, in any case, they admit that their religion as it is now practiced is little more than mere hypocrisy. The question now is whether the nature of today's Judaism really will prove strong enough to survive a revolution. . . . Where there is not enough healthy and enduring strength to withstand painful surgery successfully, the organism will perish and its individual components will return to whence they had originally been taken and will be used in the formation of other organisms. Furthermore Judaism, as a minority religion, must have far more vigorous content, for any seclusion, even if it be merely in matters of religion, must be based on a sound reason of its own to prompt one . . . to turn aside from the majority. The Christian, to cite just one example, need not pose questions to himself about his faith. Even if his religion were to be bad he could manage to remain completely unaffected by it, for his life is that of an individual within a State where it so happens that all the individuals are Christians. Not so the Jew. The Jew must always have something peculiarly Jewish about him since only his love for Judaism will keep him from becoming part of the multitude. It is precisely because he deviates from the majority that he must find a more solid basis for his faith which is his conviction. If he should fail to do so, or if he should prove unable to do so, then by this failure he demonstrates that his faith is only a morbid remnant of former times, whose disintegration is only being delayed. I have never considered it my purpose to lead toward Judaism . . . but rather toward humanity in general . . . and to have Judaism permeated at all times by humanity's concepts. Later, let things go as they may, but I will know that I have brought closer that day when God will be One and His Name One.

AZ, VIII, NO. 9, PP. 103 FF.

Wiesbaden, February 23, 1836

. . . For some time now, my dear friend, I have had a Judaism that satisfies me, a faith founded on the trust in One who guides the Universe and on the task imposed upon us to practice justice and mercy, a faith that becomes manifest in acts that fulfill this demand and that is clothed in uplifting ritual forms designed to awaken such sentiments. In my opinion, this is surely the spirit of Judaism, which, however, does not shine forth with sufficient clarity from the Bible, at least not from the Pentateuch. For just because in so vigorous a faith so much emphasis had to be placed on acts as outgrowths of these sentiments and on ritual form as means of translating them into living reality, the act lingered on as a commandment even after—due to changed circumstances—the spirit originally behind it had departed. This fossilization, in turn, effected a distortion of the spirit itself.

Such is the entire history of Judaism which came into this world with the naïveté of antiquity but at the same time with a strength of conviction which preserved it from effeteness and excesses of fantasy. But it may have been precisely because of these qualities that it fell easy prey to sober hyper-rationalizations which then, of course, would on occasion be embraced by the *individual* with all the fervor of irrational emotion. It is that pristine spirit which I would like to see revived, as opposed not only to ossified Judaism but also to any other spirit based on false foundations. I should like to revive this spirit myself. I would uproot the belief in empty forms; I would make no concessions to the false spirit, which I would fight, if not overtly, then at least by indirect methods. But, alas! at such times I realize not only my own weakness which lacks the warmth to utter my convictions in such a way as to convince others, but also my lack of such insight as would lead others to understanding. I sense, too, that narrow confinement in which I find myself and which inhibits my every step; and, of course, many a time I feel that lack of interest which every feeble attempt of mine encounters. So you see, my dear friend, I am not so completely content after all . . .

AZ, IX, NO. 10, P. 115.

Wiesbaden, June 19, 1836

. . . Here, on the Sabbath before Shavuot, with a good deal of commotion, we have done away with the *Av ha-Rahamim*. This was done by a formal resolution of the board which was announced just prior to the opening of the Ark and by a sermon of the rabbi which had the effect of a bombshell. Yet, if indeed we should be deserving of an *Av ha-Rahamim,* I hope that He is still mine, too. Ah, if only I could become utterly enrapt, with mysticism rich and deep, in the idea of a Merciful Father in Heaven, if only I could revel in it and so find peace and comfort! Yet, be calm, young man, and fight—but what for? Well, I suppose, just to let my restlessness run its course and, I might almost say, to indulge some humanitarian caprice. Let me tell you, my dear fellow, if some new era does not give birth to new convictions, things will soon come to a pretty pass. . . . Everything totters and breaks under the slightest touch of our hands, and as much as possible must be cleared away if something new is to spring up. . . . There is hardly any time left for a reformation; the only course possible now is revolution—and God grant that something new may then come forth. I am sure this will indeed grow out even of our own pain and yearning . . .

Here I am, gnawing and chewing like a dog at his bone, at the improvement of Judaism and of the Jews . . . and in the end, nothing ever comes of it. Oh, I know that I am a building-brick in the edifice, and I am quite content to be one. But I want to be that only after I am dead; what, then, is my place while I am still alive? I am afraid I must decline the honor of struggling and floundering until such time as I will be crushed into the wall, into that tiny spot in the edifice of world history where I am to have my place.

AZ, XII, NO. 12, PP. 140 FF.

Wiesbaden, November 8, 1836 (at night)

. . . Alas, we still cleave so horribly fast to the exterior works, and when the blow that will strike the religious world falls . . . we shall have to fling ourselves into the arms of the new era without having had any significant part in bringing it about. . . . There is one basic thought: *the establishment of proof, just like anything else that exists, is something that has come to be and has no binding force.* Every single piece of research, even if it should amount merely to a scholarly trifle, has worth and retains that worth. . . . But all this does not set the course for us to follow; it is just material, and who knows what its use will be, or whether we, or anyone else, will use it or will be able to put it to use? But the course to be taken, my dear fellow, is that of critical study; the critical study of individual laws, the critical examination of individual documents—this is what we must strive for. The Talmud, and the Bible, too, that collection of books, most of them so splendid and uplifting, perhaps the most exalting of all literature of *human* authorship, can no longer be viewed as of Divine origin. Of course, all this will not come to pass today, or even tomorrow, but it should be our goal, and will continue to be so, and in this fashion we are working closely with every true endeavor and movement of our day, and we will accomplish more by study than we could by means of a hundred sermons and widespread religious instruction. For the love of Heaven, how much longer can we continue this deceit, to expound the stories of the Bible from the pulpits over and over again as actual historical happenings, to accept as supernatural events of world import stories which we ourselves have relegated to the realm of legend, and to derive teachings from them or, at least, to use them as the basis for sermons and texts? How much longer will we continue to pervert the spirit of the child with these tales that distort the natural good sense of tender youth? But how can this be changed? By driving such falsehoods into a corner, of course; by clearly revealing this paradox both to ourselves and to others; by pursuing into their secret hiding places all those who could seek to evade the issue, and thus eventually helping to bring about the great cave-in which will bury an old world beneath its ruins and open a new world for us in its place . . .

AZ, XVIII, NO. 14, P. 164 F.

Breslau, August 3, 1840

. . . Munk will make other scientific discoveries on his journey,[1] and these will be its most important result. For, on the whole, that journey appears to me entirely without purpose, in an almost quixotic sense. The fact that French and English Jews should demonstrate their sense of Jewishness in this manner is not surprising to me, but it seems strange that a Jew whose outlook has been formed by true German-Jewish education should join with them. I still find it difficult to accept the idea that such acts should indeed spring from a genuine understanding of the true interests of Jewry and Judaism. Much rather, they seem to me to stem from that purely traditional, half national and half ordinary context of that wholly abstract concept of "being a Jew," without any deeper permeation with the content of Judaism. Public opinion in the civilized countries where Jews reside will be affected not at all or only very slightly indeed by such accusations emanating from either Orient or Occident; only a few newspaper articles, and the whole matter will be dismissed without leaving a trace on actual life. Hence the issue is not so much a Jewish one, since it is those nations who guide the affairs of the world who set the fashion in this instance too. . . .

We can term as "of universal Jewish concern" only whatever goes on among those Jews who comprise the upper stratum of Jewry; i.e., once again, those Jews who reside among the civilized nations, particularly in Germany, and who later will be emulated and followed by those who now are still among the uneducated. That which goes on among the Jews living in the uncivilized countries, on the other hand, is of trifling importance only, even if it were to be of general import in those particular lands. But it is not even that; this is not a case of generalized *tzarah* (distress or persecution) in the medieval sense of the word. It is simply one single arbitrary act which did not in any way affect the position of the Jews in Egypt. And as for the Jews who were murdered, no one will be able to bring *them* back to life. Of course it is a fine humanitarian deed to take up the cause of individuals who are victims of oppression; but it is not a specifically Jewish problem, and if we make it so, we distort the outlook and confuse the gradually developing good sense of the Jews. There is no doubt, of course, that Ratti-Menton, the French consul, is a scoundrel, and this is just another confirmation of what experience has taught us in the past, namely, that European Levantines are worse than the real Orientals, even as most of the merely superficially cultured, when they deal with the totally uncultured, prove to be on a lower level by far than the latter.

But of what avail is it to close our minds? The only way to salvation for the Orient would be if all the countries in it were to be broken up and dismembered; and for the Jews there is no other way except that they elevate themselves to the highest level of culture, not merely as individuals but also as members of Judaism; in other words, that Judaism should take on life, intellectually speaking. Of what avail, for either of these goals, is such a Jewish pilgrimage? Certainly, for Montefiore, who takes along a personal *shohet* wherever he goes, and whose servants wear livery with buttons carrying the legend "Jerusalem," such a move is quite in order. And it is natural, too, for Crémieux, who has only a smattering of and a sporadic interest in the civil affairs of the Jews, a man who, as vice-president of the Consistory, deems himself attorney and counsel for the Jews; who, being a lawyer, likes this kind of thing to begin with, and who, Frenchman that he is, enjoys sounding the call of alarm. But for Munk? Well, with him it is in all likelihood a case of somewhat fuzzy enthusiasm mixed with a yearning to see the Orient . . . The only thing which I hope will come of this is that Munk will bring with him a few manuscripts, hitherto unknown . . .

AZ, XVIII, NO. 22, PP. 258 FF.

Breslau, November 22, 1840

. . . And now, my dear friend, as regards Judaism's great strides forward, I am greatly dejected once again, and I do not even know whether it is possible to breathe new life into these historical ruins. The only thing alive is the rubble, which should be cleared away, and historical tenacity, which will gradually wear off more and more by itself. But living inner progress, that is, progress to an extent that would be adequate, is nonexistent, and therefore Judaism, as it is now constituted and sanctioned, will look more and more antiquated as time goes by. . . . Of what avail, then, are all our petty reforms? . . . What good is a program of religious instruction in which the teacher does not believe in what he teaches and in which the student is not supposed to believe what he is taught—a program which only passes in silence over that which should be articulately fought? I must admit that at times I totally despair of this situation. Our significance in the history of the world is a thing of the past and we are merely lagging behind. But that which is no longer a moving force in the world has lost the right to exist, and this makes itself increasingly felt in life in all its disintegrating force. . . . I therefore feel that even schism, the whole means of salvation, recedes from possibility, and hence all I can see is a slow languishing that spreads from the heart of culture outward to the extremities. . . . It is true, of course, that nature resists disintegration and thus there is a fresh impetus, a renewed spurt of energy—and I hope you will not take it amiss if I consider myself a product of this effort—but this, too, will collapse, leaving only even greater disorder for the group as a whole. What sort of heritage has the era of Mendelssohn left to Judaism? It was highly beneficial for the individual, but at the same time it has shaken the foundations of the whole without replacing it with something new and vigorous. What has been the result of the institution of temples? Sermons, good and bad; the former edify the individual, and stimulate much talk of and about Judaism . . . but they fail to reconstruct the total religious ideology and the sanctioned religious practice that is derived from it.

. . . There is no point now in discussing the Damascus Affair in detail once again. . . . I merely wish to repeat that, while it is very honorable of these gentlemen to take up the cause of the persecuted and the oppressed, it is not and has never been a specifically Jewish question. . . . I would consider even the establishment of Jewish schools in Syria a much more meritorious goal. . . . The worst thing, however, about such a type of enthusiasm is that it is being wasted on unsuccessful ventures, therefore also evaporates very quickly and cannot even be revived for sound purposes. This is the other side of the coin in an incident such as this, and it saddens me. That Jews in Prussia may have the chance to become pharmacists or lawyers is much more important to me than the rescue of all the Jews in Asia and Africa, an undertaking with which I sympathize as a human being. You may think differently on this subject, but I ask you to believe me that this is my honest conviction, intimately interwoven with the entire structure of my intellectual view of things . . .

AZ, XIX, NO. 24, PP. 282 FF.

Breslau, July 20, 1841

. . . You will understand, my dear friend, that the discontent of which I speak here is not material in nature. On the contrary, I am happy in my domestic life and well-content with my official position. But the more vigorous and gifted type of man must have something more. He must know what place he occupies in the sum total scheme of genuine human endeavor. A more profound spirit who seeks to immerse himself into the work of the intellect and into the sum total of human effort, and who seeks to find the focal point common to all struggle and aspiration, will find the true joy of living only once he has discovered that point, when he has embraced it with trusting faith, and when his every step is motivated by it. It is precisely for this reason that all my labors appear to me isolated and disjointed; it is because that one point in which all the separate aspects would find their profound cause and unity, from which they would all radiate individually, eludes me. My work, both scholarly and practical, centers in the effort to produce a Judaism that would be alive, truly spiritual, and satisfying and nourishing to both mind and soul. If only I had faith that it will indeed be possible to attain this goal, even if this should come to pass in its entirety only at some time in the distant future, when I shall be long forgotten . . . what bliss would

I then derive from any study of Semitic languages, from every historical and bibliographical study in the field of Judaism, from every Jewish endeavor and from my practical efforts. I would see them all as leading to the same goal, as so many different points of departure, all for reaching the same unclouded peak. I may regard it as a virtue that I have a comprehensive knowledge of my field and that I know how to accept and to shape it with vigor in all its ramifications. I have a fairly extensive knowledge of the linguistic, the historical, the dogmatic and philosophical ramifications, particularly of the history of our civilization and culture, and also of the strictly practical aspects of my field, and I am capable of some achievement in each. I am not one-sided, engaged in only one part to the exclusion of all others, and hence I probably do not excel in any one of them, But it may well be that my very strength lies in the fact that I can comprehend the part in its relationship to the whole and thus know how to approach it from its recognized, innermost essence. On the other hand, of course, it is this very attitude that defeats my strength as soon as it appears to me that this inmost essence has been exhausted. Then my work appears to me to be nothing but merely scholarly, the knowledge and representation of something that once lived but has since died, or, what is worse, a futile desire to effect improvements in certain given conditions of life which are basically incurable.

This, then, is what distresses me—the fact that I do not have the faith that a truly living force, penetrating the mind and ruling it, may yet well up from Judaism. And thus any concerted effort on behalf of Judaism would be outside the mainstream of life and, at best, succeed only in leading its present adherents toward this mainstream. Then, once they are in that mainstream, sucked in by its swift current, they would withdraw from Judaism altogether, actually, or at least in sentiment, as from something that has no ultimate bearing on this process. ... Any subordinate position would give me the keenest pleasure so long as it is within the main current of our age. On the other hand, even high office will only give me a sense of resignation if it is merely remotely channeled into that current but actually remains outside it. It would give me a feeling that all my life, in a sense, has been . . . in vain. Thus far I have not yet come to feel this resignation, nor would I wish to have to do so. You know that it is not praise from my contemporaries, or fame in posterity that I covet, . . . for, as it is, my name has far greater fame than I deserve. All I want is merely that gladsome inner conviction—and then I care not whether the fight flares up against me or whether my name remains entirely unknown to the generations that follow—the conviction that "I know that my Redeemer liveth." For then I would know, or at least I would think that I knew, that the idea to which I have dedicated my life is coming closer and closer to realization, and that I will thus assume a worthy position in the eyes of posterity—and I care not even if that position be quite lowly. I would know then that what I have attempted to build will not be engulfed by the waves of history, but that it will live on as a small contribution to the edifice of that which is eternal.

There you have a frank confession of my views, and I know that you can now clearly read what is in my soul. It may be, of course, that you will ask me why, actually, I should have lost my faith in Judaism, and whether this despair of a vigorous future for Judaism does not spring from subjective hypochondria rather than from objective insight? The answer to this question would lead me too far afield; therefore I will be brief here: With all its basic truth concerning the Unity of God and with all its noble ethical components, Judaism, partly due to nationalistic limitations and partly due to too great a stress on the ceremonial, has never been able to unfold a full religious life or to place itself upon the summit of religious perception. One might say that Judaism has great dormant treasures which must be held up by another hand, if its wealth is to be fully revealed for the viewer to gaze upon with awe and wonderment. Christianity is different. Despite its basic erroneous conceptions of the Trinity, the vicarious martyrdom of Jesus, and so forth, Christianity, partly because of the universality inherent in it, and partly because of the emphasis it places on the inner development of man, on faith and charity, and so forth, has succeeded in holding within itself a full, pulsating religious life and soon came to represent all of religious development. We might say that it counts sand among its treasures and that it has succeeded in using that sand as a precious thing. That sand may be discerned as such and eliminated. Nevertheless, the inner, vigorous life will remain and will continue to grow, strengthened by the treasure still remaining. But in Judaism, with only a minimum of discernment, one soon casts aside all those things that exercise so great an influence on those of little education, and one comes to reject them indifferently and scoffingly. It is true, however, that Christianity, too, has been increasingly confronted by a crisis for some time now, and we certainly do not doubt that it will come out the loser. But the struggle with Christianity is on so universal a scale, and the forces which it employs for its defense are so manifold, so rich within themselves, that it will be able to keep the interest at least of those who are part of it. And the new era and the new religious ideology that will evolve from all this will be linked with Christianity and will emanate from it. Unfortunately the same things do not apply to Judaism. This should explain why the more profound minds who are active within Judaism will react in either of two ways. They may withdraw into the field of scholarship and be utterly lost for all the practical ends of Judaism, dejectedly observing the scene from afar, like Zunz. Or else they will cling tenaciously to existing practices, persuading themselves that these forms can be rendered fluid and spiritual, as does Mannheimer, whom I had the pleasure of meeting on my most recent trip. If I were not a rabbi and if, in general, I were enjoying complete independence, I might possibly take quite a different course; I would then identify myself with the general endeavors of the time and, from that vantage point, write about Judaism and Jewish literary movements, . . . but reality is different. At any rate, I have not yet given up, nor will I do so; I continue to struggle with myself and eventually I am bound to achieve inner harmony . . .

AZ, XXII, NO. 27, P. 320 F.

Breslau, February 9, 1842

. . . I cannot very well let the mention of the Temple controversy[2] pass without comment, for the issue has aroused a lively interest. . . . Of course, I am not satisfied with all this superficiality, and I see no excuse for the fact that, in a period of 23 years, the leaders of the Temple have achieved nothing beyond a second edition of their prayer book which reflects the same lack of decisiveness as the first one did. Despite their avowed Liberal position—nay, in spite of the obligation that grows out of their attitude which led them to separate from the majority—they have done almost nothing for the proper advancement of those ideas of which, basically, the reforms in divine services are merely an outgrowth. Hence, if we were to be dependent upon the results of their endeavors, the status of the controversy would, in fact, still be the same as it had been at the beginning. The fact of the matter is that they are still beating about the bush today; they still refuse to speak out openly, and still persist in seeking to make the difference appear minute, while, in reality, the very value of this difference lies precisely in the fact that it is of great significance as part of that principle which has not yet been adequately put into practice. Fortunately Rapoport[3] and Zunz have shed some light on the divine service, and fortunately my own journal has provided building blocks with which to construct a Liberal theology. Yet, all that these gentlemen can make of these things is just a number of paltry changes in a few isolated words. Is this not a disgrace, a downright abuse of the position which they do not know how to use properly for the good of the whole? . . .

AZ, XXIII, NO. 29, P. 345 F.

Breslau, February 24, 1862

Once again I have found in my own life the truth of the adage that only the living are right, and if my decision to participate more actively in life again has earned me nothing more than the reward that my friends should once more remember me, I would consider my gain quite sufficient. You, too, my dear friend, have reappeared, and that which the sorrowing friend could not attain, the active friend has received as an unexpected gift. I cannot conceal from you, dear friend, that I was sad in those difficult days not to have heard the compassionate voice of that friend who was as close to her as he has been to me. She suffered cruelly during the last few years, and she bore it with dignity. Early in 1860 she underwent a painful operation in Berlin. On her sickbed, which seemed to be a couch of convalescence, she was quite cheerful; she had loving care and devoted friends. She left her bed and it seemed that she was cured. How radiant she was in her belief that she would now be able to return to her dear ones, and how loving the devotion with which everyone received her here! Yet, she and I, we only had a few short months left to enjoy this anxious happiness. . . . Fraught with fear, and with hope which I had abandoned entirely toward the end but which she, for her part, never gave up, time crept on until December 6, the day before her birthday. On that day she gently closed her weary eyes. It had been long expected, and yet it came with such utter suddenness. I have suffered a cruel loss. I made the pledge to myself that I would go on living, true to my children, to my office and to scholarship, and, thanks to my good constitution, I have succeeded in remaining true to this promise and am fully and entirely in the midst of life. Yet the painful void remains forever new; my home is and remains empty. I am indeed fortunate in that all my life never belonged to me but was dedicated ever to one idea, which becomes clearer to me with every passing day; I know that I must labor faithfully in its cause, and this I do. It is a blessing that I have good children, who are of an age at which they no longer require the constant care that only a mother can give but at which they are still young enough to be near me for years to come. I am fortunate, too, that I have succeeded in attaining a position that leaves me free of care, one that is respected and grows more so with each day. But ah, how sad it makes me to know that I can no longer share this happiness with her! Her love for me had deepened her understanding and sympathy for all my work and all my endeavors, and her interest in it all was so sincere. To the congregation, she was "the Rabbi's wife" in the truest sense of the word. That which her husband had to struggle so mightily to attain was freely tendered her with obvious joy. And as for the children—how proud she would have been of them—she would have grown young with them again! And how deep her appreciation, how great her joy in every little loving attention of mine! Now she is looking down on me so tenderly, even as I constantly see her before me; but she cannot express that joy in our midst—ah, my dear friend, this is cruel pain for me to bear.

You knew her when she was a lovely maiden. This she remained throughout her life; the charms of youth departed, but she remained beautiful to the very last; her womanly dignity and grace grew as time went by. Had she lived to grow old, all would have risen to do her honor even from afar.

It is only to you, dear friend, that I am speaking in this fashion; it is not that I am generally calm and composed, but that I am giving myself entirely to my work. My work claims me fully, even though I cannot say that time heals all wounds. . . . Today, more than fourteen months later, I can still only repeat those words which I uttered at her graveside: If ever I could put out of my mind this final resting place, then I would forget all that is true and right, all that is noble and good, and these sentiments will remain with me for the rest of my days.

I am not one of those who continuously probe old wounds, but it does me good indeed to be able to speak of her again out of the depths of my heart as if she had left us only yesterday. I know that this, too, makes her happy; and it is a joy to me that I may tell myself that not only was I her pride and happiness through twenty years, but that she still lives within me even today . . .

AZ, XVI, NO. 32, P. 380 F.

letters to various correspondents

TO PRIVY COUNCILLOR PAULUS, HEIDELBERG[1]

Bonn, January 16, 1831

Esteemed and honored Sir:

I have always been firmly convinced that the true salvation of any religious group lies solely in such truly religious education as conforms with reason; and this can be achieved only by stimulation and active encouragement on the part of its spiritual leaders. Looking around among those of my coreligionists who were either holding office as ministers or were still undergoing training for this purpose, I attempted to establish whether their goal was to spread light or simply to bolster vanities. To my sorrow, I discovered that nearly all of them—some because of erroneous views, others for lack of thorough learning, and still others even for no reason but narrowmindedness and pettiness—applied all the authority vested in them to the indiscriminate preservation of whatever had been handed down to them by tradition. Thus, for example, I was amazed to find, on my visit to the University of Heidelberg in the summer of 1829, that there were Jewish theologians at that institution who thus walked in darkness, showing hardly any awareness of Your Honor's stimulating presence. The reason for this, it seemed to me, was not so much hypocrisy as it was actual perversity and ignorance, and I grew bitter at the thought of my own theological studies, when I considered that I myself would have to fight against such obstacles in the future. Thus I turned to the study of Oriental languages instead, though not without casting wistful glances at that glorious, thistle-covered field of salutary endeavor. Toward the end of this summer, however, a number of circumstances as well as the practical bent of my mind impelled me to seek training at the University of Bonn for the exercise of the calling of theologian. I was highly gratified indeed when I encountered other students there who were imbued with lively scholarly zeal and impelled by a praiseworthy striving after truth. Thus I gained renewed courage, and while the shallowness of many a Jewish theologian in Baden still caused me pain, it no longer held any terrors for me. . . . I could no longer repress the desire to expose the true character of the situation . . . and to point to its shortcomings. In this I was further encouraged by the thought of you, the shining example and worthy champion of truth and light. It occurred to me that, in your own endeavor to advance the cause of the good everywhere and to defend truth wherever it may be, you might welcome such a disclosure, and that you might wish to give this essay a place in your *Sophronizon*. On behalf of all mankind, so long suppressed and led astray, I appeal to you, the great man whom I once was privileged to meet in person, to find this cause worthy of inclusion in your distinguished work. Should you find anything in it that might seem to you objectionable, I cherish the hope that you may perhaps even be kind enough to delete or correct such passages, considering that I entered the fighting arena very young indeed, called there solely by an innate drive for truth. . . .

P.S. I will take the liberty of requesting that you make mention neither of this letter nor of my name. Since this essay is open to misinterpretation in many quarters, it might have unpleasant consequences for me.

NS, V, PP. 46 FF.

TO SALOMON GEIGER, FRANKFORT[2]

Bonn, June 4, 1831

. . . For some time I have been determined not to return to Frankfort upon completion of my studies at this University . . . but rather to select another large city, such as Berlin, Munich, Vienna or Paris, where I might also have the opportunity of continuing my education in all areas. I did not think it would be difficult for me to earn a living in such a place; through recommendation, I could always find work as a private tutor, either independently or with a family. I am too well known in my native city to be able to develop my own convictions quietly there; removal to another place, I thought, might offer me the opportunity to do so undisturbed. Of course, there are conflicts of opinions in any large city. But there I would not be compelled to align myself definitely with one party or the other. At home, however, where my every step would be watched and my every word exposed to a variety of interpretations, I would be forced to take sides. A decision to adopt a middle course is judged insufficient by either of the conflicting parties; in addition, for anyone desiring eventually to achieve prominence in public life, such a decision may well be politically harmful and constitute an obstacle in the path of his future sphere of endeavors.

From one of your comments I take it that you do approve of my tentative plan to take a doctorate. It may be true that a doctorate today is no longer necessarily a proof of great scholarship. On the other hand, it seems to be required in our day and age; besides, our universities have not yet lowered their standards to such an extent that I would not derive both considerable gratification and significant advantages from an examination creditably passed.

NS, V, PP. 52 FF.

TO RABBI ULLMANN, COBLENZ

Bonn, December 20, 1831

On the whole, I now realize . . . that if Judaism, as it is now constituted, is to move toward reform, such a move can be effected only by a most cautious creeping sort of progress. . . . The minister, both at church and at school, must always fulfill a positive function; that is, he must disseminate true insights . . . and enlighten the mind of the Jews without employing a negative attitude, i.e., without seeking to destroy . . . [*At this point Geiger contemplates the possibility of defeat in the struggle with the Orthodox rabbis*] . . . I believe, however, that there is an alternative, and if my convictions remain unchanged, it will be my life's task to pursue it. This alternative is that of separation. Simply stated, the issue is as follows: All the Jews in any one country, who have rejected the Talmud in their hearts, should proclaim this fact openly and obtain permission from the State in which they reside to form a religious community of their own. Do not think that this plan is unrealistic. . . . It is only once we have rid ourselves of this ungainly colossus that now distorts us that we can be justified in looking forward to a betterment of our lot, both religiously and politically . . .

NS, V, PP. 54 FF.

TO S. FRENSDORFF, BONN[8]

Frankfort, August 15 and December 24, 1832

. . . Whatever one may say, there is still something magnificent about Jewish life in Frankfort, something which, on the whole, is deserving of full approbation even though there are things which at times may give offense to some more thoughtful minds. In all probability there is nothing that occurs in Jewish life, there is no publication of Jewish interest, and no man among the Jews who has distinguished himself in any way, but that detailed news of it does not penetrate here. I shall try to report to you something of each of the three categories I have mentioned above.

The Emperor of Austria has commanded the board of directors of Vienna's Jewish community to see to it that the honor of the Sabbath is not violated. You may imagine that the news affected various minds in a variety of ways; unfortunately, however, I have heard all these opinions only from the religious point of view. Actually, the only question justified here is as follows: Is it within the authority of the head of a state to issue directives concerning the internal affairs of any religious body so long as they do not in any way affect the state? I would answer this question in the negative . . .

Riesser's journal (*Der Jude*) is going at a fast pace and has continued to pursue its fine editorial policy. I am not sure, however, whether I am correct in my observation that his sojourn in Frankfort has somewhat removed him from his stand of absolute neutrality with regard to religious views, which, to the great annoyance of many people here, at times would lead him to defend the whole range of ceremonial law—though in a purely political sense only. The *Sulamith*,[4] too, manages to go on existing; during these past few days I have read the three last issues. On the whole, this journal still moves along the old beaten track, still pursuing that purely apologetic goal that gave it birth, without considering that it is no longer the timely thing to proclaim "Just look, dear Christians, we Jewish children also know how to behave. We're no longer as naughty as we used to be; day by day, we're becoming more reasonable and can act just like you." If we wish to talk of religion within the framework of Judaism today (without primarily touching upon the idea of civic rights to be attained, as Riesser does), this insipid, "enlightened" twaddle will no longer do. What we need now is a scientific method, and a journal in which this method prevails. We are in need of a publication which will accept anything that is presented in a scientific manner without caring what conclusions may be drawn in the individual essays, one that will have no partisan policy, but is willing to derive its future trend from the scientific study and examination of the most varied views and opinions of the present age. Such a publication is the need of the hour, and it is my hope that you will consider yourself one of the collaborators in this project . . .

NS, V, P. 59 F.

TO SAMSON RAPHAEL HIRSCH[5]

Wiesbaden, March 24, 1833

. . . It is a splendid thing to fight for one's convictions, and it is wonderful when a man's heart and mind are so closely intertwined that his thoughts are identical with his emotions, so that there is no discord within him. . . . I would like you to consider whether it may not be that you are harping too much on the righteousness of your own conviction and arbitrarily rejecting all men of differing views as wicked shepherds. . . . For my part, I welcome genuine good will wherever I encounter it. Since the ultimate goal of all of us is one and the same, then I should think that we should all want to further the cause of what is truly good. As long as it is earnest striving stemming from an earnest mind and religious emotion, this should also waken, nurture and strengthen the sentiments of true religion. Granted that orientations may differ, and that so far we have established merely those factors which will eventually lead us to the one true direction, that goal is sure of achievement in the end. Of course, it is quite true that, in my professional life, I am closer to him who, in these his earnest endeavors, also happens to share my own views, has the same ultimate goal in mind and uses the same means for attaining it; but that could hardly be otherwise. . . .

Much as my personal conviction is not a matter of mere reason, but an integral part of my very being, and much as any striving in an opposing direction may sometimes grieve me, there is, to me, at all times, this one consolation, namely, that all good will must beget some good. . . . Although I can thus lay no greater claim to being accepted without mistrust than you can, it is, after all, this difference of opinion that makes the step [*accepting the rabbinical appointment in Wiesbaden*] easier for me than it might have been for you. I was certain of my own good intentions; I had mapped out a path for myself to follow, and now I was to test whether reality would belie all my hopes—and, praise be to God, reality did not belie them. . . . You may say, "Naturally, anyone who approaches a task so light-headedly, anyone who, in his self-confidence, so grossly overestimates himself, will imagine that he sees the results of his endeavors everywhere he goes." But if you did indeed think so, you would be gravely misjudging me . . .

NS, V, PP. 77 FF.

TO LEOPOLD ZUNZ, BERLIN

Wiesbaden, August 12, 1834

I am happy to be able to send you the announcement of the first publication of my *Zeitschrift*[6] and I hope that you will approve of the spirit which is to guide it. Yielding to the importunings of several friends, I have not put sufficient emphasis on the non-partisan spirit which it is to maintain, since, as a handmaiden of scholarship, it must represent every phase and concept of true learning. However, as the editor (though not, of course, as a contributor), I shall make this policy my rule.

At the same time, I wish to repeat my humble request to you to draw on your rich store of knowledge and write erudite articles that will lend a dignified opening to my journal. Could you not possibly contribute some important items from such manuscripts as you have already completed? . . . So Rapoport wants to put out a Hebrew journal? Despite the high esteem in which I hold this worthy, ingenious and erudite scholar, and despite the eagerness with which I read everything that emanates from his pen, I still harbor many misgivings about this undertaking. Why must he do it in Hebrew? Is it in order to put severe limits on the number of people that are to be able to acquaint themselves with the learned treatises to be published in the journal? Is it so that not one enlightened word may perchance escape from the pen? . . .

At any rate, I shall approach this highly esteemed gentleman also and try to induce him to contribute to my journal. And would you, too, permit me to ask why you had your own book[7] translated into Hebrew? Were you thinking of [*readers in*] Poland? I think that with these people the fundamentals of elementary education will first be required to burst asunder the crust that has formed around heart and mind. They, too, must first pass through the initial stage of enlightenment before they will be sufficiently mature to be receptive to true scholarship, for whoever does not hold this point of view will neither understand your book nor know how to appreciate it.

NS, V, PP. 82 FF.

TO JACOB AUERBACH[8]

Wiesbaden, January 5, 1837

Fortunately there is now a book that is of sufficient significance to be used as a source of support, and also a man who is as taken with it as I am. This book is Strauss' *Life of*

Jesus.[9] It is an excellent work which simply *must* be read by everyone who does not wish to stay behind the times, a work that is not only of the greatest scholarly significance but will also have considerable influence on Christian theology. I sincerely wish you could have had the pleasure of reading the various critical reviews of this new publication. You should have seen what the insipid rationalists . . . had to say about it; the hue and cry of the gentlemen, driven into a corner, for their daily bread and the precious halo of their divine vocation—ah, how they blanched with fear lest the laurel wreath of reason vanish from their temples! Well, this man Strauss will still cause them plenty of trouble . . .

NS, V, P. 96 F.

TO RABBI E. GRUENBAUM, RABBI IN LANDAU

Wiesbaden, May 10, 1837

. . . One day we must take the step to begin to move the foundations of our traditionally-sanctioned institutions; the longer we delay, the greater will be the confusion in the congregations of Israel, and the more righteous the indignation with which those who know our convictions will view our lack of spirit. As for the judgment of posterity—we won't even think about that now. But of course it is precisely those who are honest and determined who must take such action. You cannot expect anything from the others, nor is it possible to reach an understanding with them when it comes to making decisions or a plan of action. But once others have made the decisions, they will follow the lead. Whatever we have achieved in the past we owe to the courageous pioneering of individuals; the trouble is only that in such decisions, separately made, an accord of several parties is absolutely required, and without direct personal communication such matters may take an eternity[10] . . .

Those who are to participate in this conference are by no means of such bad repute as you think. Their adherents may not be of the noisy kind; but they are sufficient in number and will stand by them with wholehearted affection and complete confidence and will not fail them in the hour of decision. At least I can assure you of this in the case of the most infamous of them all, one Dr. Geiger of Wiesbaden. . . . After the conference, everyone else will be asked to support its resolutions. Certainly, many will be asked at a later date to take an interest, but the initial steps must be taken by men who can be relied on. I believe that this undertaking will be extraordinarily successful. For, naturally, we will not let matters rest at a mere conference; serious discussions will have to be held in which everyone will have the opportunity to take a stand for or against. This is the only way to extricate ourselves from a highly difficult situation, to put an end to hypocrisy and to attract the indifferent layman . . .

This first conference should be informal in character . . . subsequent meetings, however, should be systematically organized, and I have already conceived of a plan which I believe to be very promising. . . . You, my dear friend, belong in the front ranks and I am sure you will not let anyone cheat you of this honor . . .

NS, V, P. 97 F.

TO JACOB AUERBACH

Berlin, June 13-21, 1839

Neither the authorities nor the Jews will be able to shake my determination. The former accord me treatment that is strange indeed and would like to get rid of me through all kinds of devious means. But nothing will come of that; they will have to declare openly that they do not want me, or else they must accept me. I would give one year of my life, or even more . . . to have the Prussian government make a clear and definite pronouncement on anti-Jewish measures without any evasions or subterfuges. They would love to checkmate me so that I would drop the whole thing in disgust and enable them to parade the righteousness of their cause when the occasion arises. Yes, if this were solely my own private

cause I would have left here long ago, but, as it is, I shall
see this matter through to the end. These gentlemen, even
as the faint-hearted Jews, have been mistaken in me. For I
am confronting them with an obstinacy that will cause them
considerable embarrassment for this display of weakness and
for the shrewd cunning that accompanies it. . . . Our misfortune is that, thus far, we have always been either too soft
or too weary. . . . However, I shall not be either, nor will
my congregants in Breslau.[11]

To be quite honest, literary life in Berlin has utterly failed
to impress me. The city is much too large to have any specific character, to say nothing of a literary character. One
must have access to certain circles that are closed and
private . . .

The Jews here are not to my liking. Only here can one
begin to understand the real meaning of indifference; indeed,
the strength here seems to lie entirely in negative action.
However, these experiences could not, and cannot now, alter
my convictions in the least. For my endeavors were never
directed at merely casting off, but at effecting a complete
cure which also happens to necessitate the eradication of
everything that is bad. The "vain comforters" are of the
opinion that one should not cut out the cancer entirely, but
just scrape at it a little. . . . This may look fair enough for
the time being, but the cancer will go on growing. Ah, those
fools who persists in charging us with destructiveness! It
is either because they are not capable of comprehending the
situation, in all its profound ramifications, or because they
lack the heart to sense the full magnitude of the ailment,
that they are not shocked by it and roused to action!

But of what use is all this childish prattle? It is just a
pity that even grown men occasionally join in this babble.
I am above all this now. . . . This much I know, or at least I believe I know, that I would succeed better than all these gentlemen with their "positive" chatter in curbing this indifference
and creating an interest in religion; even here [in Berlin] my
experiences in this sphere have not been altogether unsatis-
factory. It is precisely because all my demands are based on
living conviction within me, and not on mere cool consent or
accidental agreement, that I may expect to have greater influence. In addition, these gentlemen confuse long-range goals, as

set forth by the writer, with *immediately attainable ends* as envisioned by the rabbi . . .

NS, V, PP. 140 FF.

TO M. A. STERN[12]

Berlin, August 2, 1839

. . . You already know that I have girded my loins with patience; it may be, though, that this will be of no avail in the case of my position in Breslau. . . . The people in Breslau are really decent and cooperative. They spare neither effort nor expense—you can imagine that I'm not living on my income here—in order to bring about a favorable outcome, and their zeal never slackens. Now, even if these worthy efforts should fail to reach the result we desire, they have aroused so much sympathy on the part of both the authorities and the Jewish people that they will still yield fruits that will not perish. If, on the other hand, the outcome should be positive, then we have achieved something great, and I hope that so important a position as the one in the Breslau congregation will offer me an opportunity to do great things, especially since I have already acquired a good following in so many other places. But, if the decision should be negative—well, then everything will go on as before . . .

As to the *Kerem Hemed*,[13] you should not treat it with such contempt. It is a haven, if not for *Wissenschaft* as such, then at least for erudition, and that means a great deal. The Hebrew in it is intelligible and not without grace. I have already told you frequently just what I think of this modern Hebrew style; but what does the form matter if the content is valuable and if even the form is of some use in certain places? After all, Rapoport and Luzzatto still are excellent scholars with great ingenuity, who, in addition, have at their disposal the practical means which we lack. As for Reggio, though he may not be quite on their level, he is still by no means an unworthy fellow-scholar. We in Germany, who, of course, adopt a higher level and embrace a more comprehensive scope, tend too easily to lose sight of the concrete detail of that which is peculiarly Jewish, and we must therefore be most grateful to them for working for us with so much industry, thoroughness and insight . . .

I could tell you a lot about Berlin. Its basic character, it seems to me, is much knowledge and versatility without any *genuine* specialization, that is, no character and no will-power. I don't want any part of this cosmopolitanism. It may make you "human" but it also renders you shallow and colorless. I, too, can be non-partisan, but I am determined to carry through whatever I deem to be right. Furthermore, I can explain and understand why and how things came to be as they are; but I want to rise above them and control them, and not to approve of a wretched situation simply because I happen to *understand* how and why it came to be. In that case, I would rather take common onesidedness. It is therefore not particularly surprising that I should like to keep to myself in this colorless city in which, of course, the Jews are the most colorless of all. However, I'm not doing this out of my own free will but rather because of necessity. Here, if anywhere, I am offensive to those Jews who call themselves the only religious ones; to the Greek-, French-, Berlin-, or even Christian-educated, I'm a fool—so, what am I to do? . . . I still believe, however, that my stay will have some little effect in this city.

NS, V, PP. 142 FF.

TO M. A. STERN

Berlin, November 14-16, 1839

. . . By now I have become so hardened and firm in my convictions, and it has become so clear to me what I want and how I can usefully function in the service of Judaism, that nothing can deter me. Schism is out of the question, for there would not even be the slightest historical support for the seceders. Since every development is possible only within the framework of history, he who wishes to exert influence on such development within Judaism must cleave to that history even if it were to be against his will. Though I myself —typical product that I am of the present structure of Judaism and of the situation of present-day Jewry—feel inclined to protest, I can adopt this historical attitude easily, all the more so since I am tied by bonds of affection to the entire intellectual development of Judaism, from its very beginnings down to the present day . . . and thus it is a component of my personality, as it were. Since I have by now acquired the persistence of passivity to go with courage into the active fight, I will let things take their course. . . . I will remain on top.

The personal relationship with Zunz and my sojourn here I would not have missed for anything. Indeed, I have learned a great deal from Zunz. . . . I have always devoted myself earnestly and lovingly to the study of Jewish history; but now, inspired by my contacts with Zunz and putting them to use, I have embraced this pursuit with even greater eagerness. While I do not ignore everyday issues, I no longer feel a desire to inject myself into them. It was a good thing that they were given lively discussion and that no words were minced. But this has had its maximum effect, and so things may be left to the *diis minorum gentium,* if I may put it so without appearing immodest. . . . You know that, as a historian, I am no mere bibliographer, and though I do not possess the splendid erudition of Zunz or of Rapoport, I still know how to apply what little knowledge I have and to make it bear fruit. . . . It is a good idea, by the way, to display one's learning to the people, for this is the way to keep their respect. Thus, I am not discontinuing my *Zeitschrift* because I am weary of these labors but . . . rather in order to be able to achieve something more solid and enduring. . . .

Most of the rabbis, especially those who fill important positions and could exercise great influence upon others, do not have enough learning. But time will take care of that. After all, the flowering of Jewish literature only dates back to 1820. The impulses and drives within it give rise to hopes which are certain of fulfilment. At present people are busily engaged in the endeavor of unearthing buried treasures from the olden days, and if only these were presented properly— which of course is not now being done, and it is for this that my work is to serve as a model—they would soon be generally appreciated and accepted.

NS, V, P. 147 F.

ABRAHAM GEIGER AND LIBERAL JUDAISM

TO LEOPOLD ZUNZ

Breslau, March 4, 1841

. . . I still have not received permission to publish my *Zeitschrift*. Under date of the twelfth of last month I wrote about the matter directly to the Ministry of the Interior; but I still have no reply. As it is, I am far less inclined right now to write history than to make it. What could possibly save us in our present state of inner confusion? The only course I can think of is schism. How can we continue to drag with us through the centuries of world history that sordid appendage that has been attached to us? Any strength that we may possess is dissipated in trivialities, and nothing worthwhile ever comes of it or can ever come of it. How much longer is this to go on? It is impossible to reshape this entire mass. It can only be destroyed by some world-shaking occurrence. But this will not come to pass if those elements that shape it persist in their attempts to breathe new life into it. But the latter will perish, for they are constantly haggling over absurdities so that they can never achieve anything of abiding value. It is a great loss for the entire intellectual development of this century that the vigorous and unfettered forces of Judaism are not permitted to unfold freely and to take part in the total culmination of culture and learning. This, however, is not so much the fault of the State . . . as it is due simply to the present situation of the Jews, who, of necessity, will have to divide so that the one part will eventually be eroded and disintegrated as time goes on, even as will inevitably be the case in Catholicism also. The other part, small though it may be, will then have a share in the dominion of *Wissenschaft;* this is the enviable lot of Protestantism and should be, to an even greater degree, the destiny of Bible Judaism as well. Rifts such as these have ever been liberating forces in world history, for while they abolish the material integrity of one entity, they lay the foundations for the ideal unification of the whole world. I am firmly convinced that this must come to pass, and I would like to have a hand in its realization . . .

NS, V, P. 155, F.

TO REV. MAX LILIENTHAL, RIGA[14]

1842 or 1843

... You know, dear Sir, that for the past half century and more, the center for progressive endeavors among the Jews has been Germany; and it still is there today. Ever since I first began to think—and I had occasion even quite early in life to meditate most clearly and decisively on this subject —it has been my most fervent wish ... to participate in these endeavors at their very source of origin as actively as my abilities would permit. I have prepared myself for this task most earnestly; I have overcome many a scruple ... and have exposed myself to much unpleasantness in the process. Yet I have firmly adhered to my steadfast determination to be as forceful as possible a voice of progress among my brethren. Praise be to the Lord, for He has abundantly blessed my efforts. I am not conceited enough to believe that I have achieved great things for the welfare of the Jews, but I know that I have been counted in the ranks of those who seek to divorce true religion from superstition and to cleanse Judaism from the dross that has encumbered it; I have been among those who are endowed with an active mind for *Wissenschaft* and for wedding that *Wissenschaft* with life and faith. To date my name has earned far greater recognition than my feeble successes deserve, and I may be hopeful that future literary efforts on my part will yield additional fruit. Thank God, my material circumstances have also taken a turn for the better and my present position is an influential one.

However, there is still much that needs to be done even here in the Fatherland, which is the center of this progress. Would I not then be remiss in my duties if I were to leave here in order to give of my energies to another country, where at present only the after-effects of our own achievements can be felt? Would it not be better that I remain here as before as the "tail of the lion"? ...

Would not my leaving here be gross ingratitude to my brethren in my Fatherland ... and to the congregation here which labored and struggled so mightily to have me belong to them? ... And I might as well admit it—despite the fact that her authorities reject me because I am a Jew, I still love Germany. Must love have logical reasons? I feel my own being inextricably interwoven with Germany's *Wissenschaft*, with the entirety of its intellectual earnestness—and who could sever the nerve fiber of his very being with impunity? Thus, though she, in return for my own efforts and those of my brethren to enter ever more completely into her life, genteelly excludes us, I must remain in Germany. I must wage a dual fight, against the reactionary elements among the Jews, on the one hand, and against those privileged denominations who simply ignore all things Jewish, on the other; and I must wait with hopeful yearning for that day when that which has already been freely given elsewhere shall be accorded to us here as the right to which we are entitled . . .

NS, V, PP. 164 FF.

TO EMILIE GEIGER IN CARLSBAD

Breslau, August 13, 1844

. . . When you are here, life in all its aspects, which are sufficiently abundant even beyond that historical process of Judaism, still lovingly clings to me. But now it is always only this one thing that occupies me—and, O Father in Heaven, how unpleasant this one thing is! And to think that one's energies, upon which one relies and which one believes capable of contributing to an abundant harvest, are actually being dissipated in attempts to soften an impervious rock—is this not dreadful to contemplate? But of what avail are all my lamentations? This is the viewpoint that life has assigned me; I cannot abandon it, nor shall I abandon it. I must wage my battle and fight it to the end; and though the gains may be paltry, the struggle will still not have been in vain. Ah, if only one could heed one's own impulses and come forth to fight in the open! But this constant bowing and scraping, this groping and maneuvering—this is what devours all of one's energies and deprives one of all the joy of toil and labor . . .

NS, V, P. 175 F.

TO LEOPOLD ZUNZ

March 19, 1845

... In the expectation that you will be open and frank with me even as I am with you, and on the assumption that candid outspokenness will please you more than dissembling circumlocution, I would like to discuss with you quite openly something that I have found somewhat disconcerting. I do not wish to criticize, for I know that your words and your actions spring from solid conviction, but solely to ask you to enlighten me as to your reasons for doing as you did. First, there was that essay in the *Wiener Kalender* (Zunz, *Gesammelte Schriften,* II, 172-177) in which you very edifyingly expanded on the beneficial effect of the practice of putting on phylacteries. If I am not mistaken, I did already express to you my surprise at this article on a previous occasion. There is no doubt that any ceremony may take on a deeper meaning and that it is never altogether devoid of significance. But should this rite, which is based on a misinterpretation of certain biblical passages, which is linked purely with those excesses associated with charms and amulets, and which is so completely alien to our own thinking and to our own culture and sense of beauty, truly have such beneficial effects? What is dead remains dead; the spirit which was once contained within it still continues to manifest itself, but in other ways and in other forms. To seek to reawaken it now would be a vain endeavor and, even if it were to meet with success, would have only deplorable, soul-killing and demoralizing consequences.

This essay was followed by your opinion on the rite of circumcision (*Gesammelte Schriften,* II, 191-203). I was not in agreement with the *Reformverein.*[15] Its adherents were not clear as to the goals they sought to pursue, nor were they sufficiently sincere in their pronouncements, and instead of choosing a more circumspect approach to the masses and refraining from moving by such leaps and bounds, they elected to attack the rite of circumcision which was still considered the very nerve fiber of Judaism. . . . On the other hand, I must admit that I cannot find it within me to take so decided a stand in favor of circumcision, simply because it is, and has ever been, a time-honored practice. The fact remains that it is a barbaric, gory rite which fills the infant's father with fear and subjects the new mother to harmful emotional strain. The sense of sacrifice, which in days long past lent an aura of consecration to this ceremony, has long since vanished from our midst; nor is so brutal a thought deserving of perpetuation. True, in the olden days religious sentiment may well have clung to it; at present, however, its only foundations are habit and fear, and we surely have no desire to dedicate temples to either. And as for the attitude which you seem to adopt toward all reforms in general . . .

I must confess to you that, though I cannot subscribe to all his assertions and though I cannot view every one of his measures as properly timed, I still love Holdheim most sincerely. I love him because I can recognize the zeal of honest conviction and of a higher moral tone in his every word. And to think that you, with all your mental vigor, should suddenly become impervious to all this pulsating intellectual life, that you should have come to conceive of the past not just as the history of the development of thought but as the standard to be applied to our present intellectual endeavors! This was a phenomenon that pained me deeply; I lamented the loss of a man such as Zunz for the endeavors that stir ever more strongly as time goes on; I deplored the possibility that even the most vigorous of minds may become closed at a certain stage. Frankly, I feared also for myself!

And then came the news about your private life. It was said that you suddenly decided to keep a strictly kosher home and everything that goes with it. Certainly, I would respect such obligations as everyday life imposes, and I would see nothing either unusual or strange in your conduct if you had thought it the advisable thing to do under the given circumstances out of consideration for your position as head of the Seminary. But it was said that you did this, not because you felt that your position necessitated it, but out of principle. . . . I must admit that I cannot see that at all. It is precisely these dietary laws that are so void of rationale and at the same time such a hindrance to the development of social relationships. Truly, the ideal of the deeper sense of brotherhood among men should have priority over the revival of that sense of separation which is both devoid of color and is of very dubious value. Consequently, I could attach more value to almost anything rather than to this particular branch of rabbinic legal practice that has been cultivated from micrology to almost sheer madness. Thus I find myself asking the question: Can he really believe that he is serving some purpose with this? Can he really think that, in this way, it will be possible to create a healthy Judaism, one that will stimulate mind and spirit, and stir men to action, a Judaism of a sort that will include everything that is truly human? I keep searching for the answer; but much as I seek to pursue views along the most divergent directions, I cannot find an explanation that will satisfy me.

There, thank God, I've got it off my chest! This oppressed and tormented me until just now, when I told you myself about that which caused me so much anxiety. If you still have for me those feelings that you showed me in Berlin and which you have also indicated to me in your letters, you will send me your reply. . . .

Please be good enough to remember me to your wife. Even though she may punctiliously see to it that no *milchig* knife will as much as touch a *fleishig* tablecloth, and though she may push her bonnet down almost to the tip of her nose, she will still always remain my friend. As for us, we are well, thank God, both *milchig* and *fleishig*. Our kosher lunches and dinners agree with us splendidly, and in short, we are as well as all *gebenshte yiddishe kinder* should be . . .

NS, V, PP. 181 FF.

EXCERPT FROM ZUNZ'S REPLY TO THE ABOVE LETTER

May 4, 1845

. . . I detest the idea of a rabbinical hierarchy. I feel only contempt for a Reform with statutes on *milchigs;* and as for attacks on defenseless Judaism that spring from anti-religious sentiments—I leave them to those who like to cast themselves in such a role. The criterion for true religiosity can only be religiosity itself, that which is considered valid for all and universally cherished in a living tradition. . . . It is not religion, but ourselves that we must reform; it is not at inherited, hallowed tradition but at prevailing abuses, from both without and within, that we must direct our attack. The hue and cry against the Talmud smacks of apostasy ... But enough now of discussion and deliberation on these things. The more foolishness I see around me, the more I see of the stupidities which degrade us and bring us no gain, the more I am drawn to scholarship. I would rather that you write me about the things of which we talked in former days.

Remember me to your dear wife; my wife asks to be remembered to both of you. Now we've argued enough, and I close,

As ever, your friend,

NS, V, P. 184 F.

TO THE ESTEEMED BOARD OF DIRECTORS OF THE JEWISH COMMUNITY OF BRESLAU

March 19, 1846

The introductory part of this letter is devoted to an explanation by Geiger of why he had not come to a decision on a call he had received from the Reform Society of Berlin to become its minister.

... In my work on behalf of Judaism I have always thought it not sufficient merely to attempt to correct flaws by sporadic patchwork or whitewashing. Instead, I have duly recognized that the present generation is the outgrowth of a long series of distorted forms of a Judaism that has evolved through many unhappy centuries. Hence this form which is now extant stands outside the pale of Jewry; it is no longer the vital element of the religion of the Jews. There are those, few in number, who still hold on to this form outwardly, without, however, being imbued by it within. To them it is simply a matter of habit and fear. There are others who do not care for it at all and have discarded it with indifference. Such a state of disastrous confusion, of total deceit which needs must undermine all truth and morality, can only deeply sadden anyone who views religion as a vital power and who looks to its institutions for strength and edification ...

I conceive it my mission to dedicate my energies to the

endeavor to cure this ailment. However, there are only two ways in which this can be done: either the people must once again be trained to accept an ideology and religious rituals which they have long outgrown, or else Judaism must give up all outworn forms and, devoid of all its nationalist elements from the past . . . come forth in its eternal truth, in its lofty teachings and with its appeal to mankind to hallow all of life. The first course is as impossible as it is unjustified, for that which the spirit of history, in which God also manifests Himself, has cleared away and buried, no human reason can reawaken or revive. What remains is the alternative, which is what I have attempted to accomplish from the very beginning of my endeavors. I have always persisted in pointing to the sore spot in our present religious affairs; I have never contented myself with those little items that may satisfy transient curiosity and that may offer fleeting attraction because of the illusion of revival that they create. . . .

To most of them, religion is not the most profound and sacred element of life; it is not a living conviction which they gladly affirm and which they would wish to see realized in all their institutions. Much rather, it has become to them the object for exercising diplomatic skills and ingenious bargaining. Such a state of affairs can be naught but revolting to any man who sees his very being and his calling in true religious conviction, especially when one sees that religion is primarily thought of as a commodity to be tailored (but not in excess) to the needs of others, but not to one's own self which is supposed to be above such things. I hold such indifference, such apathy toward any warm religious sentiment that is so lightly cast aside, to be a more dangerous adversary than error and superstition. It is this, the more evil spirit of the two, that has taken hold in our own community.

All too frequently, the task of nurturing the seedlings of earnest manly faith and conviction has been made bitter for me. When some members of the community avowed the belief that the dichotomy between life and religion must be removed and indicated their desire to submit recommendations accordingly to the Rabbinical Conference, I viewed their declaration as a sign of good will and sincerity, without, however, committing myself on the actual practical feasibility of their proposals. My attitude was denounced as apostasy. When I declared myself in favor of introducing some

German prayers into the service, without, mind you, deeming it advisable to conduct the entire service in German, much complaint was heard. In fact, it was even considered necessary to keep my endeavors behind lock and key, as it were, by giving me a colleague (whom I honor and esteem) to serve as a sort of drag. Thus my position here has become such that I can no longer pursue my goals with that zeal and unrestrained freedom which I consider necessary. With every step I take, I glance furtively about me, in fear not for myself but for the possibility of continuing my constructive endeavors. I detect a variety of attempts to undermine the trust which the congregation has placed in me, and I must say that the thought of such a future fills me with fear. Toil without active influence, a position devoid of sincere appreciation, holds no attraction for me. I must not allow things to come to a pass where I must turn traitor to my inmost calling and pine away without doing effective work.

This is what oppresses and torments me. I felt impelled to present it to you bluntly and openly. The relationship between my congregation and myself must be honest and clear; it is only in this manner that fruitful and blessed cooperation is possible.

NS, V, PP. 189 FF.

———————⟨∞⟩——————

TO RABBI J. KAHN, TREVES

Breslau, April 10, 1856

... I must admit that I find that far too little scholarly work is being done by my colleagues, especially by those who represent the progressive point of view. I am putting it very mildly at that; the fact is, I might say, that nothing is being done at all. They believe that they have done enough through their sermons and through the practical work of the rabbinate; but both of these can be truly beneficial only if they are the expressions of sound conviction. They do not care to take the trouble to examine and improve their scholarly background. As for me, I am as busily engaged in the practical ministry as anyone else; I preach sermons and give religious instruction, more so, perhaps, than anyone else, and

I am kept occupied with weddings and funerals and with the answering of inquiries—all of which constitute essential functions in so large a congregation which at the same time maintains so great a variety of outside contacts. But I would be most unhappy if I were to abandon my studies for even one week. You have begun serious studies at the University; why not continue them? Of course I know the value of practical work. I myself have given in to impulse and edited a prayer book; but I consider such projects to be recreational activities and not duties whose fulfilment should constitute the satisfactory performance of my calling . . .

NS, V, P. 216 F.

TO SAMUEL DAVID LUZZATTO[16]

Breslau, March 23, 1857

Your letters delight me always, but this one was doubly welcome. Despite our differences in religious and ideological conviction, it is my earnest desire that our relationship should be based on mutual esteem and friendship. For myself, I can say that the warmth of my own sentiments for you will not cool, even though the differences of opinion might emerge even more bluntly in the future than they have in the past. Would this be true also of you? I must admit that at times this has worried me. It goes without saying that, nevertheless, I have always adhered to the basic tenet that Luzzatto is dear to me, but dearer still, above and beyond all else, is the truth as I believe I see it after honest and objective research. Yet, it would grieve me to lose your friendship. Your letter reassures me. True, I see in it some sadness that I should oppose you, i.e., your views, too sharply; but I also note your pleasure at our agreement on many an issue. Therefore continue to accept me as I am, and please be assured that whatever I am is the result of sincere love of truth rather than of some idle caprice. After all, why should one fail to take into account the possibility of great intellectual differences? Why must one always suspect bad faith? Whenever I hear of such insinuations, I cannot refrain from expressing my indignation; indeed, I consider it my duty to refute all charges of this sort.

NS, V, P. 218.

TO SAMUEL DAVID LUZZATTO

Breslau, September 6, 1857

... In the meantime I have received a few lines from you, and I must confess that their contents surprised me. For an expert like you, is there nothing more to say on the wealth of material in my book (the *Urschrift*)—and on the many new well-documented thoughts developed in it—but those banal phrases against rationalism? My book contains historical evidence throughout, and no mere assumptions at all, neither rationalist nor irrational. Why, therefore, this tilting at windmills? To others, I would say: "You condemn because you wish to refute but cannot"; but what am I to say in the case of a man whose love of truth and whose abilities I esteem equally?

I hope, therefore, that the bad mood in which you found yourself when you wrote your last letter, and for which my book could not have given you cause, has long since vanished, and that the New Year may bring you continued vigor and true happiness, even as I hope that it will bring me a great many interesting letters from you ...

NS, V, P. 219.

TO M. A. STERN

Breslau, December 8, 1857

... You are probably aware of the fact that I have not been idle, and I may rightly expect that, alert as you are, you must have been apprised of my *Urschrift* by now. I am waiting anxiously to see what effect this book will have. From private sources I have already heard the most contradictory reports from a variety of viewpoints. But so far, the public has still taken no notice; nor has there been any reaction from objective, truly scholarly critics. It is true, of course, that the book will encounter some difficulty in penetrating broader circles. In our Jewish circles the progressive elements do not sufficiently engage in serious scholarly studies. Those who have acquired scholarship pay slavish homage to a spurious, apologetic trend. In Christian circles this book will encounter obstacles because of its Jewish origin, but even more so because rabbinical scholarship is completely unknown in those quarters. And yet I am conceited enough to believe that it *must* be a success; my faith in truth continues unshaken. My judgment would be heavily beclouded were I to be deceived in my belief, which is corroborated by additional study every day, that I have discovered the one correct method which will both pave the way for historical insight and truly initiate a continued development based on firm foundations. I would be happy indeed if you, who are both interested in the subject and capable of passing judgment on it, were to give me your own frank opinion.

NS, V, P. 224.

TO EMILIE GEIGER IN CARLSBAD

Breslau, May 28, 1857

. . . The *Volkszeitung* has published an article . . . on my *Urschrift*. It seems that a pietist preacher in Potsdam gave a critique of Bunsen's[17] work on the Bible which he condemned in the sweetest tones. The writer of the article in the *Volkszeitung* takes the opportunity to discuss the significance of this work, and adds the following note:

In addition to the Bunsen Bible studies, there has appeared recently another work of significance that will provide biblical scholarship, for the next decade, with a vast store of critical material presented from an entirely novel viewpoint. The title of this work is Urschrift. *etc., by Abraham Geiger. It treats the history of the origin and evolution of the biblical text we now possess in a manner that leads to new information and conclusions of extraordinary nature. It is indeed comforting to know that scholarship moves forward steadily and we must content ourselves with informing our readers of that progress.*

Now the *Kreuzzeitung* has reprinted the whole article from the *Volkszeitung* to show by inference, as they put it, that the Reform Jews are working hand in hand with Bunsen; as to Dr. Geiger, they assert, his views are well known. I am quite pleased even with this article; it is important that both friend and foe should speak their minds quite openly on my book and so give due recognition to its significance.

NS, V, P. 226.

TO M. A. STERN

Breslau, December 28, 1858

. . . It is only now, almost two months later, that I begin to answer your letter of October 30. . . . May I admit to you quite frankly the reason for this delay in my reply? It is the unpleasant discussion about God in which you persist. As for me, I bear some notion of Him within myself. My own mind, whose nature—entirely independent of my body though at present linked with it—has become to me a sure fact of inner experience, is ample proof for me of the existence of an equally *personal* Universal Spirit, of the existence of a Deity who, in consonance with the mind's deepest yearnings, overflows with love. This notion, of course, does not contain the full thought clearly circumscribed, but there lies within it something that is soothing and poetic. Deprived of this poetic thought, both the world and I would be prosaic indeed. I am by no means a friend of that semi-darkness, of that affected ignorance which gropes around in vagueness, indulges in romantic self-deception, and yearns to have its own intellectual vapidity revered as poetry. I know that poetry is based on genuine emotions . . . [*which*] may very well go hand in hand with rational insight; yet it derives nourishment solely from that knowledge of intangible greatness which dwells within the human heart. It cannot seize it or dissect it, but it must acknowledge it in all its force. I will not deny that, with such a complete acceptance of a personal God and of His direct intervention in earthly affairs, we will not be able to avoid the use of at least a few anthropomorphic terms. . . . Let us, therefore, dismiss this philosophical discussion. I do not hesitate to go forward as far as I can; but I cannot exceed the limits of my own intellect or go beyond the roots from which it derives its nourishment. Thus I believe that I had best leave it at the gladsome awareness of the former and at the reverent contemplation of the latter.

NS, V, P. 229 F.

TO BERNHARD WECHSLER[18]

Breslau, April 8, 1861

. . . Is it not an ironical reflection on the entire course of our development that the Reform congregation in Berlin seems unable to find anyone suitable for them, that there seems to be no young and gifted theologian whom they could accept with enthusiasm? They are putting strong pressure on me . . . of course, no one knows about it yet. . . . The best thing would be for them to disband and bring all their influence to bear upon the larger, united religious community. In order to accomplish this, however, they would have to be propelled by some inner force; but at present their strength resides solely, or at least mainly, in their unity. What might four hundred intelligent, well-to-do families not achieve if they could exert a concerted influence on a Jewish religious community not subject to state control! But this spiritual impulse is lacking. . . . It reminds me of the reputation Judaism has acquired—that it does not seek proselytes, and that, as in Mendelssohn's dictum, it has no dogmas. It is a very respectable reputation, which fortunately is unfounded on fact and holds true only with regard to excesses of proselytism or closed and narrow dogmatism. . . .

NS, V, P. 251.

TO BERNHARD WECHSLER

Breslau, January 7, 1862

... I want you to know that, for some time now, I have been weighing the idea of publishing a journal once again. .... I have been strengthened in this intention by the annoying experience of having Hilgenfeld return my essay on Symmachus after two weeks—with profuse apologies. The sole reason for this, he claimed, was the fact that, as he had already explained in the introduction to the first volume (of his periodical), it was his policy to accept the works of Protestant authors only. If he had no such policy, he said, he wouldn't be able to keep Catholic writers away. Annoyed at this narrow-mindedness of pseudo-liberal Christianity, I took up the idea of a journal once again. I thought in terms of an annual volume dedicated to biblical and Jewish studies. . . . It seemed, however, that this would be too limited in scope and could be of interest only to a very few. ... I am still not so much in a rut that I would be able to narrow my sights to a limited scholarly field when I think of putting out a periodical. I am in the mainstream of life and must therefore look both to the right and to the left and toil vigorously alongside the others. Thus the project finally turned into a *Juedische Zeitschrift fuer Wissenschaft und Leben* (Jewish Journal of Life and Letters).... The studies are of great diversity; in addition to serious scholarly essays there are also original articles of great timely significance ...

NS, V, P. 255.

TO M. A. STERN

Frankfort, June 15, 1864

... At long last I am about to make my debut as a writer. The double issue of my journal of last year, and my lectures, with a supplement entitled "A Survey of Recent Literature on the Life of Jesus," should be out any day now, and I am hopeful that these works will be a success even with a larger audience, particularly in Christian circles. . . . My *Urschrift* has sold better during the year just past than during the previous year. The latest edition of the *Brockhaus Encyclopedia* contains an article entitled "Apocryphal Literature" in which my views on the two books of the Maccabees are cited as a matter of course. Dozy[19] in Leyden, who has already given me fulsome praise in the past, now writes me in truly extravagant terms—he is overflowing with enthusiasm, he says, he has given himself to me, body and soul; he is now a Geigerian through and through, and so forth. A new book of his, entitled *The Israelites at Mecca*, will shortly appear in a German translation, and will give me proof, as he puts it, that he is indeed a Geigerian. Since then, I am told, the *Urschrift* has become widely known and read in Holland, too . . .

NS, V, P. 289.

TO M. A. STERN

Frankfort, January 5, 1865

. . . I may be mistaken about many things, but I am not mistaken when I view Christianity as the adversary of great cultural endeavor. Christianity takes great pains to reveal the full extent of its intolerance; the papal encyclicals and the spoutings of the High Consistories, the synods and Church Days truly contribute their share in this effort. And think of the cowardice with which all of this is accepted. Every now and then someone stops to think, then bows to the Pope's judgment with regard to dogma, and merely concerns himself with the remaining areas of life (as if there were no connection between the two). In the end it is claimed that this is a misconception of Christianity; Christianity, it is pointed out, the mother and pillar of all learning, nurtures the snake in its own bosom. Such cowardice is doubly dangerous when it comes from personalities like Renan and Strauss. Then the Jews, too, allow themselves to be fooled; they join in the applause, and look dumbfounded when some unprejudiced Jew . . . finally dares to proclaim the truth. The Christians, of course, will keep a dignified silence; for, since the word has not gone forth from the sole keepers of all learning, there is no need to answer it. Then someone does come along who feels that he must vent his wrath; he will be spiteful and scornful in his folly; nor will he shrink from lies and misinterpretations. The Jews, pitifully uninformed, will quickly follow suit, saying: "Well, this man is not altogether wrong; we are fair and not at all as biased as Geiger. Even if you do give us a good thrashing from time to time, we are grateful children; for children must be whipped and, after all, you know best. And we learn from you as good children should. Why, then, don't we turn Christian? Only God knows the answer. Perhaps it is because we're stubborn, and then there are family attachments and sentimental childhood memories. Also, we're a little clumsy, you see, and can't take the leap quite nimbly enough. But you know that we do look up to you with the utmost respect." Deuce take such Jewish "enlightenment" together with Christian obscurantism; they deserve each other.

My lectures are to appear shortly in a second edition;[20] they are being translated into English in North America. . . . The kind of apologetics I pursue aren't repugnant to me. To trace motivating forces and to distinguish them from their contemporary manifestations is the task of history; this is identical neither with concealment nor with the embellishment as practiced by some others. I do not wish to preserve anything that is outworn. Those who will say that what I want is no longer Judaism have passed an unjust sentence on a religion which is by no means closed, but still in a phase of active development. Were the same to be said of Christianity, if this were possible, I would raise no objection. . . .

NS, V, P. 291 F.

TO M. A. LEVY[21]

Frankfort, March 27, 1865

. . . Our fat history tomes string together row upon row of detail without clarifying basic thoughts and their development; and with all their cumbersome verbiage they lack much that is essential. And as for the arrangement of the material. . . . Whenever I have occasion nowadays to look into Graetz' work —and usually I do that only by way of supplement to other references—I grow increasingly convinced that, with all his diligence, with all his use of new material, and even with his accurate discussion of particulars (apart from numerous errors and careless mistakes), he lacks totally that historical perspective, that insight, which would make constructive use of the subject matter . . .

NS, V, P. 293 F.

TO PROFESSOR THEODOR NOELDECKE

Frankfort, August 28, 1865

. . . It is strange, of course, that the Christian scholars of Germany, who usually endeavor to collect their data most carefully and who are wont to examine thoroughly any scholarly view that may be presented, should choose to ignore Jewish works of this nature, even when they are fully accessible to them. The fact that my more recent *Zeitschrift* is not even kept at a library such as that of the University of Goettingen, and that even my articles in the *Journal of the German Society for Oriental Studies* receive scant notice and are apparently viewed as the work of someone of no professional standing, is startling evidence of the narrowest kind of prejudice. . . . But then, of course, attention is paid there only to those German studies which have been given recognition in the place of their origin. However, I have no desire here either to complain or to make accusations. I merely wanted to express the humble opinion that men like you would do well to strive for better understanding. Let us attempt to present each other's viewpoints clearly. Let me know the nature of your objections, and you will not find me obstinate. I have no doubt that you, too, will be willing and ready to consider the arguments I will present. The book *Die Urschrift* took hold of me; it was not the outgrowth of a predetermined plan. Both the plan and the thesis did not take shape until I was actually at work on the project. In the process of writing a history of the Karaites, I came upon the Sadducees and suddenly the nature and origin of their movement were revealed to me; then, from my probing forward and backward, there evolved for me a method for the critical study of the Bible and of the development of the Halakhah. Thus it happened that, going forth from an entirely different point of departure, I arrived at destinations which I had not sought and of whose existence I had not known. The book may therefore bear the traces of that spontaneous creative process; it may lack formal organization; it may have shortcomings as regards clarity of arrangement and the treatment of the vast scope of its subject matter. But to the reader who takes the trouble to follow the studies attentively, the conclusions will be plain enough. . . . I am sure that an exchange of ideas with you will be of great benefit to me.

NS, V, P. 295 F.

TO PROFESSOR THEODOR NOELDECKE

Frankfort, November 30-December 1, 1865

. . . We are, of course, agreed on the definition of the nature of *Wissenschaft.* It is the sum total of the entire intellectual development of mankind, constantly striving for liberation from the limiting one-sided effects of transitory and strictly national phenomena. Both Christianity and Judaism have been effective factors in this process; but they have value only insofar as they have provided the human spirit with certain definite orientations, and have caused its inherent potentialities and vitality to come to fruition. If they lay claim to a permanent higher sort of validity, then they are *unwissenschaftlich* (unscientific). Of course, they are still *living* forces, and the question arises as to which of the two is better qualified to be absorbed and permeated by the general development of the human intellect. Here judgment is frequently influenced by the position of him who forms it, and even in this sense alone I may speak of a Jewish *Wissenschaft* with quite as much justification as a Christian may speak of Christian *Wissenschaft.* By the former I understand primarily a comprehension of all the intellectual and spiritual manifestations of Jewish life and it seems to me in this connection that many a Christian scholar is unable to discern its inner mainsprings because he has observed these manifestations only as they were revealed in olden times and does not know them as emanations still flowing forth continually even in the present day. Jewish *Wissenschaft,* then, as I see it, is the understanding of Judaism in terms of all its original contributions and the deeper realization of its essence; the thought that *Wissenschaft* should have a peculiarly Jewish character is altogether alien to Judaism . . .

NS, V, P. 301 F.

TO LEOPOLD ZUNZ

Frankfort, January 7, 1866

. . . We who speak to the public through our books, in the final analysis, write with those few in mind whom we may expect to have a deeper sort of understanding for what we have to say. Thus, everything that I publish is accompanied, as it were, by a tacit letter to you. Still, we remain anxious also to have direct and physical communication from those whom we hold dear. My research draws me closer and closer to the era of dim antiquity and away from the Middle Ages, although my interest in the latter, conceived in broad outlines, has by no means ceased as a consequence. I hope that you and your dear wife are both well; it would be good to talk to each other again. At any rate, I feel better for having written to you once again, and I would be happy indeed if you would send me a few lines in reply and if your dear wife would add her own postscript.

NS, V, P. 303.

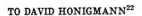

TO DAVID HONIGMANN[22]

Frankfort, June 25, 1866

. . . Ah, if only Christianity really were the religious force that it pretends to be, the source of all ennobling teachings, inspiring its adherents with conviction so deep and intense that they would bravely confront the mighty of this earth, speaking up before them with the voice of an enlightened conscience! When David played that sinful knavish trick on Uriah, Nathan the Prophet came before him and threatened him with punishment; he forbade him to erect the Temple because he had shed so much blood. Later, during bloody civil strife, Onias prayed "O God, attend Thou not the prayer of the ones against the others, nor heed Thou the curses of either against the others," and this noble martyr was stoned to death. And what do the priests of the Church do? . . . There they stand cowering in their holy vestments; not one of them dares utter a word of warning in the name of the God of Peace; not one of them feels compelled to attempt to soothe the heaving heart, or to urge upon the people the sentiments of peace as the greatest good of all for the unfettered development of the nations. . . . Why is it that they will not now unite to give testimony that force and violence, cunning and hypocrisy, are not weapons that may be used in righteous conflict? . . . There is not one word from the lips of the clergy to proclaim that today, in the year of the Savior, 1866, men should no longer resort to whole-sale butchery of their fellow-humans. Here the priests hire cut-throats and give them their blessing; elsewhere they defend slavery; and now they hide in utter servility from the din of battle. These are the representatives of a power which is supposed to serve as a moral force to rule over all of mankind, transcending all national boundaries, and certainly the tribal differences in one and the same people. Yet, they make no attempt whatsoever to wield this unifying power for the cause of peace; instead, they permit themselves to be used as tools to sharpen existing differences by inciting internecine factional strife.

NS, V, P. 309 F.

TO PROFESSOR THEODOR NOELDECKE[23]

Frankfort, June 28, 1868

The first article (on Rumania) in the latest issue of my journal will give rise to many a complaint over my hostile attitude toward Christianity. However, if, on the one hand, we see the [*Moslem*] "Ruler of the Faithful" proclaiming universal freedom of religion, and admitting both Christians and Jews to his newly-founded Council of State, and, on the other hand, note that it is not only in Rumania that we meet excesses of intolerance in the name of Christian culture, but that official Christen-

dom everywhere, including Catholicism in Austria and France
(to say nothing of Rome) and Protestantism with few exceptions, is hostile to both freedom and culture and carps at the
Jews in particular with every concession, then I must admit
that it is somewhat difficult for me to cherish love for Christianity. Why, even the non-believers cannot refrain from
spouting invective against Jews and Judaism, simply because
this hatred has been inculcated into their hearts by Christianity.
. . . Thus, for my part, I would rather cast my lot with the
second Isaiah than with Jesus. I find more pure humanity and
free spontaneity in the former than in the latter. It was in this
spirit that I wrote the second article ("Malachi and the Second
Isaiah," *Juedische Zeitschrift*, VI, 86 ff.), and I am anxious to
have your reaction to the attitude and interpretation presented
in it. I would like to have your reaction also to the essay on
anointing oil ("Anointing Oil and the Pharisees and the
Evangelists." *ibid.*, p. 105 ff.), which, in part, touches on the
New Testament. It is ignorance of the circumstances and attitudes of the Jewish people in those days that makes it impossible for even the most unbiased scholars to gain a proper
understanding of the writings of the early Christians. Let us,
therefore, join forces on the field of history; concede that
Christianity is a natural outgrowth of both Judaism and
paganism, both of which were in a state of decadence at the
time, and that for this reason both these older religions facilitated the victory of the new, while at the same time introducing
into it much that was diseased. Not pride and stubbornness on
either side, but only a new healthy development can bring us
closer to one another. The fact that I speak out to you in such
frank terms should prove to you that I deem you one of the very
few who are sufficiently objective to tolerate such outpourings
of the heart.

NS, V, P. 320.

TO THE BOARD OF THE JEWISH COMMUNITY OF BERLIN

Frankfort, October 6, 1869

I feel impelled to express to the esteemed board of directors
the sense of elation with which I received the call to the Rab-

binate of the community there. . . . I have high regard for the duties of a preacher from the pulpit; I take delight in proclaiming the sacred message from a holy place, and am confident that its effect will be edifying, encouraging, and on occasion even inspiring and stirring. . . . However, I have at least the same high regard for the opportunity to give oral instruction on a scholarly level and to provide scholarly insights into Jewish theology. In former times this was, in fact, the rabbi's most important function; it is only in more recent times that it has been forced to yield first place to the almost universally accepted practice of the sermon. Thus far it has not been revived to keep pace with the advances made in scholarly standards and insights. It is, however, precisely the nurturing of a living root of a healthy Judaism, properly interpreted, that forms the basis of my concept of the essential task of my position and office. . . . The attention I have attracted both generally and from you in particular was paid, I am sure, at least as much to the scholarly aspects of my work as to my pulpit oratory. Let me admit it to you quite frankly: the one deciding factor which could move me to make a change in my position would be the opportunity to exercise my functions fruitfully by guiding the disciples of scholarship and by paving the way for such insights as will advance the welfare of both Israel and the rest of mankind. In this connection, I must not attempt to conceal the fact that "the institutions now existing in the community (of Berlin)," as far as I have knowledge of them, could not satisfy me; I would feel content only if a theological college with a comprehensive program of studies were to be founded there, in which I could assume an active role . . .

I would have been very happy to find in the wording of your offer some statement expressing the hope that such an institution might indeed be founded there and that I would be expected to contribute toward this end by willingly engaging my effort in this direction . . .

As a matter of fact, I happen to know that preliminary steps have been initiated in Berlin toward the realization of an undertaking of this sort; that a committee has been formed for this purpose; and that, in fact, a curriculum has already been planned, circulars have been sent out and pledges of contributions accepted. . . . All this I have learned quite by accident. . . . The matter is of too great importance to me that I should sit back and wait. Therefore, instead of waiting for them to approach me first, I have acted contrary to my usual habits and addressed a frank inquiry directly to Professor Lazarus who, I understand, is chairman of the committee. I am now waiting for his reply which will have significant bearing on my decision . . .

NS, V, PP. 322 FF.

TO M. A. STERN[24]

Berlin, August 26, 1870

I know that you will hardly expect me to be happy about the present situation and the prevailing atmosphere. True, I am a German in the full sense of the word; but, over and beyond that, I am a human being, and this is why I should be willing to acknowledge the rights and merits of any civilized national entity. Particularly, I do not fail to appreciate either the contributions of the French people to the history of the world or its continuing historical calling. . . . I also duly recognize the task of Prussia and its providential mission within Germany. . . . However, I have lived outside Prussia long enough to be able to take a more objective and critical view of her role. Above all, I am a man who places greater trust in the moral and spiritual growth of mankind . . . than in violence and subtle scheming. I am not impressed by blood-soaked laurels. I recognize manliness not in martial virtue but in strength of character, and I find more significance in honesty and in the courage of truthfulness than in clever cunning and glib falsehood. Perhaps, if I had stayed on in Breslau, I would have been convinced of the righteousness of Prussia's cause in 1866; I might even have become a worshiping admirer of Bismarck. I might have joined in the enthusiasm . . . glorifying the courage of our soldiers; I might also have claimed the "return" of Strassburg and Metz, and of the whole of Alsace and Lorraine (as if a century and a half of history could simply be erased), and I might have been able to rejoice in the *de facto* completion of the union between the south and the north of Germany, though that union be cemented by blood. But now I can judge all these things quite objectively; I do not deny Bismarck's talents as a statesman and his abrupt and ruthless drive towards his goals; and I respect the strategic genius of Moltke. Above all, I know that it is indeed a historical task to overthrow Napoleonism and to chastise the foppishness of the French people. I know, too, that we have been forced into this present war. At the same time, however, I cannot close my eyes to the fact that 1870 is the direct consequence of 1866, and that the theory of "blood and iron" is abominable. It is the same mockery of "ideology" as was that of the first Napoleon, deriving from the same contempt for free self-determination, for the virile development of the nations, and from the denial of the right of every class within mankind to be taught free and independent judgment and insight. Finally, to the profound grief over the infinite misery that is sown on both sides, there is coupled the apprehension that the nurturing of unbridled passions and of mutual hatred will continue to breed disaster, even after the restoration of peace. Considering all this, whatever elation one might nevertheless sense as a member of the people will be quickly dimmed and repressed.

Yet I still remain a man with a historical perspective. I am accustomed to view the evolution of mankind in broad outlines even through its strange and manifold twistings and turnings; I do not exercise control over this course and have as little power to prescribe a path for the future as to map one for the past to follow. And I still place my full trust in that true progress which continues, all these obstacles notwithstanding. Thus I tell myself, "Let us get it all over with; but once peace comes, then you, too, must do your share to refute the erring with courage and guide them back to the right paths."

NS, V, P. 329 F.

TO REV. SYDOW IN BERLIN[25]

Berlin, March 1, 1872

On the day when tribute is paid to a man who, through half a century, has faithfully and courageously championed the right of free thought in the mainstream of religious life, it is fit and proper for even a stranger to express his high esteem and to offer his congratulations . . .

It is distressing, of course, that, even in Prussia, which is destined to be the leader of the German Fatherland both in practical life and in matters of the intellect, it should have required so much vigorous determination, and inflexible straightforwardness and selfless renunciation to remain true to the liberal trend in religion. On the other hand, as you today look back upon the past, you should for this very reason find it all the more gratifying to realize that, to the younger generation, your perseverance will be a shining example, a clarion call to follow in your footsteps.

It has been granted you, after many years of fruitful labor, to be able to continue your task with full strength and vigor. Now, at the conclusion of so long a span of unshakable determination, it seems that a ray of light has come to shine as a happy promise of the eventual victory of spiritual freedom in the seemingly hopeless struggle against the powers of darkness. . . . It gives me great comfort this day, as a representative of Judaism, to extend the hand of brotherhood in warmest appreciation to the proclaimer of Christianity. In this spirit, may mutual cooperation in spiritual freedom, even within a diversity of convictions and viewpoints, ever increase our strength.

NS, V, P. 339 F.

TO PROFESSOR THEODOR NOELDECKE

Berlin, July 8, 1872

Our complaints at the unfair treatment of Judaism on the part of Christian scholars who are otherwise sympathetic are not based on any demand on our part that they should concern themselves more with its post-biblical literature. . . . We do not have the right to prescribe the course or direction their studies should take. But we do have the right to ask that those who are not familiar with this literature should either refrain from passing judgment on it or, at least, be circumspect in expressing their opinions. We do have the right to denounce the ignorance of those who, despite such ignorance, and with boundless arrogance and spite, air their derogatory opinions on such matters; and we are justified in banning such persons from the company of fair and honest scholars. Of course, those Christian scholars who engage in the study of the origins of Christianity are not free to choose whether or not to study the later developments of Judaism. If they are to acquire the proper judgment they must be familiar with the conditions which prevailed within Judaism at that period, and it seems only fair that they should make use of Jewish sources for that purpose. It cannot be denied that it is difficult to get a proper understanding of these Jewish sources, but this fact does not exempt them from the duty to become familiar with them if they desire to voice opinions on subjects which can be understood only through a study of such sources. It is regrettable that we lack the aids necessary to facilitate such understanding, and that nothing is being done by the Jews who do possess this knowledge to remedy this deficiency. I am certain that this situation will be changed in the course of time. Here, too, however, the Jews are not to blame. To this very day, Jews are all but completely barred from unrestricted scholarly pursuits; much of the work is done either by rabbis who are already overburdened with official duties, or by dilettantes. How could one expect them to produce work of a nature that demands a lifetime of devoted labor?

You think that we expect you to view the dreadful discussions of Halakhah as something more than a waste of intelligence on subjects not worthy of the effort. If they are of no practical value, you need not hesitate to disregard them. But if they should prove absolutely necessary for the evaluation of a subject under study, an interested scholar can no more be exempted from studying them than a historian, desiring to present historical studies of that era in the light of their motivating forces, can afford to disregard the Church Fathers, the legendarians and the scholasticists.

I myself do not go along with the romantic predilection for modern Hebrew which many modern writers now use in their scholarly articles. However, one must consider that, by virtue of their way of life, most of these men are actually prevented from using a living language. It must therefore be deemed commendable that they communicate their observations in some idiom that can be understood. . . . I might add, though, that this undesirable state of affairs, too, is gradually disappearing.

I do not wish to enter into any further discussion on the point that complaints of the harshness of Christianity toward Judaism are unjustified because all Semitic religions have a natural bent for persecution. It is a sad thing that, on one hand, pride is taken in modern humanitarianism while at the same time one can, when it suits him, fall back on outworn Oriental attitudes. I am not telling this to you, but all the more emphatically to your colleagues.

NS, V, P. 341 F.

letter to leopold zunz

---◈◈◈---

(Letter from Geiger congratulating Leopold Zunz on the latter's seventieth birthday, August 10, 1864)

Frankfort-on-the-Main

My honored friend, you are now standing on the threshold of an important new phase of your life. As you look back on a career of scholarship filled with achievements of great merit and influence, you do so in the happy knowledge that your career is by no means at an end and that you can still continue, in the fullness of vigor, to create much that is noble and constructive. This knowledge is a joy also for us, the friends and admirers of your later years. . . . At the same time, in the midst of incessant activity, this milestone affords us all a pause for serious reflection. It is an occasion for us to consider with deep gratitude all that we owe you in our own education and in the enrichment of our knowledge . . .

It is not my purpose on this day of rededication to come before you with an historical account or even with a scholarl, treatise and summation of your merits. Yet, on this great day, I am most vividly reminded of that time when the force of the master's influence first made itself felt on the youthful disciple; I recall the intellectual stimulus which helped awaken my spirit, and then determined and shaped to an ever-growing degree the course I was to follow. Old, yet at the same time youthful, voices sound once again within my heart, memories of a day which, though long past, has proved to be decisive for the present. . . . Hence I may surely be permitted to speak of those influences which manifested themselves in my youth and which then became factors of great moment in my further development.

My adolescence coincided with the flowering of reaction.

In the twenties of our century any attempt of the spirit to soar to greater freedom was rigorously repressed. A national life based on a historic past was nowhere in evidence, and youth was incapable of cultivating a lively interest in contemporary developments. Religious progress born of a free inner conviction was taboo. At times efforts were made to compel retrogression to outworn religious concepts; and then again the authorities would enforce Enlightenment by decree. These mutually contradictory measures were alternated in a particularly grotesque fashion in proceedings against the Jews and Judaism. This thoughtless interference with spiritual progress and the resulting developments are matters of historical record; to reiterate them here would be superfluous.

All the more credit, then, is due those men who refused to be cowed by the unpropitiousness of the time and who indefatigably and cheerfully continued to nurture the noble seedlings of spiritual growth. Things were quiet, however, very quiet indeed around us, the young people of that day. If it is true that, as the poet puts it, talent best unfolds in an atmosphere of silence, then it was truly a most propitious time for the maturing of latent aptitudes. And, indeed, this stagnant period of quiet, unbroken by any sound from without, did have a beneficial, edifying influence on aspiring youthful minds. People concentrated on the inner life; they strove to assimilate the treasured heritage of antiquity and to become familiar with it. Delving into the splendid achievements of the classical era of German history just past, they shared its high exaltation, and drawing on the wellsprings of its vigorous élan, they nurtured their own youthful poetic drive. It was the eternal, universal human problems that fully engaged both thought and action; those current issues emanating from contemporary history, which in more productive times would have been questions occupying every mind, had receded into the background. I do not recall ever having read a newspaper prior to the July Revolution of 1830; questions of positive sympathies did not even occur. Nor did religious life offer new and stimulating phenomena; people either trod the old, worn path or else turned away from it completely. Still, these were matters of much too great spiritual concern for the thinking man not to have to turn some attention to them.

In my own native city there was a strangely rigid dividing line between those who, on the one hand, had been influenced by the currents of the new era and who made strenuous efforts to assimilate its cultural elements and those who, on the other hand, tenaciously clung to outworn viewpoints and institutions. Each group went its own way, each indifferent to the other, neither exercising any influence on the other, and yet closely linked together by the common bond of the community in which they lived. A similar division must have been evident in any larger community in those days. The drive to revitalize communal life had slackened; the stable elements lacked both the strength and the courage to make a forceful forward move, nor did they themselves deviate even one finger's breadth from the old. Generally, they remained practically unmolested in their traditional heritage so that they found no cause for battle . . .

"Let things take their course" was the adage of the day. A fusion of the ancient and the ongoing historical movement was considered impossible, even abominable. Some condemned any change, any progress, as sinful; others simply viewed such endeavors as idle folly. . . . The adolescent was not encouraged to make a personal decision; he found himself adopting a given ideology according to the orientation that prevailed in his immediate environment. He could make a change only if he himself transcended that given viewpoint by attaining independence as the result of introspection. And if he did so, he overcame the rigid narrow-mindedness that prevailed among both the parties . . .

Of course, there was a historical school; it had been accepted by scholarship and had achieved a good deal. Yet, in its struggle against the impetuous creative drive of the preceding era, when the old had been swept away without much deliberation, it immersed itself too deeply into the minor evolutionary stages of the past to be able to acknowledge the right of the conscious forces of the present day to engage in creative endeavor. The free and independent activity of man was thus subjugated to blind necessity. . . . The men who were regarded as the spokesmen of Christian philosophy sought out the old, while they fought all progress. The adherents of progress, on the other hand, would have no part of the concept of historical evolution and development; they strove to build anew solely in accordance with the demands of pure logic and reason. A higher instrumentality, such as that which genuine insight into the processes of history might have offered, was not considered.

To Jewish minds of the time, the historical approach was completely alien. On one side there were those who read the Bible through the eyes of the Talmud and of the rabbis down to their very own day. On the other side were the elements who viewed the Scriptures from the vantage point of recent findings in the field of philology and exegesis; they considered the Talmud and the literature based upon it as naiveté and perversity pure and simple; as an exercise in sheer demonic hyper-intellectualism, which had to be ignored and eliminated from the records of history. . . . They did not stop to consider what formidable intellectual evolution this literature represented, a literature in which layer had been piled upon layer and which had transformed and even forcibly supplanted many an element of earlier cultures. It did not occur to them that a healthy creative impulse had been at work to produce these forms during the course of millennia, and that this same impulse still manifests itself today, impelling the continuing creation of new forms which, rejected as daring radicalism by the one party, were looked upon as outworn by the other.

These two schools were vigorously represented also in Frankfort, where all of them influenced me to some extent during my youth. There were men who, with all their steadfast adherence to the traditional point of view, had acquired considerable knowledge of talmudic literature and certainly did not subscribe to the fanaticism typical of the ignorant. Among the champions of Enlightenment, too, there were quite a number who were sufficiently familiar with the ancient heritage to be drawn back to it over and over again. At this point I must make mention of my own brother Salomon. Early in my youth he introduced me to Hebrew grammar and to the Bible; it was he who guided me through the Talmud too, along the straight path of healthy understanding, protecting my inquiring mind from the affectations of a hair-splitting *pilpulism* not founded on truth. I am grateful indeed that I may still benefit today from the youthful mental and spiritual vigor of him who has now reached a venerable old age. On the other side, I was also strongly and beneficially influenced by my contacts with Johlson,[1] who pursued his biblical studies with great devotion, and by Creizenach[2] to whom I was drawn because of his mental alertness and moral fervor. I still recall Heidenheim,[3] that venerable old man whom, in my boyhood, I dearly loved to visit on Sabbaths and holidays at his country retreat at Roedelheim. Well-grounded in the Masorah, he was an excellent grammarian of the school of Ibn Ezra and Kimhi. He was prudent in his

selection of good manuscripts for the biblical text . . . for
the daily *siddur* and for the holiday prayer book, and he also
showed some interest in historical studies.

Thus sound instruction and inspiration were not lacking.
Nevertheless, the mind of the boy and of the adolescent remained unsatisfied. I yearned for a well-rounded, comprehensive unity of the spheres that had become separated. I
might not have been conscious of the fact, but I longed for
that Ariadne's thread which would lead me, not *out* of the
intertwined mazes, but *through* them. I sought to recognize
the gradual evolution and the peculiar characteristics of the
spirit that pervaded each era in history, and to comprehend
these things for myself, each according to its own manner
and fashion. Herder and Eichhorn[4] were my early guides
through the realm of the Bible; and if they did not satisfy
me altogether, they still succeeded in broadening my perspective. I sought to investigate on my own . . . I wanted to
try my own hand. Long before I entered the University, I
had begun work on a commentary on the Mishna, intending
to explain the Mishna independently from the interpretation
of the Gemara—it was all conjecture then, but later it
turned into full realization and has gradually become
common knowledge in the world of scholarship. I also gathered a wealth of material for a dictionary of the Mishna . . .
an undertaking that I have continued indefatigably, though
not without interruptions. Perhaps I may yet reap its full
harvest some day in the future. My historical studies in a
narrower sense were centered particularly on Maimonides
and the other Jewish philosophers, though, within the limitations of my means and my experience, they extended to wider
circles as well. Into this quiet labor there suddenly fell that
ray of light, of which I was hardly conscious, which illumi-
nated my path and prepared me for the even greater light
that was to stream forth for me later on.

That one beam, honored Master, was your own *Zeitschrift
fuer die Wissenschaft des Judentums*[5] which accidentally
came into my hands. It did not have a large circulation, nor
did it exert widespread influence, but for many a receptive
reader its contents proved to be both significant and stimulating. Its spirit and language were thoroughly steeped in genuine scholarship . . . And there I found your epoch-making
work on Rashi. It was like a mountain stream which becomes
all the more refreshing and invigorating by virtue of the

great obstacles which it has to overcome. The assurance with which you mastered the great wealth of your material, the light you shed on dark and pathless terrain, your edifying, illuminating progress through the arcades of medieval Jewish literature—all these afforded both refreshment and stimulation, though, instead of quenching my thirst, they only served to make it keener.

If those of us who are aware of the present dearth of interest in the Jewish literary movement look back in nostalgic retrospect upon the better days of yore, the period to which we will turn our wistful gaze can be no other than the middle of the thirties. The decade that had gone before, on the other hand, had been a colorless one; its creative elements had no contact with one another and they had no central point around which they might have gathered. *Bikkurei ha-Ittim,* the Hebrew journal which encompasses that decade, did not live up to its title; it failed to produce those "first fruits of the times" that would have heralded a richer harvest to come. Instead, it succeeded only in bringing forth the late fruit of a day long past. The *Meassef* of Mendelssohn's school combined subjects of higher education by means of an aesthetic treatment of the Hebrew language and the discussion, in Hebrew, of subjects of general interest. It was believed that the revival of the Hebrew language was an end in itself. However, general culture and learning had even then penetrated Jewish circles to such an extent that they could be acquired in the idiom of modern, living languages. The time when Hebrew, as the sole language understood by all, was the only key to basic education and the only tool for conveying the elements of culture and good taste had long since passed. Yet people persisted in these obsolete endeavors and in fact conceived of them as characteristic features of Jewish learning. This claim might still have been valid for eastern Germany and the Slavic nations, but it certainly was no longer so for us, in western Germany.

Hence it was both a novel and a happy experience for me when, in 1828, in Karlsruhe, I saw a current issue [of Zunz's *Zeitschrift?*] which contained the first biography ever written by Rapoport; i.e., that of Saadia, and it was there, too, that I first heard the name of Luzzatto mentioned. It was a fine preparation for what was to come. . . . The circle of men of note had widened, the aids to scholarship multiplied.

To this was added the influence of teachers and friends at the University, which I entered in 1829.

Yet I always looked in the direction of Zunz with a certain amount of impatience. He was silent too long to suit me; I had looked to him for renewed stimulation and it had failed to materialize. Ever since 1830 the fiery spark of Riesser's message had stirred me to the very depths of my emotions; I valued his effectiveness within the Jewish community even more highly than his success outside. The awakening of a vital, common Jewish interest, a closing of the ranks in the search for spiritual advancement and ennoblement, the creation of centers around which our forces might rally—all these ideals were my own goals and aspirations. I sought to win all my friends, both near and far away, for this aim; and my ideal was to have a journal to serve as the rallying point for this intellectual struggle. And again it was Leopold Zunz whom I envisioned as the founder and leader of such an undertaking. Carried away by this idea, the young man overcame his shyness and, in April 1831, he first turned to Zunz, unburdening his whole heart and laying before him all his struggles and labors, which were then still somewhat awkward and uncertain.

Permit me, Sir, to quote for your recollection some of the passages contained in that first letter.

The high regard, . . . with which your worthy aims and endeavors inspire me, has nurtured within me the desire to have closer contact with this noble man, once my own powers have developed and I dared hope to emulate him. Not merely erudition and familiarity with the literature of Judaism distinguish the Jewish scholar. He must be endowed, too, with thoroughness . . . coupled with a profundity which traces scientific contexts and extracts the spirit therefrom . . . he must have an interest in the Golden Age of Jewish literature and a desire to portray the men who distinguished themselves in that field. Finally, a genuine Jewish scholar must have a profound respect for these most valuable remnants of a unique culture. Similarly, his aim should not be to uproot the ancient trunk altogether and to plant a new one in its stead, but . . . to beautify the tree, to give new life to its roots so that it may yield new, fresh, rich and healthy fruit. Thus it is not blind reforming zeal, trimming the exterior but still leaving the interior cold and bare, but the effort to revive Jewishness and to fashion it anew from within Judaism itself that seems to me an endeavor which will bring honor to the Jew as such.

Seeing that I believe I have recognized such a man in you, would you take it amiss that I have overcome my timidity and dared to approach you?

Thereafter I gradually proceeded to set forth my request that a mouthpiece of opinion be created "for the scientific treatment of Jewish antiquities, and for the civic and religious betterment of our coreligionists," an undertaking which should unite the efforts of all of Israel's scholars of Judaism, of all men who take an interest in Judaism, be that interest religious, historical or civic. I spoke of "the great number of shallow rationalists" and then, as opposed to them, of the truly honorable "rationalists of intellect and soul." I said that these latter

stand in awe of the positive as the fruit of the human mind; they know how to appreciate antiquity in its sublime, classic simplicity. They take no pleasure in Voltairian mockery, nor do they look upon the ancient framework of Judaism with derision. Instead, they give willing recognition to the influence of Judaism on world history and proudly stress its lofty ideals. To them that which their forefathers built upon Judaism for centuries may no longer be religiously binding, but they view it as worthy evidence of that past religious life.

Among these men I placed Zunz above all; through him I wished to see my heart's desire fulfilled.

These utterances should give some indication of the mental image which the immature youth of those days had conceived of the man. . . . He believed that in this great master he beheld the guide who could lead to salvation. . . . If this was the effect of the study on Rashi, one may readily imagine the profound impression that the *Gottesdienstliche Vortraege* (Lectures on the Divine Services of the Jews) must have made in 1832 on the recent university graduate then just starting out in life. At last, a clearing had been made in the wildly tangled forest of Jewish literature; long centuries of evolution lay exposed before the mind's eye; the inner history, though merely hinted at, wrought upon the understanding.

The book had a profound and refreshing effect upon me personally. But over and beyond this it was a landmark in

Jewish history, a turning point in intellectual progress. New activity began in every field and there is none who would not gladly agree that he has received both impetus and instruction from this work.

This marked the end of the silent era; my own years of apprenticeship, too, were done . . . but I shall always be willing and ready, Sir, to learn from you. In my own independent scholarly and practical activities I have not always followed quite the same path which you have taken and along which you have continued; but I have always looked toward you with respectful attention. May I be granted the privilege of deriving instruction and new strength from your vigorous labors for many years to come.

NS, I, PP. 296 FF.

3

---·•━◆◆◆━•·---

excerpts

FROM

GEIGER'S WORKS

A GENERAL INTRODUCTION TO THE SCIENCE OF
JUDAISM
from Nachgelassene Schriften

REPORTS OF THE JEWISH INSTITUTE OF RELIGIOUS
INSTRUCTION IN BRESLAU
from Nachgelassene Schriften

JUDAISM AND ITS HISTORY
from Das Judentum und Seine Geschichte

THE ORIGINAL TEXT AND TRANSLATIONS OF THE BIBLE
from Urschrift und Uebersetzungen der Bibel

a general introduction to the science of judaism

(Lectures delivered by Geiger at the Academy for the Science of Judaism, Berlin, 1872-1874)

PREFACE

The introduction to the Science of Judaism which is to be given here aims at bringing about a full understanding of the religious thought and ideal content which pervades Judaism and which dwells within it as its unique life-giving force. The only method by which such understanding can be acquired is the study of the manner in which the idea first entered into the physical world, of the way in which it has found expression in language and literature and in which it has manifested itself in practice in the course of history. Only when the spiritual motive behind Judaism has thus been traced inductively will it be possible for us to gain a true conception of its full content and its philosophical and religio-ethical tenets. It is true that they will then be isolated from the time-bound forms in which they have been expressed at various periods, but they will still bear within themselves vital forces which have not yet achieved their full development. The Science of Judaism may thus be divided into three aspects:

1. Philological
2. Historical, particularly as regards the history of Jewish literature and culture
3. Philosophical and religious

To begin with, there will be some who will count against Judaism the fact that it has a philological aspect at all, which is supposed to be no less important than its history, and who will view this as proof of its narrowness. There will be those who will compare Judaism with Christianity. They will point out that, while Christianity has exerted some influence on the development, or rather on the style, of language, it did not make its appearance in a language of its own, but in Greek which was then the idiom of world culture. The fact that, soon thereafter, Christianity came to employ Latin, the tongue of the Romans who held sway over the civilized world, will be taken as an indication of the universal nature of this faith. On closer examination, however, one will find that what seemed an advantage for Christianity is actually a shortcoming and that what first appeared to be a weakness in Judaism is actually one of its strong points.

A new idea can originate only in a strong personality. It is only by a strong individual that a universally acceptable idea can be conceived. It will then mature into consummate expression only in one who is especially qualified and endowed for this purpose by his active participation in the general natural tendencies of mankind. Wherever a superior form of development of the universal human type is in evidence it will manifest itself in superior, distinctive individuality. In such persons the idea which can embrace all of mankind will shine forth in the form of a conviction that pervades all of that person's life; the idea will carry with it the demand that everyone else allow himself to be imbued with it to the same extent and also the awareness that this demand is possible of fulfilment especially here. This conviction will dominate such an individual. Moreover, while the conviction will, on the one hand, constitute the whole essence of that individual, his personality, sharp and distinct as it is, will, on the other hand, impress the seal of its subjective nature on the idea. It is impossible to separate the two influences from one another.

If this is true with regard to one individual, it must certainly be even more so in the case of a whole nation. It is only in a nation with special potentialities that science, art, and religion will manifest themselves in a refined form. Just because they are so completely dominated by the idea, the people, its views and its language will also impress their full individual character upon the thoughts and creations which are supposed to represent that which is universally human. Only a people which has a healthy vitality and which constitutes a closed entity will be able to produce ideas that are viable, comprehensive and of abiding value. These ideas will, of necessity, bear the imprint of the definite and unique physiognomy of that people. This physiognomy is the vessel that will contain the idea and will of necessity limit its manifestations. It will detract nothing, however, from the general validity of its contents. Thus the idea must come to the fore in full individual definiteness and in accordance with the language and concepts of the people with whom it originated; indeed, it must come forth as the particular expression of that people. Only later may it become transfigured into a greater spirituality, as it becomes independent of the soil in which it first matured. If it is not to fall victim to that curse which adheres to every unhealthy outgrowth of romanticism, it must not be the product of vague and hazy perceptions. Thus, we will not cast aspersions on the universal value of ancient Greek art just because its themes were derived from mythology and its characters bear Greek features. True, the artist of today no longer carves idols, nor does he mold his figures in terms of Greek beauty, but the fact remains that the idea of art was fully realized by the ancient Greeks and this will be understood by everyone who is receptive to it.

The strength of Judaism lies precisely in the fact that it has grown out of a full national life and that it possesses both a language and a history as a nation. The idea of Judaism was an all-embracing one. Hence, if it was not to be a drifting shadow, it had to find expression in a healthy national individualism which, on the one hand, saw all of mankind epitomized within itself, but, on the other hand, sought to embrace all the world of mankind beyond its own confines. Thus it is a strong point of Judaism that it originally revealed itself in a language which was entirely imbued with the idea and which was the noblest fruit of a full national life. Judaism was not, however, dependent upon language and nationality; indeed, it survived in all its vitality even after being deprived of both. When its vessel was smashed, its survival was not affected thereby. Because it always had to engage in violent struggle, Judaism remained a closed and separate entity; and yet it has succeeded in transmitting its basic ideals to mankind as a universal heritage. And when the artificial barriers fall, it will continue to retain its universality throughout the course of history. Let us, therefore, look back with joy on our former life as a nation, as being an essential transitional era in our history, and on our language, through which the life of that Jewish nation had taken root in spiritual soil!

Christianity put in its very first appearance as a universalist faith; but precisely in this lack of a national origin and individual language lies its weakness. Its concepts and sentiments are characterized by great vagueness; they conflict with every definite national trait. They are mere phantoms which deny all real life. Dreams of a disembodied existence, they widen the chasm between body and soul and view the destruction of all things physical as the greatest attainable bliss. Christianity arose under the influence of the disintegration of noble civilizations, the Jewish and the Greek; it was garbed in decaying languages; it had the seeds of morbidity implanted in it, as it were—a morbid state under which it labors to this day. Christianity is the true mother of mysticism and romanticism. Judaism, on the other hand, is lucid, concrete, vital and affirmative. Judaism is permeated with spirituality; it does not deny the earthly world, but transfigures it instead. It is rooted in one particular people with a language and history of its own, and yet it embraces all of mankind.

. . . The Science of Judaism is the study of the particular orientation of the spiritual life through which, within one particular sphere, Judaism was founded, developed, broadcast, and preserved in full vigor down to our time. Our interest in this spiritual force grows as we perceive that it did not operate within narrow limits and far away from the world of reality. On the contrary, its spiritual power has manifested itself almost at all times in the very midst of the mightiest spiritual movements in world history, at the very focal points of important cultural developments. It was, in fact, receptive to stimuli emanating from the centers of culture, so that it never shut them out; but it was not absorbed by them. It succeeded rather in assimilating them to its own manner, thus giving evidence of its independent vitality. This evidence is corroborated even more effectively by the telling influence which the spirit of Judaism has continuously exerted on human progress as a whole and which—as its vitality permits us to hope—it will continue to exercise in the future. At three important crossroads in world history, Judaism had an important part in guiding the development of spiritual and intellectual life. At the close of the era of antiquity, Judaism gave birth to Christianity; during the Middle Ages, it brought Islam to life and nourished it with its essential content, and at the opening of the modern era, it provided the intellectual background for Spinoza and thus the first momentum for a complete revolution in the theories of philosophy. These world-wide forces did not continue to have an effect on Judaism, but the spirit of Judaism continued to be manifest within them. It is significant, too, that Judaism survived and took root in those countries which long before had produced the first fruits of civilization: Egypt, Phoenicia, Syria, Assyria and Babylonia. Judaism maintained the closest possible ties with these countries and thus certainly was in no position to ward off their intellectual influences. Nevertheless, Judaism remained independent of them. True, at a later date, it was exposed to the influences of Parsism which it assimilated in a fashion which was its very own; subsequently, it united with Hellenism to give birth to Alexandrianism; and, eventually, it developed its own fullest potential in closest union with Arab civilization. It was in this manner that Judaism made its contribution to the cultural movement and communicated to medieval Christianity the intellectual heritage of antiquity which it had rescued from oblivion in the Arab era. Hence the hope is quite justified that the time may not be distant when Judaism will once more impregnate and so transform the world of ideas, and at the same time independently assimilate the variety of outside cultural elements to which it is exposed.

Through this highly effective activity on the part of Judaism, both in giving and in receiving, the content as well as the scope of its "science" has developed into a mighty system. . . . All of the individual parts thereof constitute member organisms of one great whole. None of these may be ignored; by the same token, no one such element may be emphasized at the expense of the others. The sole task of the specialists, therefore, is to analyze the individual facets and then to relate them to the whole.

Even as any vital and viable idea falls into a threefold organic division of its own, so this entire wealth of material, too, may be separated into three major categories.

The idea became manifest in the physical world with all the vigor and freshness of youthful strength; however, it remained confined inside the framework of the time and the space within which it was born. In naive elation at its victory it overlooked the limitations inherent in it, and, as it soared upward, it bore with it upon its wings the dust of the earthly conditions under which it had first come into being. . . . Its eyes were trained upon the Utopian heights from which it felt called upon to envelop all things below, and yet it found itself compelled to go on existing within the narrow bounds of limited lowlands. It had the ability creatively to reflect a perfect image, and yet it remained so deeply rooted in its native soil that it could not detach itself from it.

Thus Judaism became firmly consolidated. Next, it sought to penetrate all outside conditions, to transform them. But, instead, it was itself modified and influenced by the very conditions which it had sought to affect. The further it reached out, the more one-sided it became; it dissipated its strength and lost its intensity. The spiritual wealth which it gained was not always genuine, and the idea which inspired it grew superficial and was eventually spent, dissipated.

And then it attained the third phase. At this point it pulled itself together and reverted to its former intrinsic character; but with the difference that now it was changed by a wealth of experiences and acquisitions which it then purified and transfigured.

NS, II, PP. 35 FF.

. . . Language is the articulation of the national idea; history is the idea in action. Language is more vital and more immediate than history; like a garment, it covers the whole spirit at one time. However, its first outpouring is connected with a definite stage of the people's development. Thereafter it will at best no longer be the expression of the spirit but only its handy tool; in most instances it declines and becomes petrified. History is different. History does not reflect the spirit completely and all at once; it is dependent also on many factors which lie outside the spirit of the nation to which it belongs. But it is precisely by means of struggle, by development, by conflict and by victory or defeat that the strength or the impotence of the spirit is revealed. Particularly in the case of Judaism, we find that history revealing an inexhaustible wealth of possibilities for the unfolding and molding of spiritual and intellectual life.

It is self-evident that history, as an essential component

of the Science of Judaism, can only be a study of the history of spiritual achievements. The outer facets of its history have value only as substrata, as conditions under which achievements could come into being and which either hindered or furthered the growth of such achievements. It should be remembered, however, that it is inherent in the very nature of the Jews that their history should primarily be a spiritual one and, as such, a process that helped shape the entire world, and that it should not be expressed either in civic policy or primarily in political or communal life. The Jews remain in a state of inner division which in turn gives rise to inner struggle and feats of spiritual heroism. Such, in fact, is the fate of all highly gifted peoples. The empire of the ancient Greeks fell, after their short-lived world supremacy, their unity having been forged by the Macedonians, the most primitive tribe in their midst. As for the Italians, who are now in the process of being welded into one united nation by the crude Piedmontese, they have yet to prove whether, as a united nation with a capital in Rome, they will be able to regain that historical significance which we must admit they had attained during the Middle Ages. It was not despite their own inner division, but, in fact, just because of it, that the Germans were able to give birth to the greatest discoveries, . . . to the free spirit of the Reformation and to the glory of a literature of world-wide import. It is our wish that the new united *Reich*, led by its imperial dynasty, may be able to record similar achievements. Such, too, has been the history of Judaism, and it is precisely to its independence from political status that Judaism owes its survival. Anything that enters into the life of a nation as a sudden thing, instead of as a tender- sapling, gradually growing into a strong plant, is no longer history. Judaism, on the other hand, has sprouted into full bloom from the tenderest of seedlings; with this fact it demonstrates that it has a genuine history.

. . . As part of the Science of Judaism, a study of its history will, of course, remain subject to all those laws which history recognizes as science. Scientific, critical study must not be hindered by dogmatic assumptions. Judaism has no cause to fear an unbiased critical examination.

. . . The history of Judaism is wonderfully unique in that it spans a period extending from remote antiquity down to the immediate present. It is therefore not mere curiosity which acts as a spur to its study, not merely the desire to eavesdrop on the mystery of the origins of Judaism, but at least equally the desire to detect the extent to which all of its later development was essentially already inherent in the growth and flowering process of the original seeds. These beginnings are hidden, modestly and shamefacedly in dim obscurity; the scholar, however, cannot avoid this difficulty, but must remain dependent upon these prehistorical phenomena. Without the revelation which only such study of the ancient history of Judaism, even though the results may be mere approximations, afford, he can never succeed in gaining the proper insight into Judaism's subsequent history which lies more fully recorded before him.

The history of Judaism may be divided into four periods.

The first period is that of *Revelation,* of vigorous creation, unfettered and unhindered. It was an era of free, creative formation from within. This period extends to the close of the biblical era, which cannot be said to have ended at the time of Exile, for its outgrowths continued well beyond that date.

The second period is the era during which all this biblical material was processed, shaped and molded for life; it was then that Judaism took root in the spiritual heritage of the past and at the same time still maintained a certain degree of freedom in its approach to that heritage. This was the period of *Tradition,* which extended from the time of the completion of the Bible to the completion of the Babylonian Talmud.

The third period is characterized by toilsome preoccupation with the heritage as it then stood. The spiritual heritage was guarded and preserved, but no one felt authorized to reconstruct it or to develop it further. No one dared go beyond the limits set long before. This was the period of rigid *Legalism,* of casuistry, the era which was devoted to the summing up of what had been handed down by tradition. It extended from the time of the completion of the Babylonian Talmud down into the middle of the 18th century.

The fourth period, the era of liberation, has been marked by an effort to loosen the fetters of the previous era by means of the use of reason and historical research. However, the bond with the past has not been severed. What is being attempted is solely to revitalize Judaism and to cause the stream of history to flow forth once again. This is the era of *Critical Study,* our own modern era.

. . . Corresponding to the outwardly discernible course of history there is also an inner, spiritual history, namely, that of religious development. As a consequence of the growth of a sharply defined national consciousness . . . which tended more and more to work for segregation and for the exclusion of all foreign admixtures, the Deity which this nation worshiped also had to assume a unique position. This of course did not necessarily exclude the recognition of other national deities; it was thought that the god Khemosh had the same relationship to the nation under his rule as Yahweh had to the people of Israel. But the other deities were regarded only as alien gods, as hostile beings which would be overcome by the God of Israel. The concept of God did not immediately take shape as a pure ideal of one God for the entire universe, a Supreme Being who could neither be pictured nor perceived by the physical senses. Nevertheless, this idea of a God superior to all other gods already bore within itself the seeds of a more mature concept toward which it then evolved, slowly but inevitably.

We have hardly any records to supply us with information concerning that time when the Reubenites first settled in the territory east of the river Jordan. In all likelihood their religious views differed little from those of the neighboring tribes. Nor do we have any definite records of the time of the first settlements in the territory west of the Jordan. The mode of divine worship there was still harsh and cruel —crude, in keeping with the character of these tribes—but it clearly tended to weld them into one single unit. Gradually, certain places, particularly Beer-sheba, gained prominence as exclusive sites for the worship of God. We must assume that in those days such practices as human sacrifice, and the worship of wells and trees were the custom; the worship of God, however, sought to entrench itself in a form clearly separated from the religious rites of alien tribes, though without attaining complete purity just yet. Here, too, we have no reliable historical records to serve us as an introduction to the thinking that prevailed in the midst of those tribes.

In all likelihood it was only with the immigration of additional tribes, such as those of Manasseh and Ephraim, who came west from Egypt through the land east of the Jordan River, that the religious picture took on a purer form; this change may well have come to pass even prior to their movement to the west. From then on a milder character, the product of a higher civilization, came to permeate the religious views of this region. Although it still survived for some time, the practice of human sacrifice as part of the official religious ritual was now opposed, and the primitive practice of offering one's children, and one's sons in particular, to the Deity was replaced by the milder custom of circumcision. The precise extent to which the influence of Egyptian civilization made its weight felt here and in other similar instances is difficult to determine . . .

Men like Elijah and Elisha, whose personalities, though enveloped in a veil of pious legend, still rate high above those of their peers, whose excesses of sensuality were the vogue in their day, were stern in their determined fight against tyranny and lack of principle. But even greater were those prophets, such as Hosea, Amos and others, who did not stand out by virtue of miraculous acts but who had a powerful effect upon the spirit of the people by their high ideals of religion and ethics. The priestly class, too, a numerous and powerful body in Israel, was affected by this progressive process of purification. Now there came about a wonderful amalgamation of the old and the new into a single whole. The ceremonial of priesthood and sacrifices now stood side by side with religious requirements of great refinement and purity. The feeling of revulsion at any other mode of worship went hand in hand with the retention of institutions originally derived from alien cultures. These institutions were now Israelized, as it were, and were themselves rendered holy thereby . . .

The entire body of strictly historical narrative came into being at a later date, during the era of the kingdom of Judea which saw nothing but apostasy and impious idol worship in the neighboring kingdom of Israel. Next to the prophets of the kingdom of Israel, the earlier components of the first four books of the Pentateuch are the only sources that can provide us with a faithful reflection of the thinking which prevailed then in the northern kingdom. There all of ancient history becomes a mirror of the present. From the very outset, Ephraim is given a place of prominence, without, however, detracting in any manner from the historic significance of Judah. Both the migration to Egypt and the Exodus thence are recorded here as events involving the entire nation. Whatever statutes and institutions had been in force at the time of the writing of this literature were ascribed to a Lawgiver who had lived in days of antiquity. This Lawgiver, however, was in turn assisted by a priestly caste which was almost equal to him, and at times even above him in rank. With this in mind, it should not come as a surprise to us that sacrifices and the priesthood should still have taken up so much space in this important portion of Hebraic literature.

Judah's development was much more gradual; but in the long run it had greater permanence. More and more, there evolved a discipline in which the existence of one officially recognized Temple only and of a continuous dynasty of rulers forced the priesthood into a secondary position. This in turn gave rise to the evolution of simpler customs, that slowly gained in purity and refinement as time went by. It was only after the fall of the kingdom of Israel in the north that Judah developed a literature of its own, though this literature was then all the more magnificent in its maturity. Personalities like Isaiah, Micah, Jeremiah and others showed a clarity of thought and boldness of prophetic vision such as had never been given expression in the kingdom of Israel. Here we find a noble kind of nationalism which, though it emphasized the doctrine of the Chosen People, was deeply rooted in a higher mission and in the calling of that People to translate this mission into living reality. It is here that the concept of One Sole Invisible God, who cannot be represented by a physical image, acquires a stronger conviction and a more definite expression.

. . . Eventually, the whole Jewish concept of history and of religious life and law had to adapt itself to the views that prevailed in the kingdom of Judah. Along with the original literary creations which were completely pervaded by this spirit, the traditions and ritual practices already in existence had to undergo a transformation in keeping with the new spirit whch now gained the upper hand. The entire historical account, particularly that of the divided state, underwent a thorough revision, in keeping with changed conditions. The history of the northern kingdom of Israel now was represented as that of a state which had no right to exist and was torn asunder by eternal dissension because it had rejected its rightful Ruler and the one true faith. Only a very few true accounts of this era may have found their way into the historical books of the Bible as they now stand; and even there they are immured within the framework of the new interpretation. Some such ancient components have been preserved from the pre-Davidic era and from that of David and Solomon; but these are surrounded by accretions and changes from which the original accounts are yet to be clearly distinguished . . .

NS, II, PP. 61 FF.

THE PERIOD OF TRADITION

The spirit of the nation, with its intuitive genius, forged steadily ahead and created new things, out of its own resources, in ever-increasing perfection until it reached its zenith. Then everything came to a standstill: now its primary concern became, not to create new things, but to preserve the acquired heritage, to collect it, sift it, supplement it and adapt it for every conceivable situation in life, an effort which might entail complete change in one instance, and the ferreting out and confirmation of the smallest and pettiest details in another. In the history of any nation, this could be an era of great significance, in which ideal concepts receive their full embodiment and thus firmly establish the life of that nation upon a bedrock of ideals. Just the same, the original creative force will be missed, and in instances in which the times by their very nature make growth and development a pressing necessity, that development will appear to be narrowly confined . . . manifesting itself in superficial breadth rather than in the dimension of inner depth. This will be particularly true when circumstances from without do not permit spiritual progress and when, in fact, pressure from without and lack of free self-determination have an unfavorable effect on the spirit. Such was the situation of the Jews under Persian rule.

At that time, the people could lead a marginal existence at best. No impetus toward regeneration emanated from the Persian empire which, after the advent to power of Cyrus, had fallen prey itself to the spiritual indolence typical of the great empires of Asia. . . . Though the book of Esther may contain little material of actual historical value, it does serve as evidence of the things that the people recalled most clearly of the rule of Persia; their situation was precarious, dependent on transient moods and caprice, and the spirit atrophied. The language in which this book is written and the attitude which it reflects match one another. Given such conditions it was inevitable that Judea, though it did not entirely fade away, should suffer from a state of creeping paralysis.

The situation changed, however, when Greek civilization attained world supremacy. It is true, of course, that by that time Greece, too, had passed its zenith. Macedonia, which then occupied the position of political leadership, was the least cultured part of Greece. Moreover, this vast expansion of the new empire, of necessity, caused the spirit of its civilization to become superficial and to degenerate. . . .

After the fall of the empire of Alexander it was Egypt, strongly Hellenized, that exercised the most powerful influence upon the Jews. A great number of them lived there; these Jews were completely assimilated into the Egyptian state; but they maintained the closest of ties with Judea, both nationally and religiously speaking. . . . Alexandria had become a haven for the Jews who had been immigrating there for centuries from the wasted and impoverished land of Judea. Here and in other places, there came into being great Jewish communities whose language, education and ideology were a mixture of those of Greece and Egypt. . . . It was only in their religion that they remained in close touch with their native land, with Jerusalem, its center, and with the Holy Temple there. Hence these Jewish communities serve as the first example of a religion outgrowing the confines of territory and nationality. Quite the same is true of the Greco-Jewish colonies which existed during the era of the Second Jewish Commonwealth. Thus we see that this phenomenon, to which Christianity has proudly pointed as proof of its spiritual might transcending all national boundaries, had been manifest in Judaism at least three centuries prior to the birth of the Christian faith.

NS, II, PP. 86 FF.

(ON THE ORIGINS OF CHRISTIANITY)

The longing for a redeemer was universal; it manifested itself in the hope that a "Messiah" would have to come. This Messiah would be a King in Israel from the House of David, and his coming would be followed by a "resurrection" and by a new era, "the Kingdom of God." ... After John the Baptist, there came another, Jesus of Nazareth, who had considered himself to be the Messiah all along; it was as a consequence of this that John stepped into the limelight as a preacher of repentance. ... Particularly in Galilee, which had long been a hotbed of superstitious ecstasy, the waves of excitement rose high. [*Jesus*] advanced the claim that he had been called upon to be the Messiah. He was the "King of the Jews" (and is referred to as such in the legend of the Wise Men from the East); Pontius Pilate questioned him, the servants mocked him, and the high priest made inquiry. ... He claimed to be not an ordinary king but a higher kind of ruler, a Messiah; he was "Christ," as we find it written over and over again in the gospel of Matthew and Mark: the "Son of Man coming in the clouds of the heavens." According to Mark, only the possessed called him the "Son of God"; Peter only said, "Thou art Christ." It was only the high priests who questioned him as to whether he was indeed Christ, "the son of the Blessed One." But while they mocked him, they did not have this title in mind. Hence, in Mark 12.99 ff. the stress is on the unity of God, and Mark's constant references are to "the Kingdom of God," while Matthew usually employed the term "the Kingdom of Heaven." Matthew was the first to have not only the possessed, but also others, including himself, refer to Jesus by that title. The passage "no one knows the Son" (11.27) still sounds somewhat obscure. Later in the account the disciples (14.33) and particularly Peter (16.16) are more definite. Peter explicitly says, "Thou art Christ, the Son of the living God." Thus the high priests question him quite explicitly about whether he is indeed Christ, the Son of God, whereupon Jesus replies, "Thou sayest it." This is why, later on, they mock this title, and at the time of the earthquake the Roman captain declares, "This is indeed the Son of God."

This point, therefore, must be excluded entirely from the original legend. He himself does not even assert that he is the "Son of David." . . . Again, this is given stronger emphasis at a subsequent point. . . . It was for this reason that it became necessary later on to put special stress on the account that he had been born in Bethlehem, and the town of Nazareth which is given prominence in the gospel of Mark is only reluctantly acknowledged as having a role in the life of Jesus. Thus, too, the gospel of Matthew contains the genealogy and at the same time the statement that Jesus had been conceived by the Holy Ghost, while there is no mention of either in the gospel of Mark.

He is, therefore, the Messiah, but for the people of Israel only. Thus he promises his disciples that they will be seated upon twelve thrones to judge the twelve tribes of Israel, while he tells the high priests that the Kingdom of Heaven will be taken from them and turned over to the plain people who are not of priestly descent. . . . The gospel of Mark mentions the heathens only once (7.26), citing the harsh words addressed to the Canaanite woman; Matthew adopts a milder tone in this connection; but nevertheless he shows the contempt in which Jesus held idolatry. The same is true with regard to the Samaritans. Jesus has no intention of abrogating the Law; he is opposed only to the exaggerated notions of the Pharisees concerning the precepts of ritual purity. . . . He also upholds the laws pertinent to fasting, divorce and to the observance of the Sabbath.

. . . It cannot be denied that he had a sort of spiritual depth, but up to this point there is no sign of a determined personality, promising far-reaching results, of a removal of barriers within (of statutes) or without (with reference to the Gentiles), or of extensive reforms, of new ideas representing radical departures from customary paths.

. . . He warns of the scholars of the Scriptures who walk about in trailing robes, who like to be greeted in the market place, who sit at the head of the table in schools and at meals, and who intone lengthy prayers while they devour the meager possessions of the widows.

... Jesus was a spokesman of the *demos*, of the *ame ha-aretz*, as he himself points out to the high priests. Much to the displeasure of the Pharisees, he sat down at table with the common man. As such a "man of the people" he incurred the hostility of the priestly aristocracy in particular. They classed him with the Zealots and, in this manner, attempted to brand him as a rebel. . . . The Sadducees disliked him because he put such great stress on the Resurrection. . . .

Jesus was, therefore, a curious mixture of rational clarity, intellectual fuzziness, and fanaticism such as is frequently found in personalities of this type; and whether his advent would, in the end, result in the appearance of a transient sect or in the founding of a lasting religious community was only a matter of circumstances. In view of his close attachment to Israel, his belief in demons and in resurrection, and his adherence to all of Jewish Law, it is hardly likely that, under ordinary circumstances, he would have brought into being anything of greater consequence than another Jewish sect, which would continue to believe in him even after his violent death, and which would take it for granted that he, like all the other dead, would eventually be resurrected. . . . But the circumstances and trends of the times changed all that. To begin with, the Jews of Greece would have an entirely different conception of such things. . . . For with them, the concept of a Messiah coincided with another idea which they had assimilated, namely, the concept of a *Logos*. He was the mediator, they believed, between God and the world; . . . he was both unique and a native of the earth; he was something in between God and the world; he was part of both simultaneously. With the advent of such a being, the barriers between Israel and the rest of mankind, as well as the binding force of the statutes valid for Israel, would be abrogated. Paul in particular subscribed to this idea. Yet it would hardly have made any headway had it not been for the terrible disaster which was to explode all the ideologies of ages past.

The Pharisees, of course, soon resigned themselves to the loss of the Temple, the abolition of the sacrificial cult and of the priesthood. For all the other laws remained in force and, in fact, it was only under such circumstances that these precepts gained their full significance as the Law binding upon all. Nevertheless, they continued to yearn for the re-establishment of Israel's nationhood and political independence, and for the restoration of Israel's privileged position. While these beliefs became deeply entrenched within this one group, there were others who asked themselves: "What if some man, who had declared himself to be the Messiah and then was put to death, should truly have been the Messiah and should be resurrected so that he would be able to pave the way for the era of the Messiah and of resurrection?" The answer was that Israel would continue to be separate from the other nations; Israel would reign supreme in the world and all of Jewish Law would remain in force. The personality of the Messiah was something in between man and God. Such is the sum total of normative Judeo-Christianity.

The disaster that befell the Jewish state had quite a different effect on the Sadducees. With the destruction of the Temple, and the abolition of the institutions of priesthood and sacrifice and the rights and privileges appertaining to these—everything seemed to have come to an end. They were overwhelmed by despair. They gave up their sober struggle against the concept of resurrection. They faded away and their views reappeared only much later as part of Karaism. In the meantime, however, the adherents of Pharisaism had grown so mighty in numbers that the Sadducees, in their adherence to their time-honored concepts, appeared to be the literal followers of the biblical text, with views on many issues much stricter than those of the Pharisees, who allowed themselves to be guided in their thinking by changing times and circumstances. Seen from the point of view of the far-reaching ramifications of the Pharisaic system, the Sadducees appear quite liberal.

But certainly there must have been some who, deprived of the very ground beneath their feet by the catastrophe that befell the nation, clung to the belief in the Messiah. Perhaps, they reasoned, he had really been the sacrifice to cancel all other sacrifices; perhaps he had been a new high priest who, by offering himself in sacrifice, abolished the old priesthood and founded a new one. With the abolition of the priesthood, they said, all the ancient Law which had meaning for the Sadducees only in connection with a Temple, a priesthood and a ritual of sacrifices, was no longer in force. This was another type of Judeo-Christianity. To the adherents of this view, the Messiah was high priest and sacrifice, both at the same time; and once the old Law was abrogated, the New Kingdom was accessible to all men. A curious document reflecting this trend of thought is the Epistle to the Hebrews. In this manner there came into being a number of concepts which had particular appeal for the heathens; these were: a new god, a universal sacrifice, and thus universal atonement without the burden of cumbersome commandments. This concept met with resistance from the Jews, however, so that its acceptance was restricted to the heathen world. But it was from Judaism that the main teachings of the new creed had been derived; these included, not only the fundamentals of religion and ethics, but also their detailed and conceptual development in terms of contemporary conditions. The idea of the Messiah and the Resurrection was taken from the Pharisees; that of the high priest and of vicarious sacrifice from the Sadducees; and *Logos*, the "second god," from the adherents of Alexandrianism. In this form the new creed brought to the heathen world, not only enlightenment, but also new darkness: the hazy mysticism which was born out of this confusion of ideas, and the unhealthy situation, particularly the desire to escape from the world then prevailing. The result was not the infusion of the ideals of ethics into the world, but only an emphasis on the contrast between the terrestrial world, on the one hand, and the Kingdom of Heaven on the other. Had this creed taken on the form of a Judaism liberated from within and extending its scope without, it would have brought salvation to the whole world; but as a separate new religion, it came to be the scourge of freedom of thought, and an instrument of spiritual oppression. Now Christianity had become completely divorced from Judaism. With the advent of the reign of Christianity, Judaism came upon hard times such as usually result from civil war and fratricidal strife; at the same time, however, Judaism gained recognition by the fact that a whole world now fought it . . .

NS, II, PP. 120 FF.

EVALUATION OF THE TALMUD

Intellectual life at the academies of Palestine was characterized by dull languor. The Jerusalem Gemara is bare, meager and sober, though not lacking in legendary superstition. But the reliable references and reports about antiquity which it has preserved for us are of great historic value. . . . The Babylonian Gemara, by contrast, is bubbling over with life; in the academies of Babylonia the scholars plunged into their new studies with youthful avidity, though at times with a passion which overreached the goals that had been set. Its statutes and interpretations were accepted as sacred, and though they changed a good deal in both language and content during their progress through time and space, no one dared question them. For this reason the reports and traditions contained in it are much less reliable [*than those in the Jerusalem text*] and must therefore be studied with critical caution. A legalistic methodology with hair-splitting casuistry now gained the upper hand . . .

It is not known how and when the Jerusalem Gemara was completed. The fact is that it was not concluded at all; it stopped abruptly as a result of the gradual decline of the academies in Palestine, probably as early as the 4th century. The Babylonian Talmud was not concluded until the end of the 5th century. In this way everything was rigidly fixed and flexibility came to an end. For the past fourteen centuries the Talmud has had Judaism within its tight clasp and still does so, no matter how frequently modern scientific study might have tried to uproot it, nor will it lose its dominance until we ourselves have entirely outgrown the Middle Ages.

This much is sure: the Talmud is not by any means identical with the Science of Judaism, nor does it contain that Science, either basically or specifically. The Talmud is, however, an important historical document, spanning an era of approximately seven centuries, which gives a clear idea of both the evolution of Judaism and the factors inhibiting its growth. It contains, for example, a good deal that is important for a full understanding of the Bible and of its history. But the Talmud must be examined only by the light of critical study, for we are dealing here with reports which, in part, have adopted foreign components even in the process of oral transmission and, in part, have moved in the course of time into an entirely different perspective. This is an extensive task for critical study, but it is a rewarding one. Halakhah, both old and new, Mishna, and reinterpretation in the Gemara are developments within a narrow sphere. Of more basic significance than any of these is the contrast between Pharisaism and Sadducism. The equality (to which the Pharisees aspired) has deprived us of our freedom in this respect, and our longing for the restoration of the old state of affairs has almost robbed us of our liberty in theory as well . . .

NS, II, PP. 126 FF.

THE PERIOD OF RIGID LEGALISM (FROM THE 6TH CENTURY TO THE MIDDLE OF THE 18TH CENTURY)

It is interesting to note that the era of inner legalistic rigidity in Jewish Law was, at the same time, a period of lively interest and participation on the part of the Jews in general culture. It is quite true that the motives for intellectual activity did not originate from within; nor was intellectual energy free and able to work on its own heritage and to transform it. However, it was determined all the more to seize upon problems of a more general nature and sought to penetrate them in response to even the slightest stimulus in that direction.

Indeed, with the standstill in the development of the Babylonian Talmud, an era of rigidity had set in. The Babylonian Talmud had not reached a natural conclusion, but had come to an abrupt ending by a cutting of the thread, as it were, by persecution and by the decline of the great academies in Persia. The cause of this petrification lay not in any total exhaustion of Judaism's vital energy. Proof for this is the increasingly vigorous participation in the intellectual life of the world. But petrification may set in also when natural development is impeded by obstacles from without, or when the inner motivations that formerly engendered it have come to an end. For either of these makes it impossible to forge a new link in the chain of vital evolution. Tradition then continues to exist as binding, but it no longer possesses full intrinsic justification. This is exactly what happened in Judaism. Oppression weighed heavily upon it and hindered free study and inquiry. The motivations which had obtained in the older days, namely, the internal conflicts within the nation and the attainment of priestly consecration for the group as a whole, were no longer present. The statutes which had resulted from them now remained as mere time-honored customs which had to find support from tradition and interpretation and were viewed as inviolable. That which in earlier days had been a means to an end had now become an end in itself. There was nothing that could be done against statutes and interpretations which were posited as divinely handed-down tradition. Of course, some opposition to the untenable nature of such tortuous interpretation gradually stirred, but it could not make any real headway.

Perhaps, had circumstances permitted continued and undisturbed evolution, the awareness of this artificiality might have become stronger and made for change. But paralysis of thought, brought about by the force of unfavorable circumstances, did not permit such a development. Thus tradition had to remain, and it became more and more inflexible and rigid as the years went on . . .

NS, II, PP. 129 FF.

reports of the jewish institute of religious instruction in breslau, 1844-1863

From the Report for 1846

... But of even more profound importance [*than the foregoing*] is the question of the place which the so-called ceremonial laws should be given in a course of religious instruction. If such instruction is to foster a religious way of life that stems from deep conviction, then the ceremonies must not be allowed to remain mere rituals which no one understands and which cannot be associated with any specific idea or thought. They must be either potent means for arousing sentiments of reverence for God, or else they must help ennoble and intensify our sense of duty. In fact, it is only those that come under the heading of the former that are ceremonies in the strictest sense of the word; the acts under the latter category are actually duties rather than ceremonies. Hence it would be wrong to class as ceremonies those biblical laws that command us to be kind to animals—such as the ban on slaughtering cattle with its young on the same day, on removing young birds from their nest without first sending the mother bird away, or on seething the kid in the milk of its mother, and so forth. These acts are not "ceremonies," but essential manifestations of kindness such as should be shown also in our conduct with animals. As for the biblical dietary laws, insofar as they keep us from making use of such foods as are repulsive or harmful, these are part of the expression of that respect for the dignity of man which views the human body, too, as an organ of man's mental and spiritual activity which must be kept healthy and pure.

There are other statutes that are customs intended to keep God in our thoughts, devices to recall certain facts or events, or symbols meant to express some profound idea. These statutes are the true "ceremonies." How to deal with these in our course of religious instruction, given the present diversity of views on this subject, is a problem that must receive serious attention. In my opinion, the instructor would do best not to go into specific details; if he does discuss them at all in connection with the synagogue service and the observance of the festivals, he ought to emphasize that these ceremonies must be practiced intelligently and with the proper attitude. On the other hand, he should not attempt to combat those customs that have long since become invalid and meaningless, for the school is not a theological battleground. Only in those instances where custom is obviously inconsistent with the pure and straightforward teachings of our faith should the instructor explain the latter without giving attention to the former. In keeping with this viewpoint, he will—to give one example— teach his students to resign themselves to the will of God in times of trial and suffering. He will warn against violent emotional displays on sorrowful occasions, such as rending of one's garments and the like, which would imply rebellion against God's decree. . . . It would be a sin against our young people to implant the seeds of conflict into them at this early age, either by attacking that which might well be viewed as sacred in their homes, or by defending that which we may reasonably expect later life to weaken in their convictions.

From the Report for 1849

. . . The institution has always gladly accepted the authority of higher religious truth; it has not, however, submitted to the hazy whims of traditional form, to the reign of habit and absurdity. It accepted its role as an institution which must follow religion because its purpose has been to serve religion. It seeks to bring about the subordination of physical perception to a spirit that is free, not an enslavement of the spirit to life-less forms. It seeks to foster the dignity of the human spirit and not its degradation; ethical, single-minded energy and not spineless surrender to the incomprehensible. It aims at achiev-ing an intimate bond of the human soul with the Divine spirit and not at compliance with statutes which find no echo in the hearts and minds of men and owe their survival merely to servile obedience to what is deemed authority and to the dulling influence of habit. On the other hand, that theory of freedom which has grown popular of late and according to which any idea, no matter how absurd, has the unlimited right to assert itself as long as a sufficient number of people accept it, is also not compatible with the philosophy of our institution. Our institution accords complete justification only to mature reason, and accepts as free only him who will gladly accept the influence of greater insight and will unite in love with all the rest of mankind.

In view of the foregoing, this institution also grants that the ethically free state has not only the right but also the duty, by authority of the reason inherent in it, to guard and preserve spiritual freedom in religious life. As for the widespread demand for a complete separation of Church and State, this institution views it mostly as a product of those unnatural alliances which people gaze upon in bewilderment, for we have here a union embracing Jesuit cunning which would gladly rid itself of any control that would stand in the way of its thirst for power, the abstract ideals of freedom of those who believe that mankind has already attained the pinnacle of perfection, and that destructive radicalism which fancies, or pretends, that a splendid new edifice will rise of itself from amidst the ruins and that, at any rate, the historical structure must be demolished before all else. For the very reason that the medieval-romantic state so rudely interfered with the expression of free conviction, the *free* state [*of the present day*] must not be deprived of the power to exercise a benevolent and effective influence in the most important affairs of its members. . . . Nowadays the masses are, in part, radically destructive; in their materialistic strivings they look down with disdain upon religious exaltation and, in part, interpret their newly-gained freedom to mean that no one has a right to raise objections to their absurdities, foolish habits and pernicious abuses. . . . The ruling powers accept the separation of Church and State, but at the same time they guarantee the historical rights of those denominations that had previously enjoyed preferred status; and as for those who had suffered oppression heretofore—well, let them rejoice that they are oppressed no more and that they may float about as free atoms without any control whatsoever. The separation of School and Church is interpreted to mean that religious instruction in the schools is no longer to be supervised by the state, which did preserve an attitude of impartiality at least to some extent, but by the individual Church groups which, of course, are thoroughly partisan. As for those denominations which are nowhere in the majority—let them fend for themselves and see how they can manage. Thus Judaism always is relegated to the status of a Church that suffers from neglect and discrimination. . . . Nevertheless, on the threshold of a new era, [*Judaism*] must prove that it owes its survival, not to a stifling prison atmosphere, but that, on the contrary, it is only when given complete freedom of motion that its vital energy will thrive and flourish.

From the Report for 1856

. . . We have no desire for protection by force. In religious life, compulsion, whatever its nature, will kill that devotion which is free and therefore warm, and will set up cold and rigid legalism in its place. . . . Whoever would appeal to the ruling powers for the protection of his religious faith or would enlist the aid of the authorities to coerce others to follow that faith and to exclude all those who would refuse to accept it . . . shows by such action that he is not convinced of the blessed truth of his religion or imbued with trust in its triumphant spiritual strength. Such a one is serving not the holy God of truth . . . but a fetish that . . . may compel fear and obedience temporarily, but temporarily only; for the power of free conscience will refuse to be stifled and will then burst forth all the more vehemently.

Judaism has never enjoyed coercive protection of this type, and it is precisely for this reason that it has survived all oppression and taken firm root in the hearts of its adherents. As long as Judaism had a state of its own, it could have partaken of such protective compulsion and, as a matter of fact, its laws bore all those features that emphasize the preservation of the religious institutions of the state. But what actually happened was that the rulers of the state were the ones that indulged in idol worship, and that only the prophets, though persecuted and threatened, saved the precious jewel by the strength of conviction set aflame by inner passion.

It was only when the state no longer gave it support that Judaism unfolded its full power over hearts and minds and became the inmost possession of its adherents for which they gladly sacrificed all earthly glory and even life itself. When the Arabs who held dominion over Spain descended from the high cultural level which they had occupied, and the fanaticism of the Almohades in the 12th century hounded every deviation with fire and sword . . . and sought to punish Averroes, the philosopher, by exile and imprisonment for his errors, the supremacy of Islam was doomed. Averroes, however, remained the guiding spirit in the realm of science and knowledge throughout the Middle Ages.

. . . One eternal truth remains: Once a religion makes use of outward weapons to persecute other religious trends, to outlaw science and knowledge and to oppress dissenters, that religion is doomed to die, and when a state allies itself with such a faith bent on persecution, it thereby seals the doom of its life as a healthy nation. As for our own state, it is safe from such dangers; its destiny, as well as the wisdom of its kings, is proof positive of this.

From the Report for 1858

. . . The concept of "cosmopolitanism" must of necessity be confined to precise limits. One belongs to humanity by virtue of the fact that one is part of a definite circle, within which, for which and *through which* one can work for mankind as a whole. An existence in a vacuum, a mere nibble at every field of endeavor, a fickle fluttering from one thing to another is the greatest enemy of all sound ability and renders man shallow. It is not in direct effort, but in the higher purpose, which one can advance also by a humble contribution, that the true cosmopolitan spirit lies. The cosmopolitan spirit must be given recognition by a refusal to adhere stubbornly to one's own limited tendency and to declare everything else as of no significance. The feeling of one's own worth and dignity must not exclude or infringe upon a recognition of the equal worth and merit of others. It is proper that man should have respect for his own endeavors, but only as a contribution to the sum total of all human endeavor. Thus the artisan who holds intellectual labor in contempt because it does not involve creative work by the hand, the scholar who terms all other pursuits inferior because they serve merely the acquisition of wealth, the German who would deny that any other nation has a destiny equal to his own, and so forth, all dwell in a state of idle self-deception. Such persons do not recognize their task as being of service to humanity, each according to his own ability, and would make the great totality of things with its rich and far-flung relationships shrink into a narrow circle corresponding to their own short-sighted sphere.

Of all the predetermined circumstances into which man is born and which then accompany him throughout his life, his religious faith is the most important. To the mind of the child in particular, religion must be presented in a definite form which will arouse his interest and awaken within him the sense of the existence of a Higher Being by such outer manifestations as ritual, sacred festival rites and family worship. The more profound the religious idea, the deeper the religious feeling, the more vivid and concrete must be its expression, lest the religion become entirely ethereal and fade away into inaccessible heights.

Therefore *historical religion* with its rich past and its fixed ordinances established through the centuries offers such spiritual nourishment as even the purest and most godly philosophy will never be able to give. Historical religion, too, has its own definite circle of adherents and forms a closed unit into which the individual has been placed by birth. If it is to be able fully to exercise its salutary influence, a sense of reverence for it must be present and nurtured. The Jew must happily look upon his Judaism as that vessel which is filled with blessings for him, the great Divine revelation to Israel and mankind. If he should turn coldly aside from it, if he should look with indifference upon its growth and development through history, if he should arrogantly ignore it and, unmindful of its magnificent influence on the whole, should deride its abuses—he would cut off what should be a wellspring of inspiring exaltation. Thus he fosters a conflict between himself and his religious station in life which cannot fail to have a harmful influence on his psychic development. The sad condition in which our faith has been for so long, the contempt and disregard from others which it encounters so frequently even today, will lead many an adherent who relies on outside opinions to become discontented with the spiritual treasure that has been handed down to him and to despise it. This makes it all the more imperative that the value and significance of Judaism be brought home to the child through early emphasis during the process of his education.

If the assurance on the part of Jewish parents that the religious training of their children is close to their hearts is to be more than a meaningless phrase, then it is their duty to have them brought up in their historical religion, in Judaism. They ought to acquaint them early with its history and its historic documents, so that the children may conceive affection and loyalty for it and derive a happy and invigorating sense of self-confidence through it. It is therefore sad indeed that the exact opposite should be true in many an instance. Whereas everything else is taught early, religious training is postponed from year to year. . . . So long as a Jewish *sense of honor and self-respect* . . . a justifiable pride, free from arrogance, in the grandeur of Jewish history is not conveyed to our children, they will be deprived of complete inner harmony, and what would be a highly effective incentive for honesty and sound sentiment will be stifled. . . . We have swung from one kind of one-sidedness to another. Now is the time to steer in the right direction.

NS, I, PP. 309 FF.

Judaism and Its History

A SERIES OF THIRTY-FOUR LECTURES, FROM THE
SECOND EDITION, BRESLAU, 1865.

*(The lectures from which these excerpts are taken were originally
published in three volumes: vol. I, Breslau, 1864; 2nd edition, 1865.
Vol. II, Breslau, 1865; vol. III, Breslau, 1871.)*

THE ESSENCE OF RELIGION

. . . It is not enough for man to explain Nature, which
surrounds him. Man himself must be explained as well, for
he is part and parcel of nature, and this search into himself
is a challenge which he dare not refuse. But the more man
thinks about himself, the more he discovers that he is the
greatest enigma of all—to himself. Attempts have been made
to associate man quite closely with creatures said to resemble
him; certain species of apes, it has been pointed out, are but
little removed from man. It has even been claimed that many a
species of ape seems caught up, as it were, in a state of melancholy, as if yearning to escape from the restraining fetters of
form. This may be a most ingenious thought for man to impute
to the soul of a beast, but it is no more than absurdity to
interpret animal dullness as melancholy and to represent it as
such. Between man and even the most advanced of animal
species there will always be a gulf that can never be bridged.
Man may be physically inferior to other living things, which
are stronger and more supple than he in many ways. Yet it is
man that has become the lord of the earth and the master of
creation. . . . To compare him, even remotely, to some animal
that lives unto itself, remaining forever at the same level,
restricted to one habitat, living out its days without influencing
the rest of creation, and leaving no trace once it is gone—
would not such a comparison be tantamount to the spite of a
child who throws away his own treasures and destroys them?
No indeed; man is very different from the beast.
He . . . is capable of transcending time and space within

himself; he is able to project himself into the remotest of places; he can summon up the past, surmise the future, and formulate a conception of that which extends beyond the immediate present. Such things are not dependent on the body. The body is bounded by time and space, and nothing can emanate from it that would be able to conquer either of these elements. Man possesses a memory; he is able to retain within himself whatever he has experienced. . . . He has made knowledge his own; when any perception rests securely within him, it becomes his stepping-stone to the next. But where, in what part of his being, does that perception dwell? Let us utter that one word which would never have come into being if the thing it describes were nonexistent: the mind of man.

Man has a mind, a capacity which is related to the body insofar as it moves and animates it. At the same time, the mind is far more than that, for it guides man to sensible thinking and gives him a view of such things as his sensory equipment could neither comprehend nor bring close to him. The thinker who inaugurated the ideological development of our modern era put it magnificently: *I think, therefore I am.* My own awareness of the fact that I am thinking affords me the guarantee that I exist at all . . .

It is solely the capacity to think, the one ability which at the same time provides man with the means of expressing ideas and sensations, that lends form to our sensory perceptions. For it is speech, the most faithful reflection of the mind, that creates the bridge between our inmost being and the outside world. It is speech that sets man apart from all other creatures; it is only speech which, born of an inner clarity, serves to make thought comprehensible and helps it become a distinct and complete entity.

Nevertheless, this superior creature upon which the stamp of dominion is so plainly impressed . . . seems to encounter obstacles everywhere in both his life and thought. The individual may advance, but he will still be only one part of mankind, and mankind is only a part of that creation, which in turn emanates from a spiritual fount that is greater still. This one limitation cleaves to him: that being only a small part of the whole out of which he stems, he cannot so far transcend himself as to attain to ultimate knowledge. Hence man must forever carry within him the awareness that he is only a fragment, an imperfect being in creation.

Beyond that, man senses that in other respects he occupies a higher position. He acts on the basis of his own principles and decisions; he proceeds according to his own free will; he has freedom of choice. He can determine his own actions. He is not driven by compulsive forces from without. He may reflect, pass judgment and conduct himself accordingly. This is an infinite advantage which he has over all other creatures. Would that he could rejoice in all this without misgivings! But here, too, he meets with contradiction within his own being. Whatever I choose, whatever I decide to do is based on definite causes. These in turn are dependent upon the knowledge I have acquired. . . . I am not the creator either of myself or my actions. My need to discern in all things the prime law of causality deprives me of my freedom; as a result, one thing follows another by the law of necessity, as it were, until I come upon causes that exist outside myself. Nevertheless, man is deeply aware of the fact that he is free, that, in his own will, there is inherent the power to counter influences from the outside and to master them. He feels remorse when he realizes that what he has done was wrong, but he has cause for self-reproach only when that act originated within himself; he cannot blame himself for what he was compelled to do by a force from without. Thus he is free and yet constrained. Hence here, too, he is aware of his limitations; he senses that he has not attained that degree of perfection of which he has some notion and for which he yearns. This is the duality within man: he is aware of his power and exaltation; but as against this, there is the humiliating sense of his dependent nature. On the one hand, he strives to raise himself to that fount from which flows his spiritual strength, a strength that is not of his own making and therefore circumscribed; on the other hand, he senses his inability ever fully to attain that high place for which he yearns . . .

VOL. I, PP. 6 FF.

REVELATION

There are phenomena of such overwhelming force that even the most reluctant of critical minds must accept them. One such phenomenon is the appearance of Judaism from out of the midst of a wilderness, like a strong root growing out of arid soil. . . . [*In the prophets*] we behold personalities of serene grandeur and simple dignity; these were men of fiery passion coupled with calm prudence; their boldness was coupled with profound humility and resignation. They impress us, and they make us sense the breath of a higher spirit within them. The teachers of old have already said it: no two prophets utter their prophecy in the same manner. Each prophet is a complete, well-rounded personality in his own right, with a distinct individuality of his own. Yet all the prophets have one common set of characteristics; they are all motivated by the one same great ideal . . .

Generally speaking, we may distinguish in man two mental processes—a twofold attribute with which man has been favored: we differentiate between talent, on the one hand, and genius on the other. These two may touch at some points, yet they are forever essentially different and apart from one another. This difference is not simply one of degree, but of actual essence. Talent is the gift to comprehend ideas easily and quickly, to assimilate them and then skilfully and adeptly to communicate them. However, talent is based on that which is already in existence, on past achievements and on such riches as have already been acquired. It does not create anything original. Not so genius. Genius does not lean upon anything; genius is creative. It discovers truths which were previously hidden and reveals laws which have not heretofore been known. It is as if there were revealed before it in brilliant clarity, and in their context according to their orderly interplay, those forces which work deep within the core of nature. It is as if these forces were tangibly real, as if the spiritual impulses both within the individual and within mankind as a whole have unveiled themselves before genius, so that it may peer into the inmost recesses of the soul and from there single out the driving forces which motivate the human spirit. Talent may be cultivated; it may be acquired by effort and diligence. But genius is a free gift, a favor, a mark of consecration which is imprinted upon man; if it is not present in him, he can never acquire it on his own . . .

The Greeks boasted of having been autochthons, of having been born in and of their own soil. Whether this claim is justified is a moot question. But another claim, which may perhaps reflect its deeper meaning, may surely be acknowledged, namely, the autochthonous nature of their mind, the originality of their particular national tendency. The

Greeks had neither patterns nor teachers for their art and learning. They served as their own mentors and masters, and presently they shone forth with a perfection which made them the teachers of mankind in almost every age . . .

Does not the Jewish people, too, have such a genius, a religious genius of this type? Was it not also an original force that enlightened its eyes so that it could look more deeply into the higher spheres of the spirit, that it could discern more clearly the close relationship between the spirit of man and the Universal Spirit, that it could grasp the higher challenge of human existence and perceive the profound ethical quality in man with greater clarity and intensity, expressing it as its unique insight? If this is indeed so, then this intimate contact of the spirit of the individual with the Universal Spirit, this illumination of individual minds by the all-encompassing force so that they could break through their finite barriers, is—let us not shy away from the word—revelation as manifested in the people as a whole.

Not all the Greeks were artists, they were not all Phidias or Praxiteles, and yet the Greek people as such had the gift of producing great masters. The same was true of Judaism. Certainly not all the Jews were prophets; and the verse *Would that all the people were prophets!* was no more than a pious wish. Another verse, *I shall pour My spirit over all flesh,* is a promise which never became reality. Nevertheless, the Jewish people is the people of the revelation which subsequently gave birth to the select instruments of that revelation. They were scattered sparks of light, as it were, which, gathered together by those chosen to proclaim the revelation, shone forth fused into one single bright flame. There is no reference to the God of Moses or to the God of the Prophets; our literature speaks only of the God of Abraham, Isaac and Jacob, of the God of the entire race, of its patriarchs who showed this same predisposition, that of introspective vision. This is the revelation which lay dormant in the people as a whole and then found a unifying focal point in certain individuals. It is a truism of profound significance that even the greatest prophet of them all left his work unfinished. He was not to stand out like Atlas who bore the world upon his shoulders, carrying out a task without participating in it—inspirer and executor at once . . .

Truly, Judaism originated with the people of the revelation. Why, then, should we not be allowed to use this term when we speak of penetration to the deepest foundation, of an illumination emanating from the higher spirit, which cannot be explained and which, though subject to later evolution, was not evolutionary in its origin? . . .

We have no intention of limiting and narrowing the term in a dogmatic fashion. It may be interpreted in many ways; but its essence always remains the same—the contact of human reason with the First Cause of all things. Notwithstanding the high regard in which the teachers of old held the concept of revelation, they never sought to deny its relationship to human endowments. The Talmud teaches that the spirit of God will rest only upon a wise man, upon a man of moral strength who is self-sufficient because he is content, having overcome all ambitions and lusts. Only a man of inner stature who senses the Divine within himself will be capable of absorbing the Divine. He must not be a mere mouthpiece through which the message is transmitted, through which the word is spoken without his being aware of it. He must be a man close to the Divine in the truest sense of the word, and therefore receptive to it. . . . Judah Halevi stresses that revelation is a tendency that was alive in the people as a whole. Israel, he says, is the religious heart of all mankind. As a group, Israel always maintained this higher susceptibility, and the great individuals who stood out in Israel's midst were the heart of that heart, as it were. Maimonides said that revelation was to be viewed as a lightning-like flash of illumination; to some, he explained, such enlightenment is granted for a short while only; to others it comes more than once; and Moses had it at all times . . .

VOL. I, PP. 27 FF.

———————··◁∞▷··———————

NATIONALISM

. . . The entire history of Israel during the era of the First Temple, that is, during the period when the faith as such was consolidated, is replete with countless examples of defection, of the relentless struggle which great men, those truly inspired, had to wage against the backsliders.

The more this corruption penetrated the people of Israel, the greater was the danger that the worm might corrode even the healthy trunk, the fiercer was the zeal which the better men in their midst had to deploy to stave off the peril. It was necessary for them to take a decisive stand against corruption, against the danger of internal corrosion by evil, with a fiery zeal that did not merely spread warmth but actually consumed iniquity. Given those circumstances, should we, therefore, be surprised to encounter, now and then, some harsh and bitter utterance against other nations; should it seem strange that merciless determination to oppose them should be preached and also practiced? Here the die is not cast for the capture of a country, or of some earthly wealth; it is, instead, an idea that is being defended, an idea which they cherish as their chiefest treasure, one which raises them above all the other nations and which is destined to be broadcast throughout the earth by the people chosen for this purpose. Should we, then, be surprised that, since the flame blazes so mightily within them, they should become impassioned and come forth with attitudes other than pure benevolence and kindly respect toward those who seek to seduce them and to rob them of what they deem their most precious possessions? . . . It should, indeed, not astonish us to encounter many a spiteful remark, many an odious expostulation. There are much more significant factors to remember. First, the fruit of genuine spiritual strength that dwelt within the people. Then, that despite the struggle and throughout it all, Israel never lost the awareness that it embraced all of mankind and that its labors were on behalf of humanity as a whole. Amidst all the hostility which of necessity prevailed on both sides, it remained a fact that this faith had come into being for the entire world and that its destiny was ultimately to embrace the whole earth. The fact that this purity and clarity of concept has never been completely dimmed bears testimony to the profound spiritual vitality of Judaism. Hence we are uplifted when, despite occasional outbursts of pugnacity, we may breathe in that refreshing spiritual atmosphere which emanates from the words of the prophets: *Let not the son of the alien who has joined the Lord say, "The Lord keeps me apart and separates me from His people."* . . . Elsewhere we read, *It is not enough that you alone should be My faithful servant; . . . therefore I shall make you a light unto the nations.* And in still another passage we are told, *Even from among their midst I shall choose priests and levites.* All of mankind is to be embraced by this one truth . . .

THE PLACE OF WOMAN

Judaism teaches monogamy, the marriage of one woman to one man. Even if there are deviations here and there, these are mere exceptions, tolerated because the Law had no desire to take drastic steps against them at a time when polygamy prevailed among all the nations round about. But it is monogamy, the exclusive intimacy between husband and wife, that is in accordance with the deeper essence of Judaism. It is quite natural, therefore, that in a later period, when environmental influences, too, had changed, a teacher should arise in Europe who would pronounce the sentence of excommunication upon anyone who violated what was the natural law of Judaism. Even in those countries where polygamy still prevailed among the non-Jews, it soon disappeared from among the Jews living there. The law had not explicitly banned the practice, but custom, the living spirit that has always prevailed in Judaism, had long since prohibited that which actual Law still tolerated. Such are the fruits that reveal the deeper core of Judaism, and it was thus that Judaism has always cherished the ideal of an ennobled family life. Of course, Judaism did not know of such things as "courts of love" and knightly romance, but neither was it disposed to delve into the mystery of an "unconscious virginity" which can nurture maternal feelings at the same time. Hale and strong, pure and fresh has been that fountain that has poured forth from the Jewish home over all the situations of life. It is the purity of its family life that has preserved Israel throughout all time in purity and strength. . . .

VOL. I, PP. 39 FF.

THE EXILE AND THE RETURN. TRADITION.

. . . Such nations as merely found states and maintain their existence for a period limited by the mandate of world history must break up as soon as they are cut loose from the states they have established. Their lives and their functions cease and they are doomed to extinction. But not so that nation which is only a means for the fulfilment of a higher purpose, the visible manifestation of a great idea that embraces all of mankind.

True, the members of a nation such as this need time to dwell
together so that they may become a united community within
which that ideal may mature to its fullest expression. . . . But
once this is achieved, that nation may cease to exist as a state
without its inmost essence being broken up thereby . . .
The Jews returned [*from Babylonian captivity*] and once
again formed a new national entity. Why could they, of all
peoples, have succeeded in this endeavor? The answer is that
they were more than a nation; they were a brotherhood united
by the bonds of a single common ideal . . .

True, the actual, immediate creative force of revelation had
come to an end. . . . [*Still*] the creative spirit had not entirely
disappeared from the midst of Judaism. It had not come to a
full stop, so that nothing new could have been produced or
refined. The living spirit continued to pulsate through the ages.
Despite the lamentation that *there is no longer a prophet in
our midst*, that same holy, ennobling spirit still continued to
make itself felt. Tradition is that force of evolution that endures within Judaism as an invisible creative power, as a certain undefinable something which never receives its final mold
but which is continually at work just the same. Within Judaism,
tradition is the soul that animates the body; it is the daughter
of revelation, of the same high birth as the latter. It has never
ceased, nor will it ever vanish from within Judaism; it is the
fount which always fructifies the times anew, and which must
give birth to new forms with every contact with the outside
world, in accordance with new needs and situations. This was
how the Jews succeeded in founding a new national and religious life.

If ever there should come a time—but this time will never
come!—when the stream of tradition dries up; when Judaism
is viewed as a completed, closed entity; when faces turn backward only, in contemplation of what the past has wrought,
blindly seeking to preserve it—then, indeed, Judaism will be at
an end. Or, if there should come a time when Jews see Judaism
with romantic awe, with some sort of antiquarian affection, as a
ruin which must be preserved in its decayed state, while others
again pass by these ruins with haughty indifference, and no
living force breaks forth from anywhere—then, indeed, the time
will have come to dig a grave for Judaism. Then, truly, Judaism will be lifeless, spiritually dead, a walking skeleton which
may still last for a time but is doomed to certain destruction in
the end. But this is not Judaism. Judaism has an eternally pro-

creative tradition—yes, let us pay due honor to this term. Tradition, like revelation, is a spiritual force that goes on forever. It is a higher force that springs, not from man, but from the Divine spirit; it is at work within the group as a whole; it selects those individuals who would serve as its bearers; it manifests itself in ever more mature and noble fruit and thereby remains a force, living and viable . . .

VOL. I, PP. 68 FF.

HILLEL

. . . Hillel conveys to us the image of—and this term will not degrade but ennoble his memory—a true reformer. He encountered all those difficulties that have been encountered at all times by efforts at revitalization and rejuvenation. Some may have asked him, "Why should you want to make changes? Abide by that which is valid once and for all. How can you presume to take upon yourself the right to make innovations?" "If I am not for myself," Hillel replied, "who will be for me?" If only that which the past has produced should have validity, if recognition should be accorded only to that which already exists without me, without my having created it—who else but I can create for me? To this, others may have countered: "So be it, then. Keep it for yourself; you are free to see it so, and to think and act accordingly. But why should you seek to come forth and make such changes for the entire community?" As if the Idea were meant for the individual alone, as if it could be filed away in a drawer, to be studied at some more opportune moment! As if it were not a living force which rules and impels man; even as the prophet put it, *There is in my heart, as it were, a burning fire shut up in my bones; I cannot hold it in.* "And if I am only for myself," was Hillel's rejoinder, "what am I?" Do I seek anything for myself? Or is it the entire community that seeks new life? "Leave these things alone, my friend," still others may have warned him. "You are too rash." But to this, Hillel replied, "If not now, when?" Every age creates and must create, and if we seek simply to crawl and drag ourselves through time, then our future will be nipped in the bud. Such a man was Hillel, and it will be clear to anyone who has ever taken even so much as a glance into the history of Judaism that Hillel was a man who dared openly to oppose those who sought to make the Law more burdensome, and who was not at all afraid to be known as an advocate of leniency who sought to render the Law less difficult . . .

[*This is an example of Hillel's thinking on the Law:*]
According to biblical law, if a house situated in a walled town or city was sold, it could be repurchased by the former owner until the end of the year. If he had not redeemed it at the end of that term, the house remained the property of the purchaser. As a rule, the former owner would do nothing until the final day of the year. Then, however, in order not to forfeit his property for all time, he would use every possible means to raise the needed funds and the purchaser was forced to restore to him the rights of ownership. To avert the loss of their newly-acquired property, the purchasers would resort to a clever ruse. On the final day of the year, the new owner would simply leave the house and lock its doors so that the original owner would not be able to return the money before the deadline and reclaim his property. Thus the law remained inviolate; the letter of the law was observed. But this did not satisfy Hillel. "No," he said, "it is not enough simply to observe the letter of the law. If the purchaser is not at home on that day, the former owner has the right to break through the locked door and leave the money inside, or else to deposit the money in the Temple. The rightful owner must not be allowed to lose his property through the cunning of another." . . .

Such a man was Hillel; and thus he became a restorer or, if you will, a reformer of Judaism, and his labors have continued to exert an influence on Jewish life to this very day. He did not approve of "separatist" piety. "Set not yourself apart from the community," he said. Do not seek to be more pious than the others; it is not right to dismiss others as apostates and bask in the sunshine of a separatist piety all one's own. Nor was he a believer in a monastic faith; Hillel stood in the midst of active life and in many ways has strengthened and upheld the life of all of Judaism. It is futile to speculate upon what might have been if Judaism had been allowed to follow a path of peaceful development. The fact is that Judaism was not allowed to develop in peace; there were major events of world-wide import which . . . generated great upheavals . . .

the beginning of Christianity and the breaking up of the Jewish state.

VOL. I, PP. 104 FF.

CHRISTIANITY AS AN ECCLESIASTICAL WORLD POWER.
THE BREAKUP OF THE JEWISH NATION.

... Yes, Judaism has survived alongside Christianity, and in spite of it. It was fought not merely with earthly weapons, with fire and sword, with expulsion and oppression, but also with spiritual ammunition. Any good and noble trait that had been conceded to Judaism, before it had given birth to Christianity from within itself, was viewed simply as a preparation for Christianity, a Christian quality that had come into being before Christianity itself. Nevertheless, Judaism has survived; it has preserved its eternal values and has not allowed them to become tarnished. It refused to allow its belief in God to be distorted or adulterated by alien elements. It has resisted every effort to graft onto it the concept of Original Sin, which others have attempted to read into its Scriptures. Judaism has not permitted its patent of human nobility and dignity to be destroyed. It has remained steadfast in its conviction that God has given to man the power of free self-determination and self-refinement; that, despite the animal lust which is part of his nature, man also has the strength to overcome it and, by dint of his own efforts, to refine and ennoble his personality. Moreover, since the belief in original sin and the corruption of human nature has remained alien to it, Judaism does not feel the need for a redemption accomplished from without to regain its purity. Judaism has not exchanged its own concept of a God of mercy for the God of that peculiar love which, in order to appease its wrath, requires a great vicarious sacrifice on behalf of the sinful masses. Judaism has not taken the development of all of mankind to a higher goal to mean a denial of itself, and hence saw no need to fight against it. It never declared: "The time has already been fulfilled and the coping-stone of the edifice was put into place eighteen centuries ago— the coping-stone of the one world which was the cornerstone of another—and there is no other truth that can be added to the structure."

Christianity must of necessity look back upon that period as the most important in the history of the world; that era must forever be Christianity's heart and core, and the personality which brought it into being must forever represent its highest ideal. Even the most liberal among the Christians, who divest the founder of their religion of all supernatural qualities, if they are to preserve some tenuous bond with their faith, cannot escape the necessity of creating for themselves an artificial image of him, to which they then ascribe all the attributes of earthly perfection. This image, however, crumbles even more quickly before critical examination than the older, solid concept. Judaism, on the other hand, can dispense with personalities; it may give free rein to critical study as regards all of its great men, even if that critical study went so far as to eliminate the figure of Moses from Jewish history. Such an extreme step, of course, would constitute an excess of irresponsibility which we would perhaps deplore. But let us stop to consider: is it on Moses, or upon any other human participant in Jewish history that Judaism depends? There is a Torah; it is there that the faith of Judaism is imbedded, and there it will be preserved. Regardless of how the Torah came into Judaism, regardless of who gave it or what historical personality was its transmitter, whether it was a being free of sin or a mortal subject to human weaknesses—the fact remains that the Torah exists. This is why Judaism was able to preserve the character of its mission even later on; its history did not cease with the beginning of Christianity . . .

VOL. I, PP. 145 FF.

THE DIASPORA

. . . The Jewish state had been destroyed, the Jewish nation broken up and the Temple burned to ashes. . . . The Pharisees of the old school, the adherents of time-honored, strict observance, were still numerous. These Pharisees of the stringent school sought to sanctify their people by imposing upon them innumerable hardships and restrictions regarding religious observance. [*As a result, the people*] would gradually have withered away; they would not have had the vital strength needed to preserve the hallowed heritage through the centuries.

When the Temple had been destroyed, they sought to assert their bigoted mentality, looking back forever to ancient customs and precepts. "Now that the Temple has fallen," they asserted, "we must neither eat meat nor drink wine, for animals can no longer be sacrificed in the Sanctuary, and wine can be poured forth no more as a libation before the Lord." This way of thinking by Pharisees of the most stringent variety would have brought about the eventual disappearance of Judaism itself.

But on the other hand, there still were the Hillelites, the spiritual heirs of Hillel, who had more regard for inner conviction than for outworn, burdensome restrictions, and who considered the demands of the times rather than ancient statutes. These were the men who preserved the remnants and held them closely united, who did not allow the spirit to be destroyed even though the outer ties, the physical bonds, had been torn asunder. This type of Pharisaism, as it had developed through Hillel out of the inner life of Judaism, breathed the breath of new life into Judaism so that it could begin its wanderings through the world . . .

Is it surprising that [*the wanderer*] should turn his face back to the past which seemed to grow brighter the more it receded into history, that he felt that all the good and beautiful things for which he yearned could be attained only through the restoration of that past, and that he saw the future only in terms of an image of that which had long been dead and buried? Is it so strange that, as he pursued his wanderings, panting and oppressed, he should have put on a bristly coat of mail so that the dagger might not harm him . . . that he enwrapped himself in sheath upon sheath so that the chill and frigid wind that blew upon him with every word, with every breath, might not cause his body to shiver? Is it so extraordinary that he should have hung many a worthless amulet around his neck, and look to it to bring some brightness into his joyless life and at the sight of it indulge in pleasant and cheerful reverie? Wherever he went, he could build only tottering hovels. . . . And yet, wherever his new home permitted him to plow furrows of the spirit and gave him a small plot of ground on which to sow his spiritual seed, that new dwelling-place soon became for him his true Fatherland in the full sense of the word. . . .

It is significant that, according to tradition, a sage [*who dwelt in Babylonia*] during the third century should have said: "He who moves from Babylonia to Palestine transgresses a law

and is guilty of sin." So close were the ties that bound the Jews
to Babylonia and the new Persian empire. . . . Completely in
accordance with this statement is the dictum of another
teacher, who said that "the law of the State is religiously binding." Formerly, the law of the state had been viewed as an
emanation of paganism, as a work of an ungodly system, and
thus certainly not valid; in fact, it was looked upon as the
worst enemy of the Jews. Now, however, when Jews dwelt
within a Fatherland which may not have given them complete
freedom but which did offer them a stable and secure dwelling-
place, the law was regarded as religiously just. Babylonia had
become a new homeland, and Aramaic, or Chaldean, its language, became an almost holy tongue for the Jews. In former
days the term "Aramean" denoted idolatry; Aramaism was
the hostile opposite of Israel. But now the Jews lived in the
midst of these people, they held a secure and favorable place
among them, and gradually also assimilated their views and
their language. To this very day we have Aramaic prayers in
our liturgy, and these have been accepted as holy though they
are not the strains of Zion. The Aramaic translation of the
Bible, too, is generally accorded a place of preference, partly
because of its faithful and accurate reflection of the accepted
views, but primarily because it had its origins in a land that
had become the second home of the Jews. In fact, Aramaic, the
language of Babylonia, still held its own even much later, when
Arabic literature was supplying new nourishment to Judaism,
when the Arabs had already supplanted the remnants and
traces of older cultures with their own. . . .

It was with pride that [*the Jews*] looked upon Spain as their
own; they paid homage to her in their poems and clung to her
with all the fervor of their hearts. The weary wanderer had
found a new and beautiful home; he no longer looked back to
his past, because he loved his present. And even when they
were driven out of Spain, the Jews still cherished Spain and
Portugal in their memories, and to some extent do so to this
very day. In other countries, too, indeed, wherever they found
a home where they could remain for a reasonably long period,
the Jews formed close intellectual and spiritual ties with the
people. They came to love their language, to follow their customs, and continued to preserve these bonds even when they
were swept away once again by the blind wrath of the people
in whose midst they had thought they had found a new Father-

land. Today we can hear the German tongue from the lips of Jews in the most distant lands. They have preserved it in their midst through centuries and cherish these familiar sounds. The language recalls to them a homeland which, though it was drenched with their blood and never afforded them permanent and peaceful abodes, had been a place where they had had a relatively protracted breathing spell, and of whose spirit they had absorbed a good deal . . .

While bishops and knights in the Dark Ages had fallen victim entirely to a hallowed ignorance and remained alien to the complex arts of reading and writing, these scattered remnants of the Jews never ceased to strive after spiritual development. True, it was often a one-sided development which was out of step with contemporary life, but at any rate it represented an intellectual activity which kept them alert and active. Ignorance was never canonized in Israel; at times scholarship may have been somewhat distorted, ingenuity misguided, and the intellect clothed in gaudy frills; but the intellect never ceased to be active. We have before us monumental works from both darker and brighter days. These products of thought and intellectual efforts are impressive and awe-inspiring. I do not swear by every word of the Talmud, nor by everything that the medieval sages taught, yet I would not like to miss any of these things. There is in these teachings a keenness, a vigor of thought which inspires us with deep respect for the spirit that lived within our ancestors. Pouring forth from them is an abundance of common sense, wise maxims and a vitality of perception such as can stimulate and invigorate us even in our own day. . . .

The Jews are often derided as middlemen; it is said that they take the discarded clothes of one person and offer them for sale at the home of another. This is quite true. They have indeed taken the discarded garments of older cultures to the homes of the peoples of Europe—and if those peoples had not had these tattered remnants to wear, they would have been stark naked.

However, the Jews were not only middlemen; they had a creative influence as well. The more significant philosophers of the Arabic era were actually Jews, or at least a large number of them were. The name of "Avicebron" recurs in many medieval writings as one of the most original thinkers. "Avicebron" was none other than Shelomo ibn Gabirol, a Jew. His name had been corrupted from "Ibn Gabirol" to "Abencebrol" and then to "Avicebron." Ibn Gabirol was an original thinker

and at the same time an outstanding poet. . . . Moses Maimonides, that pillar of faith, a man who was creative in every
aspect of Jewish scholarship, was at the same time a thinker
who not only implanted a lasting seed into Judaism but has also
come to be acknowledged by European civilization as a great
teacher. Albertus Magnus copied the best of Maimonides in
his writings and Thomas Aquinas borrowed a good deal from
him. Who could number the great minds who lived within the
Arab realms and there developed their intellectual capacities
and gifts of poetry? . . .

When poetry flourished once again in Italy—a sense of
beauty this time rather than the vigorous spirit of scholarship
—we find, in a class with Dante, a Jewish poet, Immanuel. A
close friend of Dante, and intimately associated with him, Immanuel was full of refreshing humor, even as, indeed, despite
bitter oppression, the spirit of the Jews never grew either dull
or weary. The science of mathematics, too, has numerous representatives in the fold of Judaism. Savasorda—a name that
sounds so strange to us—was actually Abraham ben Hiyyah, a
Spanish Jew who lived in the Provence. . . .

Times are better now, and everywhere we go we can see Jews
playing an active role in everything that invigorates the human
mind and spirit. The Bible had to be rediscovered for the Christians, as it were. And who is it that has preserved the Hebrew
Bible? Who was it that has kept it through fifteen centuries
so that it could appear once again at a later date in its original
form? What with ignorance considered a holy virtue, the Bible
would have been doomed to oblivion long ago, had we relied on
others to preserve it. Had the Bible been left to their mercies
alone, it would have been lost to us. Perhaps we might now be
finding scattered fragments of it among ancient palimpsests, or
as part of some monastic breviary; and we might look upon
them, puzzled and uncomprehending, much as we might study
some Assyrian cuneiform inscriptions. It is thanks to the care
of the Jews that the world's one remaining spiritual eye has
not been blinded, that eye of Hebraism, the revealed doctrine;
it is they who have preserved it, borne it through the world as
their treasure, assimilated it with keen understanding and
communicated its spiritual aids to the rest of the world. That
proud science which believes that it is independent and that it
expounds the Bible in accordance with insight independently
gained is actually working with those tools that have been
handed down to it by none other than the Jews; we might say

that it supports itself on the crutches provided by the rabbis. Even as the rabbis provided the text with vocalization and accent marks, and even altered it here and there, so today's students have taken it over and continue to work upon it. With the beginning of the era of reawakening culture, the staff of Judaism served as a supporting rod for the new climbing plant. We might say that Reuchlin, the teacher of Germany, seized the two pillars of the spiritual temple, Hellenism on one side and Judaism on the other, and supported himself on both of them. He drew from both these wellsprings of learning. For this reason, hallowed ignorance sought to lay snares to entrap him; its adherents clamored for the excommunication of his works and its myrmidons were greatly distressed that he had not been delivered into their hands. But Reuchlin, undaunted, honored the treasures of the Jewish heritage; it may be that he even gave unwarranted attention to many a treasure that actually was specious. Of great significance, too, are the works of critical study such as was practiced by the Jews at the time; there were the works of Elias Levita[1] and the achievements of men like Azariah de Rossi.[2] Time marched on, and the Jews moved forward with it. . . .

[*In Holland*] there arose a man of Jewish birth, who, though frail of body, was the pioneer of a new intellectual epoch. Although he did not receive immediate recognition, he eventually came to be widely celebrated and has remained so to this very day. Born in Amsterdam, Baruch Spinoza was the originator of a new sequence of thought which from then on became part of the thinking world and wrought many changes. Though he never abandoned Judaism, he did not remain a devoted adherent of the Jewish heritage. But he had matured with the aid of the old teachers of Judaism; he had diligently studied Ibn Ezra and Maimonides, and he leaned heavily upon Judah Alfakar and Hasdai Crescas. He may have fought the Jewish Aristotelians, but he had found his teachers from among their midst and had inherited their philosophical discipline. He also fought the Cabala, and yet he had received much stimulation from it. . . . Baruch Spinoza laid the foundations for a new philosophy which became the mother of a vast number of modern philosophies. Firm as a rock in his own mind and character, he built a structure of thought that was of equal granite strength. . . . Did he actually discover the truth? I do not think so; but it is an irrefutable fact that Spinoza has become the teacher of mankind and delivered it from many an error and prejudice, that he profoundly stirred human minds and that he was the father of a new intellectual life and creator of a free critical approach to the Bible. The poor Jewish lens grinder of Amsterdam did not pass through this world in vain. . . .

Now, however, a new world is about to rise. We have not yet entirely outgrown the Middle Ages, but its props have become weak and that which served medieval man as a staff has today proven to be only a splinter. . . . But [*mankind*] is preparing itself for the new era; sound scholarship and vigorous thought are prepared to inquire into all things and throw new light upon them. With such sound scholarship, which will respect the finite mind and have a notion of the Infinite Spirit, Judaism, too, will be in accord . . .

VOL. I, PP. 150 FF.

THE BREAKUP OF THE STATE AND ITS CONSEQUENCES. RABBI AKIBA.

People were living in the present but with the past. They imagined that the pious men of old had been no different from the pious of their own day. The Patriarchs of the Bible were also seen in this disguise; it was asserted that they had observed, down to the last detail, all the precepts in a form in which they had not in fact developed until a much later date. Thus it was told that David and Mephiboshet had argued with scholastic earnestness over quite specific, minor details of Jewish Law; indeed, it was said that even Shem and Eber had already established houses of study such as actually did not come into existence until much later. A historical sense was totally lacking, and in the most disorderly naïveté they comingled the eras of history. Laban, Haman, and Amalek seemed contemporary enemies. The prophet Elijah was pictured as still active in the midst of Israel; he was considered to be present at the initiation of every infant boy into the Holy Covenant; he was represented as communing with the scholars in the houses of study, instructing and occasionally correcting them; frequently, in a most charming and delightful manner, he was depicted as appearing as a friend and savior, and then as visiting every Jewish home on that night each year which recalled Israel's liberation, long ago, from Egyptian bondage.

Why, this act of liberation itself was considered an event of contemporary significance! Year after year it was repeated that if our ancestors had not been liberated from Egypt we would still be slaves to the Egyptians even today. The conditions of the past were considered still to prevail in the present, and so it was quite natural that the present should be an accurate image of the past, and that people should try with all the strength of mind and soul to remove themselves from the present and to remain part of a past, which was misinterpreted to boot.

This is an important negative aspect of medieval Judaism. ... Yet, the core buried beneath all these negative aspects must have been worthwhile, for otherwise it would not have survived for nigh unto eighteen centuries under the most varied situations and despite harsh oppression. ... A mere system of laws could not possibly have preserved religion for so long a time; it was religion that maintained the Law. Nor could the concept of peoplehood have strengthened Israel's faith; it was, instead, the faith which constantly gave new life to the movements, hopes and memories of nationhood. If bent trunks, such as that of the tree of Judaism, though overgrown with climbers and freely exposed to stormy blasts, manage to survive, then the reason for survival must be that its roots are sound and its sap is still healthy. Though in dark days they may not blossom forth in their full beauty and luxuriant growth, trees such as these, nevertheless, have within them the unshakable strength of self-preservation which, despite stifling overgrowths, will not permit them to perish.

Thus, even in those difficult and troubled days, the genuine ideas of Judaism were not blurred, but enjoyed continuous care. We will find that those same men whom we view as the founders of what we today call rigid dogma were also the champions of the purest religious truths, of the most profound basic ethical teachings. Both in his own life and in his teachings ... Akiba ben Joseph demonstrated his fervent zeal for the preservation of the traditional heritage of Israel; he believed in the eventual restoration of its independence as a nation, and he fought for it; he practiced the principles of the Pharisaic school in all their outward form and consistency, and both his contemporaries and posterity have paid him homage. But Akiba also set forth principles which revealed a much more profound philosophy than might be surmised from the laws of formal observance which he advocated. He depicted God, man and humanity in the most dignified and uplifting manner. He based his maxims on passages of the Holy Scriptures and expounded the Bible in accordance with the custom of his time. . . . This is a method, or a process, which we may not regard as justifiable from the point of view of modern exegesis. . . . But if we consider these views by themselves, we find that even we cannot express them in a nobler manner today. *In the image of God He created man,* the Scriptures tell us. The question arises: Does God have shape, and is man the reflection of that image? "No," said Rabbi Akiba. "This passage is meant to be understood as follows: God did create man in a certain image which distinguishes man from all other living things; but far be it from us to presume to speak of an image of God even in allegorical terms. Let us go further. After Adam had eaten of the fruit of the Tree of Knowledge, the Lord said to him, *Behold, man has become like one of us, knowing good from evil.* How could that be? Could man really have moved into the sphere of the Divine? And should God really have said such a thing? That would be inconceivable." And Akiba proceeded to give his own interpretation of this puzzling biblical passage: "What God meant was that man became as one *within himself,* knowing good from evil." This reinterpretation may appear to twist the meaning of the words and does not fit too well into the context, but it has a definite purpose; namely, to divest God of every physical attribute and to prevent any displacement of the barrier that separates God from man. Elsewhere, it is said, *No man may look upon Me and remain alive.* How are we to understand this verse? Does this mean that beholding God involves the penalty of death? Is this possible? "Here we have another instance of mistranslation," Rabbi Akiba said. "The passage should be understood as follows: No man may behold Me, nor may any other living thing, not even the angels and the holy spirits of purity." In this manner Akiba musters all the powers of the human intellect to preserve the concept of a spiritual God in its purity . . .

VOL. II, PP. 16 FF.

THE KARAITES. THE AWAKENING OF SCHOLARSHIP.

... The Karaites were the spiritual and physical heirs of the Sadducees, and the same assumptions that we make about the latter from fragmentary reports, in part explicitly and in part inferential, we find applicable to the Karaites, even more acutely and with more telling results which, however, grow weaker in the course of time. The Sadducees had placed great emphasis upon the rites of sacrifice. This, of course, the Karaites could no longer do; for, since there was no more Temple, there could be no sacrifices.

But when the Temple was destroyed, there were those with principles akin to the tenets of the Sadduces who said, "From now on we must never partake of either meat or wine, for part of the meat should have gone to the Temple, and the wine should have been consecrated by libation." ... The Pharisees opposed them, and won out. But we know that the Karaites, soon after they came upon the scene, forbade the eating of meat for the duration of the Exile. To be sure, this did not last very long; their rigor abated in the course of the centuries; but it stood out sharply during that initial period which was closest to the historical cause of these self-imposed restrictions. Yet even after that rigor had subsided, when they no longer clung so fervently to the memories of the Temple, we find that the Karaites meticulously observed the rabbinic precepts regarding *shehita;* in fact, they even outdid the rabbis in their rigor. Why should they have acted thus? Did they not cleave to the literal interpretation of the Bible, which contains not even an allusion to specific commandments regarding the slaughtering of animals? Were not the laws of *shehita* based solely on talmudic tradition and interpretation? It is obvious that the entire procedure of ritual slaughtering is derived from the customs first introduced by the Pharisees in their slaughtering of animals preparatory to sacrifice. Actually, these practices had been derived from the Sadducees and adopted by the Pharisees in their efforts to adapt priestly sanctity to ordinary life. And so the Karaites, of course, had to consider these regulations as binding for themselves as well.

On the other hand, it would have been the natural thing, at a time when separation was still fresh, top reserve that most vigorous element of religion, the Divine service, with

all its appropriate rituals. It had not been specifically ordained by biblical law, but there was sufficiently sound basis
for it so that we might have expected it to have become a
vital necessity, the common heritage of *all* believers. But it
seems that the Karaites thought otherwise. They could not
actually reject the idea of prayer and Divine service, but they
scorned the vital contents, the very thing which had been
poured into it to give it life. Instead, they confined their
liturgy to a meager and disjointed medley of passages from
the Bible which, commingled in this manner, seemed cold
and dessicated. But Jewish prayer was a product of the
Pharisee school, and the Karaites therefore kept away from
it and it never came to life within them . . .

The Sadducees and the Pharisees differed considerably
with regard to many of the customs associated with the Sabbath and festivals; the Sadducees were stern and bigoted,
while the Pharisees frequently attempted to make observance
less burdensome. Thus, for example, the Pharisees attached
considerable significance to the idea that the Sabbath should
be rendered more beautiful by bright illumination in the
home. This is quite reasonable and logical. But the Sadducees
rejected it, harking back to the biblical injunction, *You shall
light no fire in your dwelling-places on the Sabbath day,* as
not only prohibiting the act of lighting a fire, but also making
it a sin to allow any light to burn throughout the Sabbath.
The Karaites blindly followed the Sadducee view in this matter and waged a bitter fight against the Rabbanites because
the latter permitted the use, on the Sabbath, of such lights
as had been lit prior to the beginning of the day of rest.

In many instances the Pharisees attempted to reconcile the
precepts of the Scriptures with the practical demands of life.
Frequently these attempts actually contradicted the literal
intent of the biblical law. For example, the verse *no one shall
go forth from his place on the Seventh Day* originally had
been interpreted to mean that only very short walks were permissible on the Sabbath; the statute concerning the carrying
of any burden outside the home was also rigorously observed.
The Pharisees, however, resorted to legal fiction . . . in order
to extend the "Sabbath boundary" and to enlarge the limits
of the "home" within whose confines alone any object could
be carried on the Sabbath. These modifications were based on
legal fiction, but they were appropriate for the exigencies of
practical life. The Sadducees contested them, and the Karaites

followed in the footsteps of the Sadducees, heaping abuses on the Rabbanites—as the Pharisees became known, by virtue of their adherence to the *rabbanim* or teachers of the Law—for daring to circumvent the statutes of the Bible by means of cunning stratagems.

The Rabbanites, however, did not concern themselves with the small-minded jibes of the Karaites, the antiquated literalists. In like manner, I might add to this treatise many another fact that would confirm the thesis that the Karaites and the Sadducees were essentially in agreement, thus showing also that Karaism did not grow out of the need for progress but came in response to the demands for a standstill. I might say, of course, that Karaism derived from the *needs* of stagnation, for it is quite true that the forces of stagnation, fearing progress, felt a need to be strengthened and fortified in order to maintain themselves in the face of the change and development which marked this era . . .

VOL. II, PP. 58 FF.

SAADIA GAON

. . . According to [*Saadia's*] conviction, it did not seem at all contradictory to reason that God, in His omnipotence, should be able to work miracles. In his opinion, miracles, as emanations of Divine omnipotence, did not in any manner conflict with the laws of nature, which otherwise operate with unchanging regularity, and therefore also did not represent a concept running counter to human logic. Since this is Saadia's explanation of a question which is still undecided even now, nine centuries later, we must not label him an opponent of rationalism. Nevertheless, there are miracles which flagrantly contradict all the laws of nature and reason: for instance, that of the serpent speaking to Eve or the she-ass talking with Balaam. Miraculous occurrences such as these oppose the very nature of these animals; they represent, not just a momentary suspension, but an actual overthrow of the laws of nature and of the orderly processes of logic. Now if, in a more modern day, some advocate of the Liberal trend cited these occurrences in support of his claim that the Scriptures must not be preserved literally but only in their spiritual meaning, and asked whether his opponents actually believed that Balaam's she-ass had really talked, a representative from the Orthodox camp would reply with a resounding "Yea!" But Saadia did not have the courage so to subordinate reason entirely to faith. "No," he said, "it was not the serpent that spoke, but an angel in its stead, so that it appeared to Eve as if it were the serpent that had spoken. Likewise, it was not Balaam's she-ass that had spoken; it was God who had caused a voice to be heard by Balaam, and Balaam just assumed that it had come from the animal." To Saadia Gaon, Divine revelation was not some visible manifestation of God Himself, for man must not ascribe physical attributes to the Deity. Much rather, revelation was the perception of a voice created by God, the sight of some bright light produced by Him; in other words, sudden phenomena created for the sole purpose of being seen and heard by the prophet . . .

That he was indeed part and parcel of the time in which he lived is indicated by the fact that Saadia wrote all of his works in Arabic, the language of the country which he considered his homeland. As long as religious themes continue to be treated in that scholarly idiom in which they originally appeared on the scene, the traditional notions will remain associated with them; they will be like coins which, passing from hand to hand, are given a value according to the symbols impressed upon them at the mint without anyone ever questioning the value of its actual metal content. As long as religious values are expressed in their old idiom, they will be taken at the face value of their original claim for validity, and will remain autonomous concepts on their own, set apart from any context. It is quite another thing, however, when the language is formulated from within, when it pours forth with full vigor from the pure wellsprings of the soul and is intimately linked with actual life. In that case, the ideas set forth on these subjects will be rejuvenated; then it will no longer be sufficient for the concepts to be in keeping with tradition; instead, it will be required that they be in harmony with the mode of thinking as it changes and develops in the course of life. When, at the end of the 17th century, Thomasius no longer lectured in Latin but began to teach in German instead, this change was no less significant than his fight against witchcraft. In the same manner, Saadia Gaon, when he used Arabic as the original language in which to set down his works, at least paved the way for a union of the spirit of the age with religious tradition. Indeed, he did even more; he actually worked on a translation of the Bible into Arabic . . .

VOL. II, PP. 72 FF.

IBN EZRA AND MAIMONIDES

. . . Abraham ben Meir ibn Ezra (b. Toledo, 1093; d. Rome, 1167) was a man of extraordinary versatility, keen, penetrating intellect and mental agility. He had absorbed all the manifold aspects of both the Arabic culture and the Jewish scholarship of his day. Yet it would seem that his birthplace must have exercised some negative influence upon him; for, despite the fact that he was well-versed in the Arabic language and familiar with Arabic literature, his mastery of the Arabic tongue was not sufficient for him to make use of it in his writings. He lived among a people using a Romance language so that, actually, the language spoken in these countries was not Arabic at all, and it seems reasonable to assume that he acquired it by study.

His life, we must say at the outset, was not a tranquil one. He drifted about in countries whose orientation he did not share and whose languages were alien to him; he was thrown in with men of opposing points of view. He was familiar with many places, but he never had one place where he could have enjoyed the tranquility of domestic life. He himself often voiced his sadness at the restlessness that marked his days on earth . . .

He yearned for his native land, but he could not go there. . . . True, he was greatly respected everywhere he went, and scholars appreciated him, but he also suffered many insults in his fight against ignorance and narrow-mindedness among the Jews who dwelt in the Christian countries . . .

The heart of Abraham ibn Ezra grew heavy with pain as he wandered from country to country, and this pain is reflected in all his works. Strains of sadness and conflict run throughout his writings. Even as he was familiar with every country but at home in none, he was familiar with every sphere of the intellect but never found peace of soul in his intellectual explorations. Ibn Ezra was a grammarian, a writer, philosopher, astrologer, mathematician, and poet. He displayed outstanding talent in each of these fields, but he lacked that inner concord which would have united the parts into one harmonious whole; he lacked that all-pervading ideal which would have brought him peace. He constantly jumped from one thing to another. His mind rushed restlessly from one subject to the next; it is obvious that he never derived full satisfaction from his work and his pursuits. As I have said before, one of Ibn Ezra's pursuits was astrology, which has always been symptomatic of times of dissatisfaction and of unsatisfied minds. Times and men that feel ill at ease in the present seek to lift the veil of the future, to peer into the mysteries of things to come, in search of the fulfilment, in the future, of hopes of which they have despaired in the present, and, from this glimpse into a hoped-for future, to find more peace of mind and soul. They yearn to solve the enigma of the contradiction between their fate and the justice that is supposed to prevail. They believe that they will find in the stars the solution of the enigma of the future and discern the irresistible power which guides the affairs of this world and to which men must bow without a murmur.

Ibn Ezra was the first writer to make use of wit, and he may well have owed his great popularity to his biting manner of presentation at a time of increasing confusion in taste. We must point out, however, that [*in his case*] this biting wit was not artificially imposed upon his ideas; much rather, it broke forth . . . from within him; it was the expression of his mental restlessness, of his dissatisfied leaping from one subject to the next. It seems as if he felt compelled by the use of subtle irony or gay turns of expression to burst asunder the constraints that burdened him and to cast off the pressure that prevented him from the free and full expression of his views.

For Ibn Ezra was a man of depth and keenness of intellect, and though he shed a bright light on every theme he touched, he still left more to be surmised than he actually revealed. He was outstanding particularly in biblical exegesis. It was in this field that he labored with the greatest of pleasure and with the most marked success. Here he showed daring such as had hardly been heard of before him and was entirely absent for a long time after him. At the same time, however, he

displayed that playful circumspection which seemed to disguise the daring statement or to take it back entirely. Of
the Jewish exegetes, Ibn Ezra was the one who practiced
biblical criticism most frequently and who gathered pertinent
information concerning teachers of an earlier era who had
adopted a similar approach to the Scriptures . . .
He was a commentator who probed deeply into the natural
and logical meaning of biblical passages and thus came to the
realization that, in this process, it was frequently necessary
to deviate from the interpretations [*given them by the rabbis
and the talmudists*]. He would give the most natural explanation for a passage in clear and thorough detail, but he would
always add a statement to this effect: "This is how we might
explain it if it were not for tradition. Tradition alone is
correct; the perception of our teachers was clearer and more
profound than our own, wherefore we must yield to it." Is it
not sufficient for us, however, that Ibn Ezra's lightning-like
flashes brightened the night which then darkened the horizons
of Italy, France and England? . . .

That which Ibn Ezra lacked—a harmonious, unified intellectual orientation, inner accord and hence system—was present in his younger contemporary. . . . Maimonides represents
that medieval point of view from which none of his contemporaries could have deviated. In the Middle Ages, the individual was accorded neither full rights nor freedom and
independence. The individual was a member of a corporate
unit, not so much of the State or of his people, as of the narrower circle within which he moved. This circle had its own
particular customs and rituals, its own rights and freedoms,
its privileges, its charter, but at the same time a very definitely circumscribed structure into which the individual had
to fit. Guilds, the feudal system and corporations of freemen,
even as any and all other groups that formed part of medieval
society, each had their own distinct rules and customs, and
whoever did not adhere to them existed in a vacuum, as it
were. Thus the Jew, too, had to abide by that which marked
and identified him as a Jew; he had to adhere to those things
that assigned to him his own special position as a Jew within
the framework of the society in which he lived. Any attempt
to free himself of this would have been tantamount to a
deliberate effort to pull the solid ground from beneath his
feet. Maimonides had quite the proper conception of this con-

figuration; he viewed the religious precepts as having been ordained for the preservation of the world, as a means of maintaining seemly social relationships and of reinforcing the bonds of the community. Beyond this sphere, the medieval mind simply could not go. Intellectual development might have risen to the highest level, but the confines that held the intellectual and the community of which he was a part remained fixed and insurmountable. Hence Maimonides, too, was far more concerned with purely philosophical concepts than with practical changes in actual day-to-day living. We must remember that Islam, too, which had taken a turn toward fanaticism at that time, did not favor self-determination for the individual. Averroes (Ibn Roshd), a somewhat older contemporary of Maimonides, was an Aristotelian philosopher who enjoyed great recognition throughout the Middle Ages. But he too had to submit and yield to the most conventional views and practices. Nevertheless, several unintentional, imprudent remarks which, though in themselves innocent, were quite daring for their time, rendered him suspect and exposed him to severe persecution.

In the same manner, Maimonides, too, really attained that peak which could then be attained within the framework of Judaism. He was a man imbued with the purest and most sacred zeal for a deeper understanding of Judaism and for general, comprehensive knowledge and education; he was a man who, though considerate of public opinion and paying due respect to tradition, refused to permit anything to dim his fervent passion for truth and its dissemination. He did not fail to recognize the difficulties which the publication of his work on religious philosophy entailed; he himself drew the reader's attention to the considerations and the form of presentation which he felt to be required for this purpose. At the same time, he knew that he would not be able to avoid giving offense. "In short," he said, "this is how I am. If I have a thought that clamors for expression, and I can express it only in such a way that it may satisfy and edify some one thinker in ten thousand but appear repugnant to the great masses, I will openly and boldly come forth with that message which will enlighten the man of reason, not caring whether I meet with criticism from the ignorant masses." Maimonides was a man of intellect, but at the same time one of the purest and most earnest intentions. It is true that to him the supreme goal was pure understanding and philosophical education, but he viewed these as inseparable from pure, ethical conduct in practical life; and he saw nobility of character as the indispensable prerequisite for spiritual elevation. He was forever examining his own personality, but he was entirely free from presumptuousness. Modesty and good will shine softly through his every word. In the same manner, his works on talmudic Law, save for some instances of harshness and inflexibility in the realm of dogma and metaphysics, give off a comforting moral warmth. This is the reason why he was honored in his own day, and forever after, as a man of high intellect and noble action . . .

VOL. II, PP. 130 FF.

IN GERMANY AND FRANCE

. . . Shelomo ben Isaac of Troyes in the Champagne, who lived during the second half of the 11th century . . . and who is commonly known by the initials of his name as RaShI, was a man of temperate, clear mind, thoroughly versed in his field. At the same time he was characterized by lovable modesty. His own personality was almost entirely subordinated to the subjects on which he wrote. Shelomo ben Isaac wrote commentaries on the Talmud, the Bible and part of the Midrash. In addition, he composed penitential hymns which, like all the other penitential hymns and poems of the *payetanim*, the liturgical poets of France and Germany, have no other value than to serve as a sad illustration of the conditions that prevailed at the time. He conducted a widespread scholarly correspondence in answer to the many questions sent him from Jewish communities throughout the Diaspora. His commentaries show the clear judgment of the expounder who foresees even the slightest difficulty that might be encountered by some less well-informed reader in the study of his explanations of the text. In a few short words, closely adherent to the text, Rashi succeeds in removing the stumbling blocks and in dispelling the darkness. He steers clear of digressions and avoids any discussion that is not strictly pertinent to what he seeks to explain. He sought to be nothing but an exegete, and this he was to perfection.

We can discern these qualities primarily in his commentary on the Talmud. Here he moves on familiar ground throughout, within his own climate of thought and opinion. In his commentary on the Bible his intentions must have been the same, but here the mighty stream of talmudic exegesis, of legends and derivative interpretations, seems to have overwhelmed him, so that he thought he had to set down all their conclusions in brief form, with the result that the natural meaning suffers in the process. As a matter of fact, he realized this shortcoming himself, and he added his own simple explanations to the tortuous interpretations culled from the Talmud and the Midrash; and, to the extent to which this was possible from his point of view, he sought to elucidate the meaning of each passage and to explain its syntax with such grammatical aids as were at his disposal. I say "such as were at his disposal" because the French School of that time had not gone beyond the point that Menahem ben Saruk and Dunash ben Labrat had reached. The works of these men had been written in Hebrew and hence were accessible to the Jewish scholars of France, whereas the later works [*of the Spanish grammarians*] were written in Arabic and hence remained unknown to them. Thus they remained fixed at an infantile level of linguistics and could not penetrate to the depths of the simple meaning of the text. As we have already indicated, Rashi was still very much dependent on the interpretations given him in the ancient talmudic writings, with the result that, in many instances, his own explanations led away from the simple, direct meaning rather than toward it. Given the circumstances and influences prevalent in his time, it should not surprise us that there should have been a man of this kind, who never abandoned a healthy, sober mind, and never lost his clear, unclouded perspective, yet at the same time was quite innocently reconciled to legends and to strange and curious things and accepted them all as valid and true as if they were not so strange at all. Such was Rashi and such was his school of thought.

VOL. II, PP. 161 FF.

JUDAISM AS A SPIRITUAL POWER IN HISTORY. RETROSPECT AND PROSPECT.

. . . When the mind is unable to take wing, if it is hampered in its attempt to soar toward freedom, it will gnaw at itself and turn inward more and more as time goes on. If the mind cannot transcend outer circumstances, if it cannot break through them and free itself of confinement, it will attempt to interpret them and accept them as the full expression of true spiritual life, deceiving itself that they actually represent the full expression of all deeper spiritual existence. Then the letter will not simply be the handmaiden of the idea; instead, it will assume a spiritual power of its own, [*the substitute for*] fact; and the simple outgrowth of mere sentiment will be made to intervene in the whole scheme of the world and to enter into a direct relationship with the supreme forces that rule the world. This is mysticism; it is a wandering in twilight because the light of the sun has been barred from the eye, a groping in dark mazes because the wide highway has been blocked and there is no chance for attaining the heights of lucidity. Judaism, too, had . . . steeped itself in such mysticism. In Judaism, mysticism became a decisive force in the form of the Cabala. This work was alleged to be a revelation from ancient times, a secret doctrine which set forth the most profound of enigmas in obscure but all the more pompous verbiage. Its influence on the outside world was more significant than its actual contents. At first, Judaism, by nature lucid and sober, resisted the overpowering influence of this new phenomenon of mysticism; but it could not withstand it indefinitely. Those of impoverished mind and yearning heart escaped into this chimerical wisdom, and ambitious visionaries made use of it partly to blind themselves and partly to deceive others and to acquire power over the weak. But over and beyond this, we may note the powerful influence which the Cabala exerted on the ideological structure of mankind as a whole. It was precisely the noblest and most daring minds in educated Christendom who allowed themselves to be dominated by this new mysticism of Jewish mold and to be initiated by it into the supposed mysteries of the hidden truth, since they deemed it to be the surest and most authoritative guide in such endeavors.

Mysticism is an escape for the weary mind which takes refuge in it and there composes itself once again. But then it cleanses itself and gains new strength. Thus mysticism is actually a preliminary stage for a new uplift of the mind, for a strengthened functioning of thought revived. Thus, too, mysticism was the fountainhead of the Reformation. Out of the struggle against petrified statute was born the liberation of the human mind. Within the Church there was a break between the tyranny that had ruled for centuries and the new demands which mankind, ever advancing, makes on itself and on the course of its development. Judaism did not benefit directly from this state of affairs. Whatever values the Reformation had acquired at its outset, such as liberation from the rule of the priestly caste and the clear recognition of the simple, literal meaning of Scriptural texts, had been attained by Judaism long before. All this did not now give new stimulation to Judaism. And soon the forces of the Reformation, too, set their own barriers for themselves. . . . The old forces soon gained new strength and were able to limit intellectual liberation in both scope and content and to force it to retreat. . . .

VOL. III, PP. 14 FF.

THE YOUNGER GENERATION

. . . In [*13th-century*] Spain there were Jewish communities in which the observance of the laws pertaining to the Sabbath and the phylacteries had grown lax; there were, in fact, some localities in which the phylacteries had been completely forgotten. It was only Moses of Coucy, who had come there in his travels to preach repentance, who led the people to take this precept more seriously again. His efforts were aided by unfortunate events which occurred just then in those regions and which were considered to be Divine punishment for the neglect of these laws. The fact was that attempts had even been made to effect slight reforms, reforms of the "tame" variety such as we, too, knew in the beginning [*of our own movement*]. We are told that one teacher had taught his congregation that it was permissible to omit the third service of the day, the evening service, because, according to the talmudic precept, its observance was voluntary and optional. This same teacher also pointed out that the Talmud had specified an abridged version for the twelve middle passages of the *Shemoneh Esrei* (the Eighteen Benedictions), for use in emergencies, and that this abridged version could be used in the regular service if it should be so desired. Moreover, he permitted such deviations as the consumption of cheese that had not been prepared with all the precautions described in talmudic law and even the drinking of wine which had not been zealously guarded from handling by non-Jews, and so forth. However, his views were rejected, and the old, time-honored laws and customs gradually came to the fore once again.

These were faint attempts which, however, could not attain wider significance during the Middle Ages, for medieval society adhered strictly to every statute and ritual prescribed for its every class, caste and community. . . . Gradually, all this came to appear alien, incomprehensible and senseless; nevertheless the people adhered to it with fervent rigor, seeing in it that which truly characterized their society. The same situation prevailed in the sphere of religion. Every religion adhered strictly to existing forms and diligently elaborated upon its statutes. Ideas might be flexible and subject to influences from without; but the outward forms, the religious act or symbol, had to remain unchanged.

VOL. III, PP. 29 FF.

THE FIGHT OVER MAIMONIDES, HIS WRITINGS AND HIS TEACHINGS

. . . It was felt that violence had also been done to other dogmas, particularly those related to miracles. The teaching [of Maimonides] concerning the resurrection of the dead gave offense to many. Generally speaking, Maimonides sought to gloss over this issue; thus, in his philosophical work he interpreted the tales of resurrections effected by Elijah and Elisha as simply accounts of resuscitation of patients from a death-like trance. The naïvely faithful believers did not relish being deprived of their sweet hopes for the delectable cakes and the Milesian garments which they had been promised would grow out of the soil of themselves at the time of the Resurrection of the Dead. The many accounts of miraculous events, such as that in the book of Joshua, of the sun standing still . . . were forced into the confines of mere natural phenomena, and this gave cause to much resentment. Moreover, that profusion of talmudic legend, which we today view as fairy tales from long ago but which were taken very seriously indeed in those days, erected still another tall barrier between the philosophers, on the one hand, and the firm believers, on the other, to whom every word of tradition was inviolable truth. Take the legend concerning Rabba bar Hana, who was said to have seen geese of such extraordinary weight that their wings drooped from heaviness and rivers of oil streamed from them. It is told that he asked the geese what their fate would be in the world to come. In answer to this question, one of the birds raised a wing, and another a drumstick to show that these fat parts would be served the faithful at the great feast to come. There were some who insisted that legends such as these were valid and true; the philosophers, on the other hand, would shake their heads in disbelief as they passed them by.

The interpretation of the biblical precepts as given by Maimonides also gave rise to many misgivings. If it were true that, as he viewed it, these commandments primarily constituted precautionary measures against the infiltration of pagan beliefs and customs and were merely guides to an ethical way of life, then these laws would be deprived of their independent ethical content and sanctifying power. This was true primarily in the case of the sacrificial cult. According to Maimonides, the act of sacrifice did not in itself constitute Divine worship. It just happened that it was customary among the ancient peoples to use this means for demonstrating their reverence for the Divinity. The Israelites, who had become accustomed to this practice during their sojourn in Egypt, would have found it difficult to abandon it. What, then, was Jewish Law to do? It had to permit the ritual of sacrifice, under the condition, of course, that offerings were to be made solely to the One God. Maimonides even advanced his own explanations for the specific regulations pertinent to this ritual. For instance, the use of frankincense was supposed to have had its origin in the necessity for eliminating the foul odors which were produced in the Temple by the many animal sacrifices slaughtered there. Actually, these explanations must be viewed as unimportant even from our point of view. At any rate, they did violence to the concept of the consecrated nature of the rite of sacrifice and to the higher symbolic significance of the offerings of frankincense which were performed by the High Priest as part of the most solemn service in the Sanctuary. It stands to reason that the faithful could not be satisfied with explanations such as these.

. . . Around 1232, Shelomo ben Abraham of Montpellier became the leader of the discontented. His message was disseminated by his two disciples, Jonah ben Abraham, a Spanish Jew who later became head of an academy in Toledo, and David ben Saul. They called upon all the teachers of the Law to take drastic measures to ban such heretical doctrines from within Judaism and to commit these dangerous writings to destruction by fire. However, such inciting calls to action did not meet with sufficient response in the Provence, in the south of France, which, though not immune to influences from the north of that country, maintained much closer ties with the northern provinces of Spain and readily submitted to their guidance in matters of thought and culture. . . . Hence Shelomo turned to the north for support. There the healthy spontaneity which had been fostered by Rashi, his disciples and his descendants had long since faded away. The minds were dominated by bigoted talmudic stringency; in view of the influences from without, it could not very well have been otherwise. The powers of the Church had already begun to wield both the sword and fire against heresy and unbelief, and this influence could not fail to have a dulling and paralyzing effect also upon the Jews residing in those localities. It was in those regions that Shelomo and his confreres received a better hearing. The rabbis of southern France joined in the chorus of lamentations and declared that anyone who dared give the legends of the Talmud an interpretation different from that set forth by Rashi thereby denied the actual, literal validity of their content and was subject to the penalty of excommunication.

Such statements of support, however, did not bring results of any significance; for the influential patrons of philosophy and the public opinion which they molded paid little attention to the obscurantists of northern France. Finally the opposition availed itself of the most contemptible weapon of all—that of denunciation. They came before the Barefooted Friars (the Capuchins) and the Preaching Brothers (the Dominicans), those zealots in the persecution of heresy, and said to them: "You uproot all unbelief and heresy from your midst and destroy any writings that might shake the foundations of faith. Why, then, should you not help us also to uproot from our midst the contagious evil of faith based on reason? There is Moses [*Maimonides*], that Egyptian; he left writings that undermine the faith and they are being spread far and wide through the land. Seize them, and burn them at the stake, too." What a meeting of hearts, and what an exchange of cunning looks there must have been! Here we have the spectacle of a rabbi concerned about the continued existence of Christianity, and of a shrewd monk watching with tender care over the defense of talmudic statutes and miracle tales! What touching brotherly accord! The Dominicans gave ear to the request and, by their command, the writings of Maimonides were burned. Of course, the Dominicans went just a little farther and, in addition, burned several thousand copies of the Talmud and Scrolls of the Law. And the accusers could do little but watch the proceedings in silent anguish . . .

VOL. III, PP. 40 FF.

MYSTICISM

. . . The first known writings of Moses de Leon, who dwelt in Spain in the middle of the 13th century, were Cabalistic works which differed little from other literature of this type. Bone-dry ideas were plucked apart, pretentiously presented as novel discoveries and decked out in the motley tatters of fantasy. As in all writings of this kind, presumptuousness characterized the work as well; Moses de Leon would not have created a deep impression just by his literary creations. Finally, though, toward the end of the 13th century, he made a daring and lucky stroke; he composed a Midrash on the Five Books of Moses, an allegorical commentary in which he gave full rein to his imagination. He did not, however, publish this work under his own name, but attributed it to the talmudist Simon ben Yohai, the ascetic miracle-worker and saint of a bygone day. He called the work *Zohar*, or "Radiance of Light"; it was written in pompous Chaldean and all the more impressive because of its very strangeness. De Leon knew how to captivate the minds of his readers. He knew how to blind them, too, with magnificent promises of salvation and with mighty lamentations, with accounts of celestial gatherings in Academies-on-High, where the scholars who had departed from the earth gathered and held direct colloquy with the angels and with the Divine Presence. Depicting all this in vivid colors and embellishing it with fanciful phrasing, boldly and with absolute self-confidence, he aroused extraordinary interest in the *Zohar*. Perhaps the claims of this work to such great antiquity might not have stood up before close critical scrutiny, but Moses de Leon knew how to allay such doubts as well. He had his sainted Simon ben Yohai utter words to this effect:

When the sixth millennium approaches—that would be around 1240—the gates of heaven will open and the light will shine forth. Until that day this book will remain hidden, and only at that time will it become known to mankind. At intervals of six decades this light will increase; and after ten times six decades have passed—in the year 5600, or 1840—its wisdom will pour forth in mighty torrents and will gather force until the end, until the sixth millennium has been completed. Then, in the year 2240, the Kingdom of God will be revealed in all its glory.

Whether the fullness of light really did pour forth in 1840, perhaps in the guise of romantic transfiguration for all of mankind, must be left for the individual to decide. And whether the Kingdom of God will indeed become a reality in the year 2240 will have to be determined by our remote descendants . . .

VOL. III, PP. 75 FF.

———————⟨∞⟩———————

THE 16TH CENTURY

. . . With this work [*the Shulhan Arukh by Joseph Caro*] the Judaism of the Middle Ages, the Judaism of law and statute, was set down in its final form. No new work of this kind has appeared in three centuries now, and, in fact, its like will never come again. The Middle Ages and the inflexibility that is associated with it have come to an end. True, mankind, and Judaism in particular, still suffered from the effects of the oppression of the preceding era for the greater half of the three centuries that followed; and it is only in the latter, smaller, half that attempts have been made to cast these off. Yet it is a fact that life, spirit, scholarship and research have outgrown the confines of the statutes and have found new dwelling-places. Our task today is different from the one which we have perceived in this last manifestation. We, too, want to take life into account; but not that life and that way of living which prevailed in Cracow three hundred years ago. Much as we may honor his memory, we no longer wish to heed the voice of Moses Isserles; it is our task to become independent sons of Moses and Israel and give expression to this new spirit in both scholarship and daily living. . . .

VOL. III, PP. 156 FF.

the original text and translations of the bible

SECOND EDITION, FRANKFORT-ON-THE-MAIN, 1928

The Bible is now and has always been an ever-living Word, not a dead letter. It has spoken to all generations and imparted its teachings to them; it expressed the fullness of its spirit in the living, spontaneous phrase. It has ever been an immediate presence among men. It never was a sealed book of antiquity, whose meaning the student had to unlock in order to acquaint himself with the ideas of a day long past, while he himself could feel free to pursue a path of his own that might well be quite at variance with its teachings. In reading other works of antiquity, men have undertaken to interpret them in accordance with the ideas that prevailed at the times in which they had first been written, and attempted to correlate these writings with such views as they themselves held and as were prevalent in their own day. In the case of the Bible, the exact opposite has always been true. The Eternal Word was never considered part of any one era; its validity could not be dependent upon the time at which it was composed; by the same token, it could not be construed to lack any of the newer truths and insights. This is the reason why every age, every movement and every personality in history has brought its own ideas to bear upon the Bible; hence the multitude of elaborations, interpretations, and typical and symbolic attempts at explanation. All efforts notwithstanding, it seems impossible to achieve an objective interpretation of the Bible, and even the non-believer will infuse his own feelings of aversion into his attempts to explain this work. This may result in a good deal of instability in exegesis, but at the same time it points up all the more clearly the significance of the Bible as all things to all men.

In the days before the final redaction of the Bible, however, that which in later eras was accomplished by exegesis was achieved by means of textual revision. The Bible encompassed the entire spiritual life of the people and expressed it fully; every man who studied it found within it the expression of his own higher ideals. In the vigorous renaissance which characterized the first years of the Second Commonwealth . . . in the fervent endeavor to have the Bible become truth at long last, to have the contents of the Bible become fully identified with its own attitude, the national consciousness also had to find its complete expression in the Holy Book that had become its heritage. Thus the national consciousness [*of the Jewish people*] quite innocently supplied into the text that which appeared to be lacking and artlessly impressed its own stamp upon that which was already part of the original version.

No one holding an unprejudiced conception of history, no one able to transpose himself into the conditions and views that prevailed in those ancient days and to appreciate the vital force of the creative urge and the might of the spirit of revelation—though the latter was on the wane—will take exception to such textual revision. On the contrary, such a person will deem it essential and justifiable by analogy alone. He will admit that in those days entire new works were composed which then were considered equal, or almost equal, in significance to the older literature; this category, in fact, includes a major segment of the Hagiographa. He will acknowledge, too, that entire works which were composed at that time were ascribed to authors who had lived long before. The book of Ecclesiastes and the Song of Songs were not written by Solomon, nor is Daniel the author of the book bearing his name. Instead, these works were written by other authors who were fully convinced that they were speaking to their people in the spirit of these men and hence did not think it amiss to place the names of these famous personalities upon their title pages. He will also accept the fact that the latter portions of the books of Isaiah and Zachariah, a large number of psalms . . . and a major part of the book of Proverbs are of more recent origin and had only been incorporated into the older collections of biblical literature at a later date. He will understand, too, that older works and facts appear in newer writings in a completely revised form, with thorough changes in both language and conception. He will not close his eyes to the fact that, judging by a large segment of their contents, the books of Chronicles are actually revisions of the books of Samuel and Kings, and that in this case, fortunately, the older versions have also been preserved. He cannot deny the historical testimony that in those days, indeed even throughout the era of the Second Temple, and even for a century after that, there still existed complete freedom of judgment as to which of the writings should be viewed as sacred and which should not be so regarded. He will know, too, that for a long time there was considerable doubt as to whether books such as Ezekiel, Ecclesiastes, Song of Songs, and Esther should be included in the canon, until the decision was finally made in their favor. On the other hand, there were books which, though now no more a part of the biblical canon, were highly valued at one time. One such work is Ben Sirah. Particularly those Jews who lacked familiarity with Hebrew judged many books now classed with apocryphal literature as equal in sanctity with other biblical writings. Nor will a person with a broader conception of history be able to ignore the historical evidence that certain minor changes were made in all the books of the Bible, quite deliberately and from highly respectable motives, not only in olden times but long thereafter as well. . . . The religio-national consciousness [of the Jewish people] had fully entered into the spirit of this treasured heritage; for this reason it assimilated it also emotionally and remodeled it in accordance with its own sentiments . . .

First of all, it was deemed a matter of urgent concern at that time to represent Jerusalem, or "Salem" (as it was then called, probably to imply that it was a "perfect" city), and Melchitzedek, the "King of Righteousness" or the Kohen l'El Elyon, the "Priest of God the Most High" who reigned therein, as sanctified from the beginning of time. Jerusalem was said to have been the seat of such a priesthood even in the days of Abraham. When Abraham had fought the kings and set Lot free, it was not sufficient to have the king of sinful Sodom come forth to thank him. Nay, Melchitzedek, King of Salem, brought forth bread and wine, and he was a priest of God the Most High. And he (Melchitzedek) blessed him (Abraham) . . . and he (Abraham) gave him a tenth of all (Gen. 14.18-20).

PP. 72 FF.

The extreme care taken in more recent times to preserve
the biblical text inviolate should not induce us to draw conclusions *a posteriori* that the same care was taken also in an
earlier era. In olden times the text was often dealt with in
quite an independent, even arbitrary manner, and the care
exercised subsequently was simply a healthy reaction against
this long continued process of summary text revision. There
were available copies of the text which had been preserved
from earlier times and others which were copied from these
in turn and perhaps preserved in the Temple. But it is certain that the ordinary "circulating" copies were treated quite
arbitrarily; they were re-edited and given supplements, and
their style and language were corrupted. Actually, only a
small number of such corrupted passages have persisted and
stood their ground in spite of the keen critical study to which
the text was subjected at a later date. However, there is still
a goodly number of traces of such corruption in our own
text as it now stands, and the Septuagint and the Samaritan
version bear full testimony to the copies of the earlier eras.
For the text which the former suggest through their translation is not an Egyptian or an Alexandrian text, nor is that
which the latter presents to us by way of a critical revision
of the Pentateuch a Samaritan version. As long as the illusion persisted that this deviating text was an authentic
one, that the Egyptian Jews had preserved an ancient Bible
text in a form in which they might have taken it along into
the First Exile, and that, in the same manner, the Samaritans
had received the Pentateuch from the hands of the Ten
Tribes and preserved it in that form, while the Palestinians
of Judea had revised their text, these words might indeed
have made some sense. In our own time, however, it has been
recognized that, on the whole, those deviating revisions are
worse and less accurate than is our own version of the text. It
becomes increasingly clear that the Jews of Egypt and the
Samaritans . . . had close ties of religious dependence with
the Jews of Palestine . . .

As regards possible motivations for discrepancies [*between the Septuagint and the Samaritan versions*], these
were not so extensive that they should have given rise to
such great differences as exist between these versions on
one hand and our own present-day text on the other. . . . The
earlier trend [*in scholarship*], which subordinated our own
version to that of the Septuagint and of the Samaritan, ex-

plained this textual agreement simply by the fact that it viewed the revision differing from our own as the original text, and that therefore our version would, in general, tend to conform to these older testimonials. Once, however, one has convinced oneself that this view was in error and that, on the whole, our own version is the more authentic one, and most of the textual deviations can be attributed purely to local, individual arbitrariness on the part of the Alexandrians and Samaritans, nurtured by sectarian zeal and ignorance, there still remains one question: Considering this complete separation of the Jews of Egypt from the Samaritans, between whom the Jews of Palestine served as the communicating link, how could there have been such an accord between these two sides while the communicating agent stood aside in utter isolation? The answer to this riddle lies simply in the fact that in those days the Bible text in general, and thus also the copies then "circulating" in Judean Palestine, read very differently from the version we know today. It is true that, for the most part, we are now in possession of the more authentic and original text. However, at the time when one group was in the process of translating its text and the others were engaged in formulating it, that text was circulating in the altered version, and it was only at a later date that the Jews of Palestine made a careful, critical study to make their text conform more closely to the original version . . .

P. 97 F.

THE SADDUCEES AND THE PHARISEES

With the valiant rebellion and struggle of a strictly nationalist party under the leadership of the priest Mattathias and his sons, the social structure of the Jewish people underwent a change. The Zadokites now were no longer viewed as the ruling families. Their place was taken first by the Hasmoneans (or the Maccabees) and later by Herod and his family. The Zadokites, however, though thus forced to give up their position of rulership, still were a priestly family and hence occupied an important place, for the people identified the religio-national uniqueness of Judaism with the institutions of Temple and priesthood. It is true, of course, that

Simon the Hasmonean adopted the title of High Priest, in addition to his royal prerogatives, and that for the most part his successors followed suit. It is true, too, that, after putting a violent end to his ties with the Hasmoneans, Herod elevated to the high priesthood priests to whom he had become related by marriage, a maneuver to unite the two great powers of his people beneath his scepter as much as possible. The fact remained, however, that this, the highest institution in the nation, had been hereditary with the Zadokite family ever since the start of the new Commonwealth and had become identified with that dynasty. Of course, some of the holders of that title who had come from this family had indeed proven unworthy of the office, but this fact did not erase in the eyes of the people the stamp of consecration which had been firmly imprinted upon the Zadokites. Even the zealous nationalist party, whether it approved of the individuals or not, had to remain loyal to them as the natural representatives of their Sanctuary. . . . Some individual Hasmoneans, who, after all, were a priestly family also, were forgiven for taking on the prerogatives of high priesthood either because of great personal merit or because of their religious zeal. However, they were watched with jaundiced eyes and even the slightest failing on their part, any slackening in the rigor of their religious observance, caused them to be viewed as vile usurpers.

It was for this reason that the Zadokites—or Sadducees, as they were called in Aramaic and Greek—remained the actual or deputy holders of the office of high priest. They were the old high priestly nobility in whose hands lay power and high offices. They were joined by the old and new aristocracy, the priests and the noble Judean families, particularly those to whom they had become related through marriage [*to comprise what was now known as the Sadducee party*]. The Zadokites had thus ceased to be the regents of the people. They were no longer the *Malkei Tzedek* the "Kings of Righteousness" or the *Tzaddikim*, the "righteous ones"; they no longer ruled over the land. The Sadducees, of whom the Zadokites formed the nucleus, were now a party within the people. They formed an exclusive, aristocratic group which, by their exclusiveness, kept the masses away from their own ranks. But they were still a noble party which enjoyed the greatest influence in the land either by virtue of their ancient lineage and priestly sanctity or as a result of newly acquired importance; they were a small group, but a powerful one . . .

The opposition was formed by the nationalist party which represented the more democratic element. They were as much incensed by the arrogance inherent in the aristocracy as they were angered at the careless manner in which these families, who sought to conform to the ruling classes both at home and abroad, represented the interests of the nation. All this notwithstanding, they had to follow them, for these were the hereditary ministers of the Sanctuary and therefore the nucleus of national life. This was a dual position whose inconsistency vexed them and inevitably involved them in constant friction with one another and continuous conflict within themselves. Even before that time, the nationalist party had already been considered the one which had "separated" (*nivdal* in Hebrew) from the peoples of the other lands and from their impurity. The Aramaic term for this characteristic now came to be the name of the party; the adherents of this faction came to be known as *Perushim* (the Aramaic form is *Perishin*), or Pharisees, as we say today . . .

In principle, the differences between them and the Sadducees could not be of great consequence. The aristocracy was even more concerned than the Pharisees with the preservation of tribal purity, that is, with the avoidance of intermarriage with foreign peoples; and the Sadducees were at least as meticulous as the Pharisees in their observance of festivals and Temple ritual, and in the apportionment of tithes for priests and levites, for they felt that these things would assure the preservation of their position of honor. However, in any nation where religious life pervades the entire organism of the state, but where religious nationality is represented in hereditary fashion by certain families . . . some contrasts are eventually bound to emerge. [*In priestly families*] the consecration of their personalities is of the utmost importance, since the interests of the family are valued according to the cause it represents; the innate pride of status and office breeds sternness in personality and bearing. The plain people, on the other hand, retain a religious awe for the hallowed institutions and honor the representatives of these institutions only to the extent to which they are able to identify with them. The sanctity of the individual who holds the office becomes of secondary importance, the claims of the priestly families for themselves meet with opposition, and their peremptory, arbitrary conduct becomes the object of attempts from the other faction to limit it. With the passing of time, religious demands and religious aspirations grow still further apart. The priestly aristocracy feels complacent in its position of power, seeks solely to preserve the existing institutions and regards with profound suspicion any new development, even unusual zeal on the part of the people. The people, on the other hand, are driven by a restless yearning; they seek to refine their ideal, to bring it closer to perfection, and to have it grow and develop as a vital force. To apply an analogy from a later era, the Pharisees were the Independent party, the Puritans, as opposed to the "High Church." Such is the picture of the Pharisees and the Sadducees as we can reconstruct it from reports which in part are fragmentary and in part adapted to conceptions from a later period.

The formation of the two parties, with their ascetic appendage, the Essenes, had already become somewhat blurred by the time of the end of the Second Temple. All that Josephus has to say about them is that they had originated "in very ancient times" (*Antiquities*, XVIII, 1, 2). Epiphanius gives a little more information, including the correct, though uncritical, explanation for the origin of the name of the Sadducees. According to his version, "they call themselves Sadducees, having derived this surname from the word 'righteousness,' for *tzedek* means 'righteousness.' In addition, there once lived a priest whose name was Sadduk" (*Contra Haeres*, I,1,14). The Talmud has nothing whatsoever to say about the date and manner of their origin; however, it is the only source from which we learn of the existence and the name of the Boethusians. It is only in the *Abot d'R. Nathan*,[1] a later outgrowth of midrashic literature, that we find a statement concerning the origin of the parties. The passage is an Aggadah, in chapter 5, to the saying of Antigonus of Socho who insists that men must serve God without any thought of personal reward: "Antigonus had two disciples who taught this saying to others, and thus it was passed from one group of disciples to another. Finally . . . the question was asked, 'For what purpose did our ancestors teach this? Should not the laborer who did his work all through the day receive his reward in the evening?' Truly, had our ancestors known that there was another world and that the dead would all rise again, they would not thus have taught. In due course they separated from the Torah, and thus two different sects arose, the Sadducees and the Boethusians; the former were called after Zadok and the latter after Boethus. They used vessels of silver and gold, not because they were arrogant, but because the Sadducees said: 'The Pharisees themselves have a tradition that they must languish in this world, and nevertheless they will have nothing in the next . . .' "

This patrician aristocracy which was composed chiefly of priests formed a fellowship, a Senate, which, immediately after the high priest and, later, the kings, stood at the helm of the state. Each such association of priests which shared in the government of the nation was known as *hever*, and they were found also in neighboring Semitic countries, particularly in Phoenicia. . . . In the early Bible era such priestly societies in neighboring pagan states were branded as exorcisers, interpreters of signs, and so forth. The people were warned not to participate in their gluttonous sacrificial feasts (Prov. 21.9, 25.24) and it was forbidden to consort with such heathen fraternities. . . . With the restoration of the state (the Second Commonwealth), however, the Semitic term *hever* was given currency also among the Jews, and the priestly Senate of the new commonwealth came to be known by this name. Thus we find on the so-called Maccabean coins, not only the high priest, but also the *Hever ha-Yehudim*, the Senate which ruled jointly with him. As the aristocracy gradually expanded and the Pharisees began to assume similar claims to distinction, these "societies," whose members had strong ties with one another, all practiced the same sacred rites and partook in joint consecrated repasts, developing still further. The fellowship of priests, whose members distributed the priestly functions among themselves and also jointly accepted the priestly tithes even if they were not themselves currently on active duty, was called *hever* or *hever ir*, the "Society of the City"; an individual member of the group was termed *haver*. At the same time, the Pharisees, too, formed a similar union and anyone who joined their ranks, that is, one who complied with the laws of ritual purity and separated the priestly tithes from the fruit of the harvest, was called *haver*. The confederation itself was known as *haverut*. These expressions occur repeatedly in the Talmud.

After the destruction of the Temple, the "Society of the City" lost its exclusive priestly character; these groups now became pious brotherhoods which performed ritual and philanthropic services within the organization. They would gather together for worship and took charge of works of charity, at first only for their own membership, but later for the community in general as well.

The Pharisees, more idealistic but also fanatical in their piety, were not satisfied simply with [*a belief in reward in the world to come*]. The bond which tied them to God, they felt, should be a more intimate one; it should work wonders in their midst, give them the strength for supernatural achievements and enlighten them by divine visions (of angels). In this close communion with God they, the pious people of Israel would have to reach that high moral plane upon which the nearness of God would be manifested through them. Since the present situation of Israel did not approximate that ideal, it was believed that this glory would have to come to pass in a new age on earth, in a new period during which world conditions would be completely transformed. This, and not some world in the Great Beyond, represented to them the world to come, in which they believed. When this great change came to pass, those who even now had been so close to God would all rise from the dead. This was the ideology formed by the Pharisees who were imbued with ardent, nationalist aspirations. The Sadducees were more moderate; they regarded such questions as secondary, without, however, categorically rejecting the dogmatic tenet posited by the Pharisees. When this estrangement between the two factions in the nation was wiped out as a result of the destruction of the Second Temple, the differences, too, quickly came to an end. Now all the Jews were united by hopes for the restoration of their state, and this new situation of necessity brought about a rapprochement between the Sadducees and the Pharisees. In general, the Sadducean movement now took entirely new directions. The Talmud, which contains information pertinent to its own era only, pays hardly any attention to these differences. Aggadic literature, however, has preserved them for us, together with many another recollection from ancient days ignored in earlier writings because such information had not been relevant to the era in which these older writings had been composed.

In their position of priestly and judicial leadership, the Sadducees also continued to expand the statutes pertaining to priesthood, ritual purity, tithes and the maintenance of justice. They are, therefore, responsible for the basis of the entire extended system of Judaism. It is true that their elaborations are based primarily on the Bible text, particularly on that of the Pentateuch, but in all other respects these elaborations represent independent legislation emanating from the exigencies of national life and from the status of the priesthood in it. They are extensions of the law which became so much a part of the people that they were generally viewed as tantamount to biblical command; they were not subject to question and did not require justification. The Pharisees, however, being an opposition party and seeking to outdo the Sadducees in religio-nationalist zeal, originated institutions of their own. Some of these were comparable to similar institutions in the Sadducean movement, but most of them were innovations which were not accepted by the Sadducees. It was these innovations only which in the course of time were termed by the Pharisees as traditions received from the hands of our ancestors. . . . Generally speaking, it was the Sadducees who adhered to the older standards. The ancient Halakhah and tradition is primarily their work; the more recent form and expression is that of the Pharisees. Only the fact that we receive our information of this ancient era solely from the latter, who remained in the fighting arena, makes our own conception of the whole situation nebulous and confused . . .

PP. 101 FF.

As regards criminal procedure, Josephus reports that, in general, the Sadducees had been stern and harsh; the Talmud expresses much the same criticism by the use of the epithet "robber judge" for "criminal judge." From time immemorial, opposition parties have hurled accusations of this type at the party in power, though they themselves show no more clemency once they take over dominion. When the Pharisees were temporarily in power during the reign of Salome Alexandra, their rule was so merciless that the Talmud can justify their rule of violence only by citing "the needs of the hour"—a legal term implying the abrogation of all legal procedure in certain emergency situations. The Talmud is compelled to refer even to Simon ben Shetah,[2] a hero of talmudic literature, as a man "with hot hands" . . .

P. 139 F.

... The differences [*between the two groups*] are based more
on political and partisan viewpoints than on diverging religious
principles. Gradually they became two different sects in matters
of religious observance. ... Both parties held the same views
with regard to the plain people who, concerned only with their
day-to-day needs, were not strict in their observance of national-religious precepts, did not belong to the "societies," and
politically would incline first to one party and then again in the
direction of the other. In the main, quite in keeping with the nature of ordinary people, the people in general did not look with
favor upon the aristocracy and gave its affection instead to the
Pharisees, who were the more zealous of the two parties. These,
the plain people, had adopted a name which had been derived
from history but had undergone some modification. When the
Second Commonwealth was first established, the Zadokites
and those "who had separated themselves from the peoples and
their impurity" had to wage a hard struggle against the alien
elements in the land, in order to preserve the customs of the
nation. Gradually, and particularly after the victories of the
Maccabees, the national parties became stronger; the alien
elements were then either turned out of the country or else
assimilated into the national life of the Jewish state. But the
aliens thus incorporated into the new Jewish Commonwealth
did not observe all the commandments of Judaism; they were
lax especially in their observance of those precepts that per-
tained to purity and tithing. Thus there were now two elements
against which the customs and morals of the Jewish nation had
to be upheld with firmness and rigor: the foreign nations on
one hand, and the "naturalized" aliens and even compatriots
who observed the commandments only partially, on the other.
The two terms, *goyei ha-aretz* and *ammei ha-aretz,* which
formerly had been used interchangeably to refer to the alien
elements in the land, now became subject to distinction, with
each term having an exclusive connotation of its own. The
alien nations were referred to as *goyim;* while the elements
within the Jewish people itself, who had not completely assimilated to Judaism, were known as *ammei ha-aretz.* From these
terms were derived singular forms to refer to individuals in
these two categories. An individual member of an alien people

was called a *goy*; while an individual from the Jewish masses who had not yet become a part of the more rigorously observant "societies" was referred to as an *am ha-aretz*.

P. 139 F.

Although . . . law and legend developed independently in accordance with principles of their own, they were of necessity based on the Scriptural text. They sought to explain the simple Bible precept or Bible story in accordance with their own more advanced concepts, and so the variations in Halakhah and Agaddah naturally had a significant effect on the interpretation of Scriptures. But whereas in earlier eras later assumptions were permitted to go side by side with the actual Bible text, it is a typical phenomenon of later procedure that every effort was made to find contemporary views definitely reflected in the text of the Bible, that is, to interpret the text in such a manner as to make it appear to set forth that same more recent concept. Scholars of an earlier age did not treat the letter of the Bible with such great respect. They based their assumptions on their own views; they were not disturbed by small variations that did not alter the meaning of the whole text; indeed, they did not even shrink from making minor changes here and there in order to make the wording of the Scriptures conform more closely to their own assumptions which they regarded as firmly established. Later, however, things changed. The Bible scholars of more recent eras had to bend every effort to establish a final biblical text that would be complete and accurate. Every letter and punctuation mark offered a chance for interpretation; hence even the most minute adulteration could give rise to major variations in the construction of the biblical text. It was during that time that the correct text was established with greater care; it was then that the masoretic studies first began, and, to the extent that earlier textual changes had not become too deeply entrenched to permit the reconstruction of the original version . . . we may now assume with certainty that the text which corresponds to this more recent development is the authentic one as against the older version which had been changed by arbitrary action. This more recent text, the masoretic text, is the one which, by and large, is in our hands today.

The variations in interpretation and determination of the biblical text come to the fore most clearly in the translations dating from different periods. Even at the beginning of the Second Commonwealth, readings from the various books of the Holy Scriptures, particularly from the Pentateuch, had been introduced and it was soon deemed necessary to have some learned man provide a translation to supplement each reading. The number of those possessing an accurate knowledge of the language was not large, and even such knowledge would still not have been sufficient for the understanding of difficult passages. More than that, the actual contents, too, required interpretation—and, in fact, revision—partly in accordance with the requirements of contemporary thought, and partly out of consideration for the people as a whole. Outside of Palestine, where the vernacular had nothing in common with the language of the biblical text and thus offered no aid toward an easier understanding of that text, the translation soon became so firmly established as to supplant the original version altogether.

This happened in Egypt where a Greek translation became canonical itself, as it were, so that, eventually, its authorship was attributed to an established authoritative body of seventy (or seventy-two) elders and the work itself was surrounded by an aura of sanctity all its own. This story, however, is no more than poetic conjecture and embellishment from a later date. The same is true also of other theories concerning its origin: for example, that "five elders" had written it or that it had been composed for one of the Ptolemies, and even more so of later hypotheses which do not even have support from tradition. Briefly, the so-called Septuagint version is a translation which first was communicated orally by Greek translators, but was soon set down in writing and eventually came to be the standard text for all Greek-speaking Jews. It is therefore not the product of a deliberate literary effort; instead, it came into being in response to a definite need which it satisfied. It is an expression of the manner in which the Bible text was then understood, and, insofar as this was not prevented by translators' tendencies then prevalent . . . it faithfully reflected that contemporary interpretation. It was a faithful rendition, hewing closely to the original biblical text; yet, in many passages it proceeded with a good deal of freedom. Now the Egyptian and other Greek-speaking Jews, who used this translation as a standard original text, were remote from the center where Scriptural interpretation, legalistic discussion and Aggadic explanation continued to flourish and develop. However the new findings that went forth from Palestine, particularly insofar as they affected practical life, penetrated to them and were probably accepted by them to a large extent. Thus the Greek-speaking Jews were satisfied to accept Palestinian scholarship as authoritative. Nevertheless they still retained their own version of the Bible, namely, the standard Greek translation.

In the second century of the Christian era, however, a veritable revolution took place. The national-religious life in Palestine could no longer serve as a pattern for those living in the Diaspora. The scholars in Palestine now resolutely proceeded with the critical arrangement of the original text, and every letter in the text attained major significance because of its value in the interpretation of the whole. Besides, Christianity began to lean upon the Greek translation of the Bible and adduced from it evidence in support of Christian views. But one glance into the original Hebrew text sufficed to show that this evidence was, in fact, non-existent. Only then did it become clear how far removed the Greek text actually was from the Hebrew original. It was obvious that the old Greek translation would either have to be revised or entirely replaced by a new one. This was the cause of the work of Aquila and Theodotian. Aquila made an entirely new translation that was in accordance with the more recent point of view. Moreover, in order to preserve even in the translation the same possibilities for interpretation as were contained in the original text, Aquila proceeded with a cautious literalness that did violence to the genius of the Greek language. Theodotian, on the other hand, based his work on the Septuagint, adapting it to the newer text and to the newer viewpoint. The Jews, however, could no longer be satisfied with this one translation, and particularly not with a translation in a language of such confusing character [as was that of Aquila]. The Christians, for their part, looked with suspicion upon this product of the "modern" Jews. Greek Jewry as such, moreover, decreased in both numbers and importance. Hence only fragments of these later translations have been preserved, whereas the Septuagint is still with us even today.

PP. 159 FF.

CHANGES WITH A PURPOSE

The most effective changes in the Bible text were those which were made intentionally in order to render the naive language of the Bible less offensive as religious views changed and became more sophisticated, or in order to eliminate misunderstandings that might have resulted from an artless manner of expression. When the Second Commonwealth was established, Judaism was faced with a great internal challenge, namely, to instill into the entire people, as a living conviction, the faith in the Unity of God and the duty of the entire nation to worship Him—two concepts which had attained a prominent place in the nation's consciousness during the final years of the First Commonwealth and in the Babylonian exile. This meant fending off all the influences emanating from neighboring nations and, especially, countering the attacks of heathen Hellenism, tinged with philosophy. It also meant placing added stress on the importance of Israel, despite its political weakness at the time, and protecting its Sacred Scriptures, its religious and national heritage, from misinterpretation and ridicule. What with the obvious and imperative demands of mere survival, it was only natural that one no longer stood zealous guard over the preservation, intact, of every single letter in the biblical text. Indeed, it seemed sacred duty to set the text aside if there was any chance that it might obscure the clarity of the thought which it was meant to express. Hence the generation of that early era proceeded here with a good deal of freedom. Not only did it recast the meaning by an extensive use of the paraphrase, but it even altered the text itself, by changing single letters or even entire words, all in order to obviate difficulties of dogma or remove expressions that might otherwise outrage sentiments of patriotism or feelings of delicacy and morality.

This challenge was not posed to the same extent to the generations that followed. For by that time Judaism had already made its way in its finished form and had been firmly established. No longer was there danger that a single expression might be fraught with peril or arouse fear of wholesale defection. Indeed, such expressions now no longer even seemed objectionable. On the contrary, by that time any far-reaching attempt at independent textual change, even if it was made only in the translation without affecting the original text, was looked on askance. It was feared, and rightly so, that the Word of God might be deprived of its objective security and fall prey to subjective caprice, and that, under the influence of carelessly flexible interpretation, the commandments might evaporate into vague generalities. Sectarian disputes, and particularly the rise of Christianity, lent added emphasis to these scruples. Hence there was a return to reverent literalness, and any attempt at arbitrary revision of the text was severely castigated. Nevertheless these methods had already become so firmly entrenched that the fight against them was not successful in every instance. Indeed, contemporary views were so strongly influenced by them in many respects that, subsequently, the new generation went even farther than the old. That is why in several instances our own text, the product of a more recent philosophy, makes changes in the original even in those passages where the translations reflect it faithfully . . .

PP. 259 FF.

THE DESIGNATIONS FOR GOD

. . . Once the belief in One Spiritual God had been attained and, after a long struggle, had at long last become the most precious possession and at the same time the one distinguishing feature of Judaism, it had to receive clear expression also in all the documents of that faith, and every statement in them that might even appear to deviate from this belief had to be eliminated or at least altered. Special attention, of course, had to be given to that designation for God which belonged to Judaism exclusively; that is, the name spelled YHWH. All other designations for the deity express merely some aspect of the relationships between God and the world or between God and mankind; they refer to Him in terms of some quality inherent in Him, such as Almighty, Lord, King, Father, Compassionate One, and so forth. The designation YHWH alone was deemed to express the full essence of God, reflecting His infinity, His inexhaustible abundance and the fullness of His majesty. We cannot be sure whether this name was derived etymologically (as Exodus 3.14 has it) to denote eternal being or to refer to God as the "Unchanging One." Nor can we be sure of the pronunciation the name was given at that time. Suffice it to say that this was the full "proper name" for God as opposed to all the other designations which were merely generic or conceptual in character. For this reason this Name had to be treated in the same manner as God Himself. The majesty of God had to be respected also in the one Name which was most intimately linked with it; the Name, like its Bearer, was remote and ineffable. Hence, in public readings of Scriptural passages in which it occurred, this Ineffable Name had to be replaced by some other designation. The Greek translators accomplished this by using the term *Kyrios* (Lord) for the Hebrew *Adonai*, which had the same number of letters as the Tetragrammaton and which was considered the most sacred designation for God immediately after that of YHWH.

This, however, did not work in Palestine, for there, in the original language, it was not permissible to make promiscuous use even of the designation *Adonai* in passages where it did not actually occur in the text. Besides, the exchange of the Ineffable Name for another designation which occurs quite as frequently gives no indication that this name for God is only a substitution for the Name which actually is written down in that particular passage. It was considered a better plan, in such instances and for this purpose, to read *ha-Shem*. This term, literally, "The Name," was quite a harmless expression, but yet quite clearly indicated that it merely served as a substitute for the actual Name of God which could not be pronounced. The custom was adopted by the Samaritans for the public reading of the Pentateuch and also of their later literature . . .

The Palestinian Jews followed suit. They made use of the paraphrase not only in everyday life, whenever they desired to make emphatic reference to God; in such expressions as, for instance, the sanctification or the desecration of God, and also whenever they meant to make explicit reference to the Tetragrammaton . . .

The ancient tradition that, after the death of Simon the Just,[3] the priests had ceased to pronounce the "Name" in the priestly Blessing is quite in keeping with the evolution of the substitute designation. Obviously, the tradition means to indicate to us that, after a certain period, even the priests and, in fact, the high priest himself during the most solemn service of the Day of Atonement, no longer pronounced the actual Tetragrammaton. It is certain that this tradition, which has persisted despite obvious contradictions with later assertions, is based on historical fact, namely, that in olden times the actual Divine Name was never pronounced, not even during the most solemn services in the Temple. The same tradition appears to be reflected also in the statement of Abba Saul that he who "pronounces the 'Name' in all its letters has no share in the world to come" (Sanhedrin 10.1). This assertion, however, was not accorded universal validity at a later date. It is, instead, assumed by the Halakhah that the high priest actually did pronounce the full Tetragrammaton on the Day of Atonement, when he read the thirtieth verse of the sixteenth chapter of Leviticus after the brief prayer which he repeated three times (Mishna Yoma 6.2). It is reported there that, when the priests and the people heard the "Ineffable Name" (*Shem ha-Meforash*) they fell upon their faces. Legend adds further embellishment to the tradition by claiming that when the high priest pronounced "the Name" on the Day of Atonement, his voice could be heard as far away as Jericho (Tam. 3.7).

[*The passages that follow trace the vacillations in the attitude of the Halakhah toward the pronunciation of the Tetragrammaton; it is pointed out that, at times, it assumes the common use of the term even in everyday life, but then reverts to the stricter attitude of Sadducee tradition.*]

PP. 261 FF.

And so it was that they reverted once again, with fearful reluctance, to pronouncing the Holy Name. It was claimed that, even though in times of yore the high priests and the priests in general had pronounced the actual Name in unison during the priestly blessing, the priests were bidden to make use of the paraphrase, and did so use it, whenever they gave the blessing outside the Temple. [*The Gemara*] reports that, at a later period, even the high priest pronounced the Name only softly or even "slurred over" it . . . and that, even when the high priest had actually pronounced it ten times at the top of his voice, so that he could be heard as far away as Jericho, those present would forget it as soon as they had left the scene. It was only much later that we find a definite assertion to the effect that the Name might be spelled YHWH, but must be read as *Adonai*. (Note: Several passages in the Babylonian Gemara speak of a name for God which consisted of twelve or forty-two letters. But this seems to be based on a misunderstanding, which came about because of the many contradictory statements concerning the Tetragrammaton. At one time it was declared permissible to pronounce it and it was said that it had actually been pronounced in full; at another point it was asserted that the Name was the supreme mystery and could not be pronounced. In the end, an attempt was made to reconcile the conflicting claims; it was pointed out that the former claim applied only to the Tetragrammaton while the latter referred to another name of twelve or forty-two letters which was even holier.)

It was only then that the Jews adopted the custom which the Alexandrians had already followed in their translation but which in all probability was not accepted before in Palestine with regard to the original Bible text . . .

PP. 265 FF.

Thus, by and large, after a struggle against an older, arbitrary procedure, our own text has regained its original form. Nevertheless it is not unlikely that, at present, there are in the Bible text certain passages where other designations for God have taken the place of the Tetragrammaton. Certainly, passages discussing some type of blasphemy must have clamored for such paraphrasing. For instance, the passage (II Samuel 12.14), in which David is reprimanded for blaspheming God, sounded much too harsh in its original version; for this reason the word *oyevei* (enemies) was inserted before the name of the Lord. This, of course, expressed the very opposite of what was originally meant, for this alteration made it appear as if David had blasphemed the *enemies* of God. The context, however, conveys the true meaning of the passage and the translator, therefore, used the future tense in his forced interpretation, so that the text now said that David had caused the enemies of God to utter blasphemy. In other instances, particularly with reference to Naboth who was murdered through the cunning of Jezebel, and with reference to Job, the "curses" which were shrewdly attributed to these personalities, or else were assumed to have been uttered by them against their will, are turned into "blessings," the very opposite of what had been meant in the original. . . . Moreover, even in passages which did not deal with godly men but which might have horrified the reader by reason of the association of a "curse" with the Holy Name of God, identical or similar attempts were made to mitigate the expression of the curse . . .

P. 267 F.

INAPPROPRIATE TERMS

We have observed the manner in which the desire not to profane the Name of God has given rise to any number of textual changes. We now understand that these motivations had their origin in remote antiquity and have been redoubled in the course of time. Conversely, we know that whenever such changes threatened to undermine the definitive character of the law, they were eventually disregarded and the original phrasing was restored to the text. We encounter the same procedure also in any instance where the literal construction of a verse would imply something improper about God, either because it would offend the majesty of God or because it is couched in terms with a definitely inappropriate physical connotation . . .

P. 308 F.

Examples of abstraction or spiritualization by translators of terms with obvious physical connotations occur so frequently in the biblical text and for the most part are so well known that we will confine ourselves here to mention only those which had a direct effect on the construction of the text. . . . Let us first consider passages which seem to infringe upon the reverence properly due God by representing Him as standing before a human being. It was reasoned that the inferior should stand before the superior, not the superior before his subordinate. For this reason the original text of Genesis 18.22, which read "And the Lord stood yet before Abraham," was changed to the version which we know today: *And Abraham stood yet before the Lord.* Not only the entire context (cf. verses 23 and

33) but also the Talmud and the Midrash confirm that the original version was, in fact, the more accurate one. For the explanation to the biblical verse, *Thou shalt rise up before the hoary head . . . I, the Lord,* as given in tractate Bikkurim 3.3 reads as follows: "I, the Lord, was the first to perform the courtesy of rising before the hoary head," with obvious reference to the passage mentioned above from the book of Genesis. Moreover, it is explicitly stated in the Midrash (Berakhot Rabbah, ch. 49) and elsewhere, that this is an instance of *tikkun soferim,* a "correction by the scribes"; in other words, it was indeed the *Shekhina* that had waited for Abraham.

In some other passages in the Bible, the phrasing is not so conspicuous that an actual change in the text would have been considered necessary, but the passage was nevertheless reinterpreted in the translation. In the biblical account of Jacob's dream (Gen. 28.13), we are told, *And behold, the Lord stood beside him,* with the Hebrew *nitzav alav* denoting *stood beside him.* But many authorities claim that *nitzav alav* should be interpreted as "stood above *it*" [*i.e.,* "and behold, the Lord stood above *it*" (*above the ladder*)]; others again would render *nitzav alav* as *stood above him* [*i.e., that* "the Lord stood above Jacob"], thus denoting the majesty of God above all other living things. In translating the words which God spoke to Moses, *Behold, I stand before thee, there upon the rock* (Ex. 17.6), the Septuagint renders *before thee* with the connotation of time; that is, as "before thou camest to stand there." . . .

Reverence for God requires also that no evil or injustice may be imputed to Him, not even by implication. Actually, when Moses said to God, "Kill me, I pray to Thee, so that I may not see Thy evil . . ." (Nu. 11.15), all he meant was that he, Moses, did not wish to live to behold the evil, or the punishment, which God would inflict upon the people of Israel. However, the verse, left in this form, would sound as if it were speaking of some evil inherent in God. For this reason, the original text and the translations all have changed the offending word to read *be-ra'athi* "my evil." Only the fragmentary Jerusalem *Targum* indicates a trace of the original reading in its paraphrase . . .

P. 331 F.

The expressions referring to "beholding God," or "beholding the countenance of God," were deemed particularly objectionable. In this connection, Luzzatto calls our attention to a number of passages in which the punctators have made slight changes in vocalization, thus changing the *kal* (active mood) into the *nif'al* (passive mood), so that the verse is given the meaning of *appearing before God* which, however, is not entirely correct from the grammatical point of view. An even more radical change in meaning results when *ve-nir'eh*, "and we shall behold," is changed in this manner to *ve-nir'ah*, i.e., *and he shall appear*. Thus, in the first book of Samuel (1.22), where Hannah says "Until the child be weaned, when I will bring him, and then we shall behold the countenance of the Lord," the last part of the verse was altered so as to read, *and then he shall appear before the Lord*. The expression *nir'ah*, in the *nif'al* mood, to describe an appearance on the part of the Lord, seemed less objectionable, for this term is the one most frequently employed in connection with incidents of Divine revelation to Moses and other prophets and godly persons. But in the instance where it is stated that God's Presence became visible to the Israelites as a whole, and where this fact is expressed by the participle *nir'eh* which, in a public reading, might cause the verse to be misconstrued as indicating an appearance at this very moment, the punctators remedied the situation by slight alterations in vocalization. Moses tells the people of Israel to offer up sacrifices because "the Lord appears (*nir'eh*) before you today," but the punctators changed the verb to *nir'ah* so that the verse now reads *the Lord* has appeared *before you today*. In this manner it is not possible to construe that verse as implying that the Lord is about to appear to those now listening to the reading from the Scriptural text . . .

P. 337 F.

OF ISRAEL, ALIENS AND THE GODLY

We have already noted . . . that outright insults to sentiments of patriotism by harsh threats and abusive predictions against the people of Israel in the biblical text caused certain changes to be made in that text. This same course was taken also by the translators; and our own text, too, has undergone minor changes in more recent times due to this attitude. Tradition informs us that in the olden days such harsh criticism of Israel was felt much more keenly and that consequently there was some hesitation as to whether such verses should be read aloud in public. At the end of Mishna Megillah, ch. 4 (3), we read, "Eliezer (ben Hyrcanus) says that the sixteenth chapter of the book of Ezekiel should not be read as the concluding portion of a lesson from the Prophets." As Mordecai Jaffe[4] correctly notes, the objectionable part in this chapter is not merely the enumeration of the sins of Israel, but also and particularly the statement in verses 3 and 45 that Israel is of Canaanite descent: *Thy origin and thy nativity is of the land of the Canaanite; the Amorite was thy father and thy mother was a Hittite*. The verse *the Amorite was thy father, and thy mother was a Hittite* which occurs twice in this chapter, is disguised by paraphrase to a point past recognition not only by the *Targum* but also by Symmachus, where we read, "... you art guilty enough to bear their punishment, for you appear before the court as their daughters"; in other words, Israel is not physically descended from Canaanites at all; it is just related to them in sinfulness. . . .

P. 345 F.

In Numbers 10.31, Moses asks Hobab not to leave because he, Hobab, is familiar with the camping sites in the wilderness, and tells him, . . . *thou shalt be to us instead of eyes* . . . This remark seems strange, since it would imply that Israel, which had been guided by columns of smoke [*sent by God*], was nevertheless in need of a guide. For this reason all the translators (save the Syrian) and Sifrei have made changes in the interpretation of that verse . . .

P. 347 F.

With the return from exile, when the country had been overrun by neighboring peoples and the worship of the One God had been greatly endangered by this foreign infiltration, sentiments of nationalism became intensified and the returning exiles sought to displace the alien elements. Intermarriage with them was especially condemned, and children of such mixed marriages were considered bastards. However, the complete expulsion of the foreign element proved impracticable; moreover, it turned out to be not even essential for the attainment of the basic purpose which it was to serve. The concept of national life was a religious one, so that, by adopting the religious ideas of Israel, any foreigner could become naturalized, for by becoming a Jew he had accepted for himself the basic condition of Jewish nationhood.

This was a major step forward in world history. Though the traces of nationalism had become deeply imbedded in religion, religion had now won over nationalism. To the ancient world the stranger was either an entity which gradually lost his identity by becoming absorbed into the nation in the course of time, or else a slave forced to drag with him through the centuries the shame of his foreignness and his position of inferiority. But now religion had become the instrument by which the stranger could be delivered from what used to be a distinct, permanent stigma, a stain which in the olden days could have been erased only by accident. Now the stranger could automatically rise to a status of equality by his own free choice. Religion now was not merely something acquired by birth, but the result of choice and conviction, though of course this conviction was sometimes produced by force. Thus the legal status of the stranger underwent a complete change. The non-convert had no rights whatsoever, but the convert who adopted the religion of Judaism became equal in every respect to him who was an Israelite by birth. There was only one difference, the maintenance of which the ruling patrician aristocracy claimed as their privilege, namely, that these novice Jews should be barred from such high offices as had been reserved for patrician families; and that converts should not be permitted to marry into their select family groups. Marriages contracted by other Jews with converts and their families were considered entirely legal. Marriages with a non-converted member of a foreign nationality, however, were unthinkable; they were regarded as invalid and children from such unions were not viewed just as *mamzerim*, or offspring of a type of marriage forbidden by Jewish Law, but as actual bastards of unknown paternity who were identified with the mother only. Thus, in a mixed marriage, the resulting issue were considered Jews if the mother was

Jewish, but Gentiles if the mother was the non-Jewish partner in the union. Originally, the old Halakhah had employed the term *mamzer* to denote the offspring of a marital union between a Jew and a non-Jew, but later legislation never employes that designation in this particular connection. A *mamzer*, it was pointed out, was by definition a child of a marriage forbidden by Jewish Law for other reasons, but he was not considered illegitimate, because the marriage had been contracted by Jews who were officially recognized as such. The issue of a marriage between a Jew and an unconverted non-Jew, on the other hand, was branded as illegitimate without consideration of extenuating circumstances.

The history of pertinent semantics is in keeping with this historical development. Originally a stranger who had permanently settled in the midst of Israel was called a *ger*, a "sojourner," a vassal, as it were, who had permanent residence rights upon his property in the land of Israel, but never actually owned it. The term was used also to refer to Israelites who dwelt in a foreign country, such as Abraham among the Hittites, and all of Israel in Egypt. As a matter of fact, even the Israelites living on their own soil, and mankind the world over were regarded as mere vassals or sojourners on earth, who had received the land on which they dwelt as a temporary holding from the hands of God. . . . The Chronicler uses the term *gerim* to denote the subjugated remaining members of the peoples who had originally dwelt in the land of Canaan and who were later employed to do heavy construction work for the Israelites. . . . When, however, the stranger in permanent residence was compelled to embrace Judaism by a formal act of conversion, but in return for this became a Jew with all the rights pertaining to his new status, the term *ger* came to assume a new meaning. As used in later Hebrew dialect, it denotes solely that person who has become a Jew by formal conversion . . .

P. 350 F.

The accounts from Bible times of marriages with aliens were especially embarrassing. . . . After all, even the patriarchs were supposed to have fulfilled in their own lives all the commandments and precepts which their descendants did not receive until centuries later. Thus we read in Genesis 38.2 that Judah had married the daughter of a Canaanite. But the *Targum* changed this reading to "the daughter of a merchant," since, after all, the Canaanites and Phoenicians were regarded as merchant nations. . . . Indeed, the Jerusalem *Targum* that is now in our possession found it necessary to note explicitly that Judah had converted his wife to Judaism. It appears that similar motives led the Septuagint to turn the Adullamite friend of Judah (see Gen. 38.12, 20), *re'ehu*, into a shepherd by changing *re'ehu* into *ro'ehu*. . . . In I Chronicles 2.17, Amasa is described as the son of Jether, the Ishmaelite. But it was somewhat embarrassing to admit that this famed general who had served in the armies of King David should have been of Ishmaelite descent and that Abigail, his mother, the daughter of a distinguished Judean family, should have married a mere Ishmaelite. Hence the Septuagint already changed *Yishmaeli* (the Ishmaelite) into *Jezreeli* (a man of the city of *Jezreel*), while the translator of the book of Chronicles, which is less widely read, leaves the original text unchanged . . .

P. 361 F.

In view of the aura of sanctity with which [*the priests*] were surrounded, there was good cause to tone down or disguise any passages in the Bible which might cast some aspersions upon either the priests themselves or upon their ancestors. One example of such procedure is found in tradition in connection with the biblical account of the casting of the golden calf. . . . We are entirely justified in assuming that certain mitigating changes were attempted in those passages which it was felt might show Aaron in an unfavorable light. This is true especially in those passages that do not deal with him in particular, but where, of necessity, there are allusions to his person. In those instances, all references to him were omitted wherever that was possible. We may note this special consideration of Aaron even in the account of the golden calf incident in Deuteronomy 9.11 ff., where Aaron's participation in the affair is not mentioned specifically at all, but only implied by the account of God's wrath against him and by the prayer of

Moses in his behalf (9.20). His name is not cited at all in Psalm 106.19. . . . Even the account in the book of Exodus has obviously been toned down. According to Exodus 32.3 it is to Aaron that the people brought their golden earrings. Aaron accepted them, fashioned them into a calf, and evidently it was also he who said to the Israelites, *This is thy god, O Israel* . . . Then, we are told, Aaron built an altar and proclaimed that *tomorrow there shall be a feast unto YHWH* (32.5). This cannot mean anything else but that Aaron proclaimed a feast, to be held on the next day, for the idol that had just been made, a feast which (see verse 6) actually did take place as promised. But in view of this, it is hardly likely that the original version of the account should have used the designation YHWH with reference to the golden calf. In all probability the term used for the deity in the original version was *la'Elohim*, meaning "to the god," or some other expression of that order. However, it was not thought proper to admit that Aaron should have arranged a feast in honor of the calf. Hence the Midrashim and the Jerusalem *Targum* explain that, though he seemed to have yielded to the pressure of circumstances, Aaron had actually intended the feast to be, not for the calf, but for the One True God. Hence the appropriate term in the text was changed to YHWH, *the Lord* . . .

PP. 382 F.

4

---

sermons
AND
lead articles
from Nachgelassene Schriften

excerpts from sermons

DELIVERED AT THE GREAT SYNAGOGUE IN BREASLAU

July 21, 1838

... Assume that the time has come when you will stand before the Judgment Seat of God, and that He will say to you: "I have made known to you through My prophets the profoundest essence of the Word that was revealed to you: *It hath been told thee, O man, what is good, and what the Lord doth require of thee: Only to do justly, to love mercy, and to walk humbly with thy God.* And He will ask you now: "Have you truly dealt justly with all men, even with those not of your faith? Have you been mild and forbearing? Have you not, in smug self-righteousness, overrating your own worth and your own piety, forgotten about Me, your God?" If you must then answer (since there can be no concealment of guilt before Divine Omniscience): "O Lord, I have adhered to many statutes and have kept them with scrupulous care—but I have not always been just," would you not then realize that you had neglected eternal values for the sake of transitory things? There is an ancient tale about a dispute among straw, stubble and chaff. Each of these three boasted that the field had been sown for its sake alone. The grain of wheat, however, listened to the quarrel from afar and said, "Wait until the owner of the field comes, and then we shall see for whose sake the seed has been sown." And behold, at harvest time the owner came; he cast the straw to the ground, he burned the stubble, and threw the chaff to the winds. But he gathered the grains of wheat and guarded them carefully ...

So, too, my Israelite, be very mindful of the pure and genuine grain of wheat in your faith, of the pure fear of God, so that you will work in behalf of the welfare of mankind. The outer shell, the ritual forms, are but bearers of the spirit in which that spirit becomes visible and by which it may mature; but do not forget that they are of no further use to piety once they no longer bear that spirit within them. Times and circumstances change, and necessitate many modifications and new institutions which, in keeping with contemporary circumstances, are needed to keep our religion alive. O pray that the Lord will not have to say to us also, *They have forsaken Me, the Fount of Living Waters, and hewed them out cisterns, broken cisterns, that can hold no water.* The living water, ever fresh and new, constantly flows forth from the fountain. But if you collect that water in a cistern so that it may be sure to remain the same, that none of it may escape and that new water cannot enter, then the drops may indeed remain the same, but the water will soon grow stale; the taste will be different; the spirit will have fled. Thus you too should not seek to disturb the Divine order of things. The outer form is subject to change; and if it should seek to assert itself independently, without concern for the spirit, then, alas, it will be stale and meaningless. But that which flows forth, eternally new, from the inexhaustible Wellspring of Living Waters will forever remain healthy and living throughout.

Therefore, my Israelite, do not complain when it seems to you that things are changing. The truth is that nothing has really changed. All that changes is the outer shell, only some outward forms undergo modification; the essence of things remains intact. Do not fear and be not misled by the talk of the foolish who view a few concessions to the times as tantamount to a collapse of the faith. . . . But neither must you allow yourself to be misled by those others who reject the whole faith of Israel merely because some outward forms are no longer to their liking, and who would say with the Israelites at the time of Ezekiel: *Our bones are dried up, and our hope is lost; we are clean cut off.* No, our hope is not lost; the true faith of Israel remains unshaken. . . .

NS, I, PP. 364 FF.

ON THE ADMISSION OF JEWS TO CITIZENSHIP: DELIVERED IN BRES-
LAU TO COMMEMORATE THE ROYAL EDICT OF MARCH 11, 1812[1]

March 7, 1840

. . . The eleventh day of March marks the anniversary of that
occasion when, twenty-eight years ago, the king of Prussia
uttered that noble-minded message, "Emerge, O you captives
who dwell in darkness; come forth into the light." Once again
we mark the anniversary of that day . . . which introduced
Israel into the ranks of the citizens of the state, removed the
stigma and lifted the curse which had weighed upon Israel
theretofore. Rejoice, particularly those of you who can still
vividly recall the old order and recollect with horror the contempt in which you yourselves once languished . . .

The prejudice and hatred of centuries, that seemed to have
been so firmly entrenched and so closely interwoven with a
pattern of thought and ideology, were beaten down. . . . The
widespread belief, proclaimed by men ֊and lisped by babes,
that Israel must forever be oppressed and remain the lowly
slave of the nations, was recognized for the falsehood it was—
exposed as such and swept aside. Perhap a few scattered off-
shoots of it may have remained behind, but the axe has been
put to the root and now it can no longer bear the noxious fruit
of persecution as it did in days gone by. . . . Thus I call unto
you: *Hearken, O Israel, and attend—on this day you became
a congregation before the Lord your God!*

Ah, how greatly we would prefer to cover the past with a
heavy veil. But if we are fully to appreciate the wondrous
favor that has been bestowed upon us and to sense the full joy
of it, then we must nevertheless review the major aspects of
that past before our mind's eye. There we behold Israel in
misery, even in that country which we proudly call our Fatherland, groveling on the ground like a lowly worm, in fear for its
very life, forever concerned about its possessions—bent, and
unprotected by the power of the law . . . exposed at all times to
unjust calumny and unfounded suspicions. No censure was too
harsh, no unkindness too severe, no accusation too improbable
to be directed against it; Israel had to be steeled against such
barbs at all times. No life was so spotless, no conduct so blame-
less as to be immune to abuse. Rejoice, O my brethren and
sisters, for now the eye of the law watches over you even as it

does over all the others who dwell in this land; the law protects you now even as it protects all the other sons of the Fatherland. Secure and free in the happy knowledge that your worthy way of life will win the recognition it deserves, you may dwell upon the soil on which your foot has come to rest; and you may be at peace, beholding yourself and your loved ones dwelling in security. In the radiance of Royal benevolence there is life and security, shelter from all danger and protection from any attack.

You have become a community, O Israel, for you have been granted space in which to move freely; you may spread out in every direction and you are admitted to every trade and craft. You have emerged from those narrow lanes that made up your world and limited your horizon. You have gone forth into the wide avenues and into the market places; you beheld the broad universe and your eye was strengthened thereby. In the days of their infancy, the nations each selected a calling. . . . And once a nation, in noble zeal, seeks to advance in every direction, its every talent will clamor for development, and its individual members will joyously work together in manifold spheres. It is sad indeed, therefore, if higher powers then draw a narrow circle around this collective force and say: "This far and no further shall you go!" Sad, indeed, it is when all manner of minds are fenced in and by higher decree are assigned one narrow sphere of activity. Such was the case with Israel. They all had to crowd into commerce, there to eke out a meager living for themselves and their families. But in this process the mind was stifled and the growth of many a talent that had been given by God in His infinite love was stunted. . . . But now all these energies may move about freely, all occupations are open to all, and each one may cheerfully engage in his chosen pursuit. . . . Ah, our gain is great indeed. Our hearts must beat quicker with joy when we behold the men who have earned respect in every field of endeavor, and when we see the young men who go freely wherever the prompting of their hearts and the bent of their minds may lead them.

Let us not be afraid, then, to recall that there was a time when the authorities did not care how we earned enough money so that, in addition to the barest sustenance for ourselves, we might raise the funds the state demanded of us, the taxes which were exacted from us out of all proportion to those levied upon free citizens. Could our ancestors, then, in all conscientiousness, be discriminating about where they might hunt that prey of which they would then be robbed immediately? Yet the germ of goodness, of true ethics, of the innate traits of conscience never died, not even in our darkest days. This, more than anything else, bears witness to Israel's religiousness and to the code of ethics which it always cherished. It bears out the answer that our ancestor Abraham gave to God when God asked him: "Which do you prefer? Shall your sons in days to come succumb to sin or to oppression by earthly powers?" Abraham chose the latter alternative. To be sure, this sad state of affairs gave rise to many unfortunate conditions; but no one outside of Israel's ranks has the right to censure us for this. As for the others, they would do much better to search their own souls and try to put themselves into the situation of those who, though given only limited opportunities for earning a living, were expected to cover the vast deficit in the ledgers of the state. . . . Let us shed a tear of sympathy for our ancestors who had to forgo not only the joys of living but also the sense of pride derived from the knowledge that one is earning one's livelihood by methods beyond reproach . . .

Over and beyond all that, this day is one of even more joyous remembrance. Is not being hated, and being forced to hate in return, the greatest grief that can befall man? . . . Yes, indeed, we were hated with a bitter hatred, and we ourselves were forced to hate with equal bitterness. The lips that should have uttered praises poured forth lamentations and accusations; the mouths that should have prayed for peace were opened only to cry for help and vengeance. To be sure, kindness had not departed from the heart of Israel; brotherly love was natural to this people. But, ah, how much truth is there in the saying of our sages that "There are three categories of creatures who love each other within their own group; these are the strangers, the slaves and the ravens." Strangers do not share the interest of the other inhabitants in the Fatherland and its welfare; they are not rooted in the same spiritual life; and they are indifferent to the joys and the sorrows of the others. This lack of interest draws the aliens together and they cling closely to one another, a group apart. Bonds of shared oppression and suffering unite the slaves, weaving strong cords of mutual love that bind them to one another. Ravens, too, have no share either in life or in its happy progress. They feed upon death and decay, and their mutual cohesiveness is an outgrowth of a shared hatred of the life of other living things. We were strangers in the land of our birth because we were condemned to be such; we were slaves in our own dwelling-places, and we panted under the yoke of ill will and wrongs of long duration. We were forced into the position of the ravens. We were not to have any part in life with its pleasures, such as our masters enjoyed; we were to derive satisfaction only from their refuse and decay.

Rejoice, O children of the present day, for the sun of loving-kindness shines upon us now and gives us warmth and life; the poisoned arrows of hatred that were aimed at us in times of yore have lost their sting, and the muffled rage with which we repaid them has vanished from our hearts. Mutual good will and love, which swell the heart and uplift it, have taken its place. Rejoice, for the gently wistful sentiment that brings tears to your eyes now bears testimony to the peace of Israel among the nations; it is the seal affixed to the covenant of friendship between them. . . .

. . . In proof of the divine, consecrated nature of our rejoicing, let us not simply seek selfish gain from these newly-acquired advantages, but let us apply these larger means now afforded us to noble endeavors in dignified ways. We want to prove to be true, genuine Israelites, adhering loyally to the faith of our fathers, while at the same time cherishing close ties to that community which has dealt so nobly with us. Would you have it otherwise? Our fathers remained faithful despite oppression and suffering; they willingly bore the burden of contempt solely for the sake of bearing witness to the truth; they forwent the pleasures of life and shunned no danger. Should we now lightly cast off all that for which they fought and suffered for so many centuries—merely to pander to convenience, to satisfy arrogance, and to be able to climb even higher? . . . This would be evil reward indeed for the Ruler of Destinies, a sad lack of gratitude for the favors we have received. . . .

. . . But thanks are due also to the Fatherland that has received us, to Frederick William III,[2] that magnanimous king who was the first among the princes of Germany to proclaim for us the golden message of freedom . . . and to the late Chancellor of State, Prince Hardenberg, that noble counsellor of the king, and to all those who followed him. . . . Now we shall cleave closely to the Fatherland, and give it support in every way by loyal obedience to its laws and by respect for its authorities and their ordinances. "Why," asks the Talmud, "did Moses yearn so fervently to enter the Holy Land? Did he yearn to taste of its fruits or to enjoy its riches? Not at all! He said to himself: There are many obligations that Israel can assume only once it has settled in that land. O would that I may live to enter it so that I, too, may fulfill these obligations!" Such should be our own sentiments today. Let us rejoice that the sphere of our responsibilities has expanded, and that we have an opportunity to put to use, for the benefit of a wider community, those talents with which the Lord has favored us.

. . . Dear friends, our era boasts of the attainment of higher knowledge and perception. New clarity penetrates all things, and preconceived notions are fast disappearing. Should the remnants of old prejudices then prevail against us undisturbed? No, worthy friends! The day cannot be far off when this cloud, too, will be dispersed. The day will come, and soon, when we will no longer be a religious community that is merely tolerated, the only religious community not enjoying official recognition from the state. Things will and must change. The spirit will be able to unfold freely and will receive both recognition and status in the society in which we live; the houses of worship will no longer be forced into hiding; our communal affairs will then be deemed worthy of protection; the teaching and the teachers of our religion will be given generous encouragement, and progress within Israel will no longer meet with opposition. The day cannot be far off when we shall be given that which we are now still lacking, be it as payment of an ancient debt or as a gift of kindness, and Jew and non-Jew will joyously stretch forth their hands to one another saying, "Praise be to the Lord! The strain has been lifted, the discord has vanished, the heart is free. Come then, let us go forward, each in his own way, but all of us in the path of love and glorification of the name of the Lord; peace and happiness below; grace and blessings from above."

NS, I, PP. 372 FF.

ON THE OCCASION OF THE FIFTIETH ANNIVERSARY OF THE BATTLE
OF LEIPZIG[3]: DELIVERED IN FRANKFORT-ON-THE-MAIN

October 18, 1863

. . . Indeed, we recall the glorious victory that German strength and German courage won, and we recall the heroism which our fathers showed in that battle. And yet the message still resounds in our ear, *Not by might nor by power, but by My spirit, saith the Lord of Hosts.* . . . To be sure, the hour of victory was one of great exaltation and profound emotion in the hearts of those who waged the fight. But we, dear friends, are their grandchildren; can and should the same sentiments be stirring within our own souls today?

Our sages tell us that when the Egyptians drowned in the sea—those stubborn, arrogant Egyptians who had kept Israel in long-lasting bondage—the heavenly angels who served the Lord wanted to join in the hymn of victory that the Israelites were singing. But the Lord said to them: "And you too? How can that be? Should you really sing a hymn of praise while the work of My hands is drowning in the sea? That Israel, liberated, should burst into jubilation, is understandable; but as for you," said the Lord to His angels, "who look down from the open heavens, should you feel joy at the thought that men rage against men, that a people must fight to attain freedom? Should you, indeed, exult while corpses are piled high?" . . . The nobler spirit of mankind grieves at the sight of men and nations torn by strife and discord; it covers its head in sorrow at the sight of the maimed, of the tears of the families of the fallen, of destruction and of the smoldering habitations where peace and prosperity formerly dwelt. We shed a tear for those who gave their lives for the independence of the nation, and for the fathers and mothers who were robbed of many a precious hope. But at the same time we proclaim: Away with hatred and jealousy! Let us look with human compassion also upon the enemies who fought the battle in those days. Even they, against whom we had to draw the sword of battle, were human beings, imbued with what is noble and divine; let us then shed a tear even for the fallen foe.

Our memory, then, is not concerned with might or with power. But what about the results of our victory? . . . To be sure, the independence of the Fatherland was regained, and the German people whose name was to be expunged from the annals of world history has risen again. This is a great and uplifting thought. We may raise our heads once again in the full awareness of our strength. . . . And yet . . . it is indeed a resurrection that we celebrate today, the resurrection of the German people and Fatherland; but was this a restoration to a full measure of strength and vigor? Our sages of old in their clarity of perception say this of resurrection: "The dead who will someday rise again to renewed life will rise with those imperfections and infirmities with which they were afflicted during their lifetime; but then they will be healed forthwith." ... The German nation, too, has risen again, but its imperfections and infirmities have been resurrected also. And now, my dear friends, will it, too, be healed in the near future? Would you say that the hopes and expectations that were cherished then, half a century ago, have been fulfilled, that those justified aspirations have actually been realized? History answers this question for you, and I fear that only a few will be satisfied by its answer. . . . Has our Fatherland become united, great and powerful? Has freedom gained happy entry into all its provinces? Are all its people joined together in vigor of spirit, in a new spiritual life? . . . Often, alas, free and noble sentiments have been subjugated, and the noble-minded have had to wrestle with the basest of passions and the most selfish of motives, which all too often rise to power. In our recollections there is many a sorrowful memory. No, exaltation does not stem from the might we have gained. Let us shed tears for those men who went down to their graves with broken hearts because their noblest aspirations were scorned, their high-minded endeavors despised; tears for those noble men and youths whose inmost being was blighted because, in the face of the powers which then held sway, they dared write upon their banner the device of liberty for their great Fatherland. . . . No, my friends, our festive joy derives neither from might nor from power, but solely from the thought that, through the spirit of God, all things will lead to victory in the end. . . .

What was it that distinguished the man whose defeat we commemorate today, which had given him power over the nations? Was it the support of the seasoned veterans who followed him, their warriors' courage and the ceaseless striving after the glories of victory? Or was it all due to his mind, to his strategic genius, or to the unconquerable power of his will? Certainly, all these things had a part in it; but this was not all. He was the heir to great ideas derived from the Divine spirit that pervades mankind. It is true that these ideals were often abused, and, besides, he soon suppressed them altogether. Nevertheless these ideals of liberty, equality and fraternity exerted a liberating influence among men and introduced a new era in that country where, though often misused, they had first attained acceptance. It was with this spirit that he swept through the world; it was this spirit that opened for him the portals to both hearts and minds; and when the fortunes of war opened the cities for his conquering armies, it was actually these ideals that had won the victory . . .

But what was it, on the other hand, that so profoundly oppressed the German people? This was a people that had come of age long ago; it had already produced the most glorious creations, already awakened to a new and vigorous culture, and already shone forth among the nations in the full luster of its spirit. And yet the spirit of God did not rule in that people's midst; it had been suppressed by pettiness and trivialities. A caste system, setting people apart from one another; distrust and class prejudice; medieval oppression inhibiting freedom and independence—these were the forces that prevailed. The genuine spirit had to escape into spheres where no despot's decree could reach it. The spirit of the Divine was lacking in the people . . . hence the people had to go down. The teachers of old said that, if a people suffers defeat, its God, above all, is defeated; then its spirit is extinguished and all the good and noble things within it must be suppressed. This is how Germany fell despite its multitude of armies and its innate strength. And this, too, is how her mighty conqueror was vanquished in his turn. He fell because he mocked the spirit and reduced liberty to servitude; because he sought by tyranny to destroy the ways peculiar to each nation and to force everyone into the garment of silent servility. He fell because he suppressed the work of freedom, wanting only slaves and not free men around him. What was it then that raised the German people up once more? It was the fact that the spirit within it reawakened to a new and independent existence; it was a spirit of active noble-mindedness, of moral discipline and conscious forcefulness. When Deborah sang her song of victory . . . she enumerated all the tribes that had taken part in the struggle, and she gave special praise to the *men of Zebulon that handle the quill of the scribe*—a somewhat peculiar way in which to describe a valiant host of warriors. And then again she mentions Zebulon as *a people that jeoparded their lives unto the death*. Herein lay the consecrated nature of this struggle: men of intellect, of profound and peace-loving scholarship, were gripped along with the rest by zeal for the freedom of the Fatherland. They turned the war into a battle of the spirit. In like manner, a higher spirit had come also upon the entire German Fatherland: not only the professional soldiers, but all the noble youths and mature men went forth to free their precious Fatherland, to safeguard the great treasure and to preserve the genuine, living spirit . . .

Hear this today, O my people, and do not be faint-hearted, even though all your wishes have still not been fulfilled, though strife still prevails today and your just hopes still meet with opposition. . . . When, another fifty years hence, another generation is assembled here, may they mark this day as a celebration of brotherly conciliation, the brotherhood of all peoples, a celebration under this device: One God, accepted and humbly worshiped by all; one human race, united in love; one great and mighty German Fatherland! . . .

NS, I, PP. 399 FF.

EULOGY IN MEMORY OF THE LATE BARON JAMES DE ROTHSCHILD: DELIVERED AT THE GREAT SYNAGOGUE OF FRANKFORT-ON-THE-MAIN, ROTHSCHILD'S NATIVE CITY.

November 29, 1868

. . . They went forth, these brothers, sons of a worthy father, from a crowded, tiny home, from the gloomy alley whose ruins reflect shame upon us even today; they went forth from the confines of this Free City. Breaking through every barrier, they have become a power in the capitals of the world, a major power by virtue of the potent influence they have exerted by their participation in the affairs of the world.

With this man, the last of the Rothschild brothers has departed, and a new generation takes their place . . .

We do not bend the knee before wealth, nor do we grovel before earthly glory; but we revere the Divine power which has manifested itself so marvelously in the life of one man and of an entire family. It is not our doing that now, in the century following the life of Mendelssohn and his great and talented disciples, the Jew should still not be measured according to his talents and achievements, but weighed in terms of his treasures. . . . Since, however, both the high and mighty of the earth, and the history of the times, have chosen to apply this yardstick, we may well derive gratification from the fact that our own native city should have brought forth such a power, which has wrought fruitful changes and has wrested recognition from those who hold sway in proud palaces.

That princes in the sphere of the spirit and princes in the realm of commerce should have come forth from this small Free City is no mere accident. . . . Let us be gratefully aware of the fact that the eye of God's grace rests upon this city, from whose genuine civic virtue and glorious history the minds of men have gathered strength. It was here that a broader view of the world unfolded and sons matured who moved away from their native city when its horizons became too confining for them. Many are those who have had their roots here, and under whose shade the whole world has found fresh vigor, for they have put to use for the good of all mankind those talents and that inspiration which they received from the place of their birth . . .

It is our duty, dear congregants, to keep this memory alive. Even as it was once said of Joshua ben Hananiah: "Happy is she who gave him birth," so may we say today: "Happy art thou, O Frankfort, that the cradle of this family stood in thy crowded alleys; happy art thou, O congregation of Israel, in which this power grew; and happy art thou, O Israel, which implanted its spirit into this family!" For they have all remained faithful to the Covenant of Israel and have loyally adhered to it. Even as they paid due and proper honor to their natural parents until the very end and then cherished their memory in their hearts, so, too, they also dearly loved their venerable Father Jacob and never despised their old Mother, the Congregation of Israel. . . . They all reverently cherished their ancient faith which nurtured them and which remained alive within them at all times; he who has now departed was a shining example of this.

Thus they were living and accusing witnesses against all the intolerance which still was shown the sons of Israel's faith, against the base passions that sought to exalt themselves as religious truths, and against that medieval narrowness which sought to clothe itself in the rich drapery of the cloak of religion. While the Jews in general were still confined to certain streets in which they would be permitted to breathe, no districts were closed to this family. Every door, including the portals of the proudest of princely palaces, was opened wide for them. As princes of peace they were welcomed everywhere, even while their coreligionists were still viewed with contempt. They were exalted not only above their own race but above all other citizens. While Jews as such were denied all recognition and, indeed, it was made impossible for them to develop their nobler spiritual potential, these brothers were barons and as such considered the equals of the noblest families.

The southern sun casts its rays upon a delightful spot of ground [*Naples*], a veritable garden of God. Tyranny has not been able to destroy it, but it did dull the spirit of its people, so that until very recent times that bright sun could not shine upon the face of a Jew. Nevertheless, even in that place, there stood the cradle of a new branch of this family, and newborn sons of this house were admitted into the Covenant of the fathers. In the west [*in Spain*], in a country where the spiritual vigor of our ancestors had brought forth many a magnificent flowering, political and religious oppression had joined in an unholy alliance for the purpose of casting fetters for the mind. . . . To this was joined that religious hatred against the Jews which, centuries ago, had cast out the benefactors of the nation, the guardians of her spirit who had advanced her industries, and which since then has not suffered the foot of even one of our brethren to come to rest there. But the ambassadors and representatives of the House of Rothschild were not only tolerated in this land but actually honored along with the grandees of the nation.

. . . Yet, with all their power, they never grew arrogant. Even as Moses, who had been bred in the palace of Pharaoh, went out to his brethren and was moved by their misery, so they, too, never denied their close bond with all their brethren in Israel. Their hearts were quick to sense the sufferings of their fellow-Jews and, wherever possible, they sought to alleviate them. A bountiful outpouring of blessings flowed forth from their homes to quicken the meadows stricken with the drought of poverty; they built hospitals for the sick and clothed the naked, and he who has now departed gave generous support also to learning. . . . They did not descend to wallow in their wealth; they remained imbued by the Jewish spirit. They were humble before their God and paid grateful tribute to His bounty. Their homes were maintained in purity, and noble domestic virtues are the blessed heritage which unites all the members of this family in close harmony . . .

A breath of greater freedom animates our own day, and Israel, too, no longer gasps in such stifling confinement as doles out the breath of life in miserly measure. The rotted barriers have fallen, and in those places where they still manage to linger on they are so worn away that they will collapse at the first strong gust of wind. . . . The bodies are oppressed no more, and the minds have been freed. Recognition is now accorded also that son of our faith who knows how to make the rich natural potential of our race bear fruit. But as a result, our task has grown greater too. We must not merely enjoy what the course of time and progress has given us; instead, we must freely utilize, for the common good and for the spiritual edification of all, that treasure which we have borne with us throughout the millennia and which we have safeguarded throughout our sufferings. It is from us that the spiritual, religious fountain of living waters has gone forth. . . . It is now our task to maintain this wellspring in all its refreshing vigor.

. . . Shining before us from days of old is the radiance shed by the names of men who, braving death, offered their bodies as a guardian wall against the foe, of men who distributed all their worldly goods among the hungry in order to feed them. Yet it is said of only one of these that "Truly, the name of this man shall be remembered for good always." The name of that man was Joshua, the son of Gamla. Joshua happened to have been a high priest, but it is not by virtue of this exalted office that his name has been preserved for posterity. He acquired office through the great wealth of his wife, Martha, the daughter of Boethus of noble Jewish lineage. But it was not his wealth that gave permanence to his memory. He set himself a lasting monument at a time when education was threatened with utter neglect; he founded institutions of learning in which a religious spirit and noble learning were implanted in the young. At a time of savage warfare, the young generation was to learn not only how to wield weapons but also how to gain the upper hand in the struggles of the spirit. And, indeed, when the Jewish state was destroyed and countless citizens were dragged into captivity, Israel's spiritual vigor remained alive. It was this spirit that steeled their bodies to suffering, and preserved their purity, their cheerfulness and their moral serenity. Blessed indeed, be the memory of Joshua the son of Gamla!

. . . A short time ago we marked the 100th anniversary of

the birth of Israel Jakobsohn. His abundant wealth would not have given permanence to his name. He is remembered because he was a shield and protector of his brethren . . . Lavish in charity, he founded a school in which the new educational requirements of our time were linked with our traditional heritage for the education of the rising generation. He built houses of worship in which the faith of Israel was to shine forth in purified form and to be preached in messages of inspiration. Therefore his name will live forever.

Herein lies your challenge, O Israel of this present day, you wealthy ones in Israel who vainly seek to link your names with worldly goods, you noble men in our congregation so receptive to all that is good, and, above all, you of the new generation of the House of Rothschild. May you see to it that the ancient spirit remains alert in youthful vigor and that the wellspring which watered the millennia, and which must never dry up, shall be preserved. Here, at the cradle of your power, in our own native city or in its vicinity, at the seat of an institution of higher learning where all the rays of the spirit meet to form one mighty beacon, let there arise a school of higher studies for Israel's heritage of wisdom and learning. We do not wish to pick up crumbs from alien boards; it is our desire to offer our own rich contribution of intellectual nourishment, so that all the forces of the mind and spirit, whatever their viewpoint, giving and receiving in mutual interchange, may strengthen one another in noble rivalry! Let the name of him who has now departed be associated with a new institution of this type. And let this ancient verse come true in our own day: Great things hast thou wrought when thou still wert Jacob (James); now thou shalt continue in thy achievements as Israel, the fighter of God, for thou hast not only wrestled with men and been victorious, but hast also striven for the Divine and wrought Divine things in peaceful endeavor. This will be a new radiance to illumine the bright escutcheon of that house and to give an everlasting memorial to its name. . . .

NS, I, PP. 425 FF.

ON THE SPIRITUAL LIFE OF ISRAEL: DELIVERED AT THE NEW SYNAGOGUE OF WIESBADEN

August 24, 1869

Inasmuch as Israel is and should remain unique, it is a spiritual bond that unites Israel. It is a spiritual life all its own which embraces all its members, and which will remain unchanged even under the most diversified circumstances— through all the changes of rushing events which crowd one upon the other, in the most distant lands and in the midst of differing ideologies and varying convictions. But if you should ask me: "What is the content of this ideal that binds us together with so indissoluble a bond?" I will have to answer you that man has not been endowed with the ability to give an exhaustive portrayal of a spiritual life. . . . What is true of the knowledge of God applies here also. Who would presume to set forth what God is, to seek to confine His essence into one single exhaustive concept? All we can say is that He exists and that He is the original cause of all of life. He is the All-Wise One. But it is only the traces of His infinite wisdom that we behold in that masterpiece which is the world. He is the Almighty. His rule is evident everywhere. It is he Who maintains the Universe and provides it with power to continue growing and developing. Thus you may see God even if you are not capable of grasping His essence.

. . . Of Israel's spiritual life, too, we can only say that it exists and that it manifests itself as a basic force. . . . An emanation of the Divine spirit, Israel was imbued with a creative spirit all its own and has been so to this very day. The other religious creeds are its daughters . . . and the best that is in them they owe to the spirit and tradition of Israel. Israel worked as a basic force in history. Israel exists; at first it was a small family, then it grew into a tribe and thereafter it became a whole state. And when its spirit became separated from the political state, might one not have assumed that it would vanish and that its body would disintegrate into its original components? But this never came to pass. It was only then that Israel's soul truly blossomed forth and entered into all parts of the world; and now the strength of Israel has proved itself everywhere. Even as it did not cease to grow in days of oppression, so it will not disintegrate in freedom; it will not dissipate itself into atoms to join alien configurations. To the outside, of course, in civic affairs, it will join with other elements and merge into the national life that surrounds it; but it will always retain its own spirit: it will continue to exist.

Of course, Israel is not like a stone which endures through millennia, rigid and unchangeable, which then is smashed and broken apart when the elements sweep over it. . . . No, Israel is wise; its life is a life of knowledge. Its faith, likewise, is not fixed, bound or rigid—for that would not be wisdom and eternal spiritual life. No, Israel heeded the call: "*Know* the God of your fathers and serve Him." Listen and choose for yourself; test it and see for yourself. It was not the outward, rigid law that made Israel indestructible; it was the winged message of the prophets that rendered Judaism inviolable. The lightning flashes of the spirit did not emanate from Sinai only; they flared forth also from Israel's great men, the prophets. In a world of paganism and idol worship, their message became a life-giving spiritual sun.

In later times, too, Israel remained loyal to that spirit and to knowledge, never attempting to confine freedom. . . . To be sure, the sons of Israel were part of the times in which they lived and could not rise above the level of their contemporaries in knowledge and perception. . . . But even in the darkest days, there was an inner strife and stirring which preserved the real life of Israel in strength and vigor. . . . and was it not in the darkest ages that the brightest luminaries shone forth from Israel, of all peoples? That which a great medieval thinker plainly set forth was felt by all, even unawares: faith is not an empty phrase, a formula or an assertion which you must accept unquestioningly. . . . No, faith is an idea which, rooted deep within your heart, must constitute the foundations of your spiritual being, the flower of spiritual life, the noble fruit of genuine conviction. . . . Israel never gave recognition to any belief that would not be consistent with understanding; it never worshiped as a sacred mystery that which was in contradiction with what could be comprehended by human reason.

"Faith and Reason are two beacons," each shedding its own light, but both ultimately meeting and fusing into one bright beam. This is the doctrine of Israel; this is its wisdom and this is the guarantee for its continued survival. In our days, much that blossomed in times gone by has faded away, and minds frequently are divided. But do not despair, my friends, for Israel's spiritual life remains unified. Scholarship may move along the most divergent paths; trends may split up into a host of shadings and partisan factions; yet, do not lose courage; only *one* spirit is now and shall ever be within Israel . . . Spiritual life undergoes manifold changes in its outer manifestations, and the Divine spirit, too, reveals itself in many different forms. But it is precisely the varied nature of its manifestations that marks the existence of a genuine spiritual life in the midst of Israel.

Thirdly and lastly, my dear friends, Israel is "mighty." Israel is endowed with a vitality that ensures its survival. By this I do not mean the kind of might that relies on the strength of the arm. . . . Israel's vitality has always consisted in the endeavor to fight for that which is Divine. . . . It has given its all, and suffered without flinching or hesitation for its God and for its faith . . .

Israel's vitality is derived from its readiness to make sacrifices when it is called upon to defend all that is great and good. . . . A testimonial of this ready devotion is also this new House of God in all its splendor and magnificence; it is a testimonal of honor for Israel, a badge of honor for this congregation, and a memorial to the noble and cheerful spirit of those who gladly gave of their own possessions for its construction.

. . . Israel has always distinguished itself by its good deeds and will continue to do so in unflagging zeal. In this respect it always was one whole, one unit, and has remained so to this day. No call for help from afar is allowed to go unanswered. All hasten to stretch forth the hand of brotherhood; the warm heart does not grow cool along the way, nor does it ever cease to beat. We are one, and we belong together. The good Jewish heart is the bond that unites us. Many things may have departed from our midst; many an outward ritual, many an obsolete statute has vanished from the scene. But the fountainhead still remains in full vigor; the good heart is still beating and will not die. And as long as you, my people of Israel, can say of yourselves: *Even when I seem to be asleep my heart is still awake,* then you, too, will live and survive, inviolable, eternal. . . .

NS, I, PP. 436 FF.

lead articles

———————◆❦◆———————

FROM *WISSENSCHAFTLICHE ZEITSCHRIFT FUER JUEDISCHE THEOLOGIE* (6 VOLUMES, 1835-1847)

PRESENT-DAY JUDAISM AND ITS INTELLECTUAL TRENDS

Religious life, at a time when independence of thought has attained such dominating influence, must of necessity present some highly peculiar manifestations and forms. The struggle is being fought with all the weapons of well-armed warriors. On one side is the intellect, destroying and negating, the critical evaluation of the documents of history, and much theorizing; on the other side is the preserving and fortifying effect of reason, the deep yearning of the soul for the poetic transfiguration of religious form and legend, and deep-rooted prejudice. At first, a gulf is revealed that seems unbridgeable; the opponents refuse to recognize the legitimacy of each other's weapons; they deny the wounds they have inflicted and each claims that the other has violated the rules of combat. Gradually, however, there is a rapprochement between the opposing parties. The weaknesses which each has discovered in the other lead them for once to attempt to see things from the point of view of the other side . . . and then, almost despite themselves, it occurs to them that their original procedures may have been somewhat one-sided.

The result is the growth of a school of historical criticism which examines the forces of history from two different aspects. . . . For one thing, it shows us that the phases, ideas and phenomena of history did not spring all of a sudden from the brilliant fancy of some ingenious human mind, like Athena from the head of Zeus, but that all things stem from quiet origins and lie dormant until they are stirred up by the strong hand of a gifted man or by the shock of some mighty occurrence. . . . This way of looking at things teaches us, too, that salvation will be found, not in a violent and ruthless break with tradition, but in careful research into the deeper decisive factors in history. Whatever has been formed in the process of history we, who ourselves are organs of history, must continue to develop, inhibiting here, furthering there, moving along with the wheel of time at one point and seeking to accelerate its motion at another. Such is the conservative function of history.

Viewed from the other side, the historical method is primarily critical. Not everything that has been handed down to us from ages past stems from hoary antiquity or from the very beginning of time. Later periods have grafted many a twig onto the ancient trunk, and have added many a new link to the chain of tradition. Only a dull and simple mind can believe that things have always been as they are now. The fact is that not everything which we see before us as an apparently completed structure is a pure development of the religious idea. . . . Accidental causes, tragic or overwhelming contemporary events, misinterpretation or distortion often alter the true picture beyond recognition. The mind which lives only in the present sees the structure only as it is now, apparently complete and grown together into a homogenous whole, and views it as composed entirely of essentials, so that anyone who would dare touch the sanctuary thereby violates it. But truth upholds its rights and gradually all intelligent and sensible people must gather beneath the banner of historical criticism. . .

Within Judaism, we are still for the most part engaged in the first phase of the campaign of historical criticism. Many are still in the grip of a destructive sham enlightenment. A select few allow themselves to be guided by a penetrating and illuminating criticism. But seeking as they do to combine this method with the requirements of deep reflection, they are often led to a point where everything dissolves as in a haze. Their religious concepts are tied to forms and views which, in commendable reverence, they regard as sacred relics of their youth and would not like to see disturbed. Elsewhere in our ranks there still exists a rigid bias which effectively closes the door to all thought and to independent inquiry. Nevertheless it cannot be denied that, for the past fifteen years, men like Bernays, Zunz, Jost and Rapoport have been hailed jubilantly by the disciples of scholarly research. . . .

It is the wish of this journal, too, to dedicate itself with full devotion to the cause of endeavors such as this.

. . . Judaism in its traditional form presents a difficult challenge to an organic union with the demands of our times. Christianity, since it has been the religion of entire peoples and nations, has been of necessity subject at all times to the influences of forces from without. . . . True, it has not itself created religious art, but the genius that inevitably stirs within the human breast has given of its own creations to [Christianity]. . . . It is true, too, that science has slightly wrought changes in Christian beliefs even if, at the same time, it sought to corroborate many a doctrine of religion with all the weapons of the intellect. . . . But the fact is that the scientific attitude acquired its real power not in the Catholic South but in the Protestant North. Thus in the end it called for a complete reform in all of religious life, such as became evident in Protestantism. . . .

Judaism has lived its sad life under circumstances that were highly inauspicious, not only for its followers, but also for the survival of its idea. A tiny band in the midst of a mass of believers in other faiths, oppressed by them on account of their religion, the Jews have always had to rely on that religion. Among the Jews the spirit freely developed, not independently of religion, but in close contact with it. In Judaism art could not take wing and allow the faith to benefit from its vigor. . . . The spirit, oppressed, could not rise to happier heights. . . . Thus form itself lost beauty and dignity. For this is precisely the strength of any positive religion—that the concepts that lie submerged in it are brought to life through its outer forms, and that the forms as such serve, by the power inherent in them, to exalt the spirit and to consecrate it. But where cries of fear resound round about us, where anxiety fills the spirit, where the dimmed eye no longer perceives beauty, where the ear has grown deaf to harmony, where men desire only to sigh and to beat their breasts so that the God of mercy may withhold His chastising hand . . . it cannot be expected that, even in more tranquil times, the ritual forms should be able to retain their ancient beauty and reverence through dignity, solemnity and edifying strength. It is for this reason that we have so many customs in Jewish life which, though in themselves meaningful and dignified, present an outer aspect that frequently makes them the butt of scorn and ridicule. Thus the shame of former days, which has not yet been overcome even to this day, has cast a gloom also over our own faith by blighting its spirit and distorting its form. This, then, is the battle which must be waged all the more fiercely in Judaism since, in Judaism, the gulf between things as they are and things as they should be is greater than anywhere else.

Nor is this all that is involved. Wherever tradition is so far removed from contemporary views, there must be, of necessity, two opposing parties, strictly separated from one another. One group would like to leave everything as it is, because they deem it all to be sacred. No one would seek to rob them of this belief. However, they defy history and all progress as absurdities. But more than that, they also defy the true spirit which gives life to Judaism; they do so without knowing or realizing it, for proofs to this end fail to convince them. The party at the other extreme declares that, since Judaism as it exists today is afflicted with shortcomings, there should be no Judaism at all. According to this point of view, everything must be cut down to the roots save for one puny sprig that hardly bears more than a few meager leaves, to say nothing of fruit. Is this one tottering reed to be a substitute for the tree, so firmly rooted, which spread cooling shade for so long and bore refreshing fruit, a tree which grew luxuriantly even though it might have been just a little bent? ... There is still another factor which the present has added to the balance of the rash advocates of destruction, namely, the striving after civic equality. Civic equality should and must be won, but not at the price of religious independence. If you are willing to pay that price, that would be the easiest means for attaining what we seek. Thus there are those who are afraid to utter even one word that might displease some Christian, and who abandon any custom that seem to them to jeopardize their chance for reaching this goal. In a zealous effort to create an enlightened impression, certain circles are seeking to ape Christianity in a way of which we do not know whether it is more ridiculous than sad or more sad than ridiculous.

... This state of affairs weighs most heavily on the theologian who within his own heart must fight out to a successful conclusion the struggle to reconcile the past with the present. The one party exhorts him not to give even one inch of ground. The other party admonishes him to press forward with giant steps lest he be labeled a Jesuit, a hypocrite, an obscurantist, an Orthodox, and so forth. The layman offers well-meant advice, but he does not know this terrain—and, anyway, fault-finding is such a pleasant pastime.

And what of the theologians? If they were thoroughly familiar with the entire marvelous, well-built structure of our religion and, at the same time, had acquired a maximum of modern education, then they alone, through scholarly and practical work, would be able to advance the welfare of Israel. But they have failed to do so for the past fifty years. They have either nervously held back and withdrawn, or else yielded leadership to men who were far away from religion and indulged in the shallow prattle of sham enlightenment. . . . But God grant . . . that men may now come forth who have the spirit needed for leadership, who know the age in which they assume that leadership, and who clearly see the goal toward which they are to lead. God grant that it may not come to pass that, as Maimonides complained long ago, the rabbis, in their anxiety to find a position, force themselves to remain silent and by their air of ambiguity make their every act and their every utterance seem vacillating and vague. We are in need now of men who will show how Judaism gradually came to be what it is today, men who will not shrink from the realization that many things in Judaism owe their existence neither to tradition nor to rational interpretation, and that, even as it was time that has given rise to custom, so time can also abolish it. We are in need of men who will know how to refute both the arrogance of ignorant reformers and the malicious mockery of those holding different beliefs.

NS, I, PP. 445 FF.; CF. VOL. I, PP. 1-12.

ON THE LACK OF RELIGIOUS FERVOR IN PRESENT-DAY JEWRY
(REFLECTIONS OF A LAYMAN)

It is not merely the divergence in religious views that has brought about the wide gulf which separates Jews from one another. . . . It is quite posible to differ on the question of whether certain religious statutes or rituals are absolutely essential for salvation or not, without necessarily compelling those who so differ to go separate ways in their entire religious attitude. That which seems essential to one may be deemed beneficial or helpful by another who may be edified by observing that particular ritual without, however, feeling that he would be jeopardizing his salvation were he to neglect that observance. But such mutual understanding ... is possible only if the practice of religion as such fills the heart, if the outer forms affect the soul and have an ennobling and heartwarming influence, regardless of whether they are viewed as indispensable or merely optional. It is certainly not a commandment of the Jewish faith to listen to a sermon; nevertheless the sermon has brought many to the house of God, not because they thus fulfill an obligation toward God, but because they seek stimulation and edification. Many people find that it is not the ritual of the Day of Atonement that inspires them; they crowd into the synagogue because the thought behind this day, on which man recalls his sins, fills them with a certain inner wistfulness and healthy self-abasement.

Religion is closely interwoven with the inmost life of the soul. ... The inaccessible Power on High that rules over us, the realization of our own minuteness, the benevolent guidance that comes forth to us wherever we go, the yearning of our heart, the calm and pensive longing of our soul for the unfathomable—all these motivate the religious stirrings of the heart. But the more deeply this emotion is rooted in our being, the more must religious practice be attuned not to weighing down this delicate fabric but to stimulating its growth. ... The more closely religion is related to the poetic feeling, the more must its outer form bear the impress of all that is beautiful, uplifting and appropriate to the emotions of the soul ...

It is not sufficient to cultivate an attachment to tradition by a welter of customs and ceremonies, if all this ritual is not touched by the refreshing breath of spiritual and emotional impulse. ... Only true religious fervor can break the fetters of doctrinaire rigidity, and it is the fire of ardent emotion that will melt the crust of ice with which a petrified past has surrounded the heart. In such a felicitously educated heart, prevailing custom will merge with symbolic significance without any initiative on the part of critical reason; on the other hand, such practices which lack all ideology will recede into the background and eventually disappear altogether. For customs that serve to illustrate religious concepts are subject to change. Frequently such customs are bound not only to yield to the advances in enlightenment and civilization but also to lose their original charm and edifying character.

Now if the synagogue were to possess such religious fervor, . . . all its religious expression would have an uplifting effect on the spirit. . . . This is indeed the aim toward which many leaders in Jewry are striving, the goal that many who are guided by their inmost feelings would like to see attained. But within the two groups, into which present-day Jewry has been sundered, such views have not as yet acquired sufficient force. Both of them seem more eager to accommodate reason than to give due consideration to the demands of the believing heart.

The believers in form, who adhere strictly to tradition, do not possess the warm faith of the heart. For how else could one explain the fact that they oppose every reform that has as its purpose to exalt and edify? How else should one explain the fact that they oppose the sermon, congregational singing, musical accompaniment in the services, and prayers in the vernacular . . . and that they are repelled by dignity and order, the basic conditions for spiritual concentration both during the synagogue service and on other religious occasions such as weddings and funerals? Why else should it be that the planting of flowers on cemeteries, and other graceful innovations designed to inspire the heart with solemn reverence, prompt hateful petty fights? Almost all of these things do not even appear to be in conflict with tradition to one who lives in the present day. But even if there should be some inconsistency, should we not be mindful of the splendid maxim that "It is a time to work for the Lord; this is why thy Law is made void. . . ."[1] But, of course, such considerations have no weight where only lip service is being given to God, while the heart remains far removed from Him and the deference paid Him is merely human law, carried out by rote.

. . . Thus, that which formerly was the vigorous product of religious awareness has turned into a rigid mummy—Egyptian, but not Israelite. . . . The inner religious life of these believers reveals, not joy in the fulfilment of the commandments, but only fear of giving them up—all of which, however, does not silence grumbling and scoffing at the religious practices. There is no sentiment of holiness here. . . . In home life. . . . where even every familiar, day-to-day activity should be given an aura of higher consecration, where every piece of bread that is broken, every joy of which we partake and every sorrow that befalls us should be uplifted and ennobled by the awareness of the higher destiny of man and of his relationship with our Father in Heaven, there is truly no trace of a temple of God. Do we have any right to deplore the indifference that prevails in our day and the sad fact that our children have succumbed to an alien spirit, when we ourselves are filled with the same indifference? . . . Indeed, the mouth will murmur in dumb resignation, "Well, God will make things turn out right." But the fact is that everyone knows for certain that things will not get better, and we adopt for ourselves the heartless, selfish motto, "Just let there be peace in my own lifetime." However, where there is no faith there can also be no spirit; only desperate hopelessness still struggles on, attempting to stave off utter ruin, at least for the time being, and not strong enough to raise itself to the true and living spirit . . .

But even in those who fight against such rigidity we do not always find that strong *religious* interest which feels repelled by the synagogue simply because it does not find enough life there. . . . They do not search for inner life and outer stimulus; their delight is only in deadening doubt. It is not the warmth and the sacred ardor that they miss in the synagogue, for they have no desire for such things. It is not that the bond with the Higher, Invisible Power seems to them to be too loose in the present atmosphere of routine and tepid indifference; quite on the contrary, they are fighting solely against the fetters. Thus they have no definite goal; they seek only to destroy but not to build. They do not demand institutions that wil lsatisfy religious sentiments without doing violence to the aesthetic sense and flying in the face of reason. Nor are they seeking to purge the entire religious system; they are bent solely upon eliminating anything that might disturb or interfere with their personal convenience and complacency. For how else could one explain that those who are not wanting in means, authority and intelligence should be willing to put up with a type of synagogue life that is in utter contradiction with their views? . . . If they truly realize that religion as it is at present is inadequate for both their own needs and the future welfare of their children, should they not press for far more extensive reforms? Should they not zealously see to it that only those men should be leaders and teachers of religion in Israel whose views will not serve to banish all genuine inspiration from our houses of worship?

But we see no evidence of any such endeavor; at best, there is patchwork, just to maintain outer appearances. Often, indeed, attempts at improvement are scorned. The best they seem to be able to do is break with the faith altogether; this is negative action, deriving, not from love for true religion, but from hatred for the spurious belief that exists by its side. . . . It almost seems as if our time were too weak to put up a fight. . . . Wit and derision, the weapons now in use, are poisoned arrows which drain off healthy vigor with the sore' spots they inflict. Indifference is hailed as a cure for superstition; but what indifference actually does destroy is true faith, while the latter's dregs of fear and superstition continue to spread . . .

NS, I, PP. 456 FF.; CF. VOL. I, PP. 141 FF.

POETRY, FROSE, AND PERPLEXITY

There is no doubt that among the most beneficial religious institutions are those customs that are direct outgrowths of the poetry of folkways, when the soul itself clings to the religious institution and adorns it with graceful offerings. Who would wish to deny that such beauty, in which joy and intimate communion with God vie with one another, is inherent in our festivals? Neither the public celebration in the synagogue service nor the explicit religious statute affect the spirit so strongly as the poetry of the home observance in the intimate circle of the family . . .

It is essential here, however, that this emotional expression does not lose its free form; much rather, it must be permitted constantly to gain new inspiration and rejuvenation. Thus, for example, the concept of liberation is given felicitous expression on the evening of the Passover festival. . . . The head of the family, with the patriarchal dignity of the free householder, recalls the fatherly love of God which has stood at the side of our ancestors and the present generation. Seated at the Seder table adorned with imaginative symbols, the family partakes of wine that cheers, and joins in happy song that expresses both reverence for God and the true joy of living. Cheerful banter with the children serves only to heighten the enjoyment and pleasure of the holiday. Then there is the festival of Sukkot, when booths are decked out in rustic beauty with the best that field and larder can offer, the abundance of lights on the days of Hanukkah, and the exchange of the gifts on Purim. All these should serve to generate a spontaneous gay and festive mood which springs from unfettered devotion.

Unfortunately, this free outpouring of emotion has been turned into rigid statute. It is painful to have to find fault with that which is most beautiful in religious life. But perhaps it is only by this procedure that whatever is truly inspiring can be brought to the fore once again. Of course, it may be that the Seder with its pillows for reclining, the narration of the plagues of the Egyptians, be it two hundred or two hundred and fifty, the drinking of the four cups of wine, and the strange songs chanted in an alien tongue which are even more repellent when badly translated, still gives joy to some. But in those circles where direct immediacy and devout acceptance are no longer present, the whole ceremony will in all likelihood give rise to boredom rather than to joyous conviviality. For that which is now missing is the very element that renders such customs truly effective; we no longer have free and unfettered expression, since the customs have become commandments. Had it not been laid down in precept just how one must sit, what one must recite, when one should drink and what must be chanted; had precept not set down in detail for every Israelite that he *must* rejoice in just this manner and in this manner only, the healthy poetic intuition of the people would have always found meaningful and appropriate ways for the celebration of such days of release. We do not intend to place the blame for this on anyone in particular, but the fact remains that it was an error on the part of the past to deprive us of the poetic value of our festivals.

The same is true of the festival of Sukkot. This holiday is being celebrated in a way that gives no consideration to family life which alone could lend it a more profound significance. It is nothing but the barest fulfilment of commanded ritual if one removes a portion of the ceiling from some room of the home, and indulges in self-deception with a few leaves and the wind that blows through them. But here too, the outer, formal precept is strictly observed. Close attention is paid to the shade cast by the booth, to the construction of the walls and the roof, and to the material that must be used. In this manner all the charm of the observance is eliminated . . .

We could go on and on with other such laments. But I think we have proven our point; namely, that the fragrance, bloom and color have vanished from where poetry should reign supreme; all that has remained in their stead is an artificial flower, crushed and soiled. Thus the delicate plant of poetry which is in need of tender care within religious family life has been crushed. The prose of statute has laid rude hands upon it. As a result it reluctantly withdrew its petals and we are left in a state of perplexity. Who will reawaken the blossom from its slumber?

NS, I, PP. 488 FF.; CF. VOL. IV, PP. 161 FF.

THE WRITER AND THE RABBI: TWO DIFFERENT APPROACHES

From among the many different approaches to the study of present-day Judaism, this journal has chosen that of historical evaluation. This, in turn, involves two main aspects. On the one hand, that which now exists must be viewed as something which came to be through a gradual process and which, based on an eternal foundation, has undergone manifold changes in the course of time. It must be remembered, too, that Judaism in particular has often been hindered in its free development because of the unfortunate position in which its adherents found themselves. On the other hand, every element that is added in the course of history is entitled to *relative* recognition. For regardless of greater or lesser age, every such element deserves recognition as a revelation of the religious consciousness of the religious community.

Which of the two above aspects of this approach will be given greater emphasis varies with the attitude of the scholar who makes the study. The calmly assaying historian who is far removed from contemporary issues will attempt to trace the development of ideas, forms and statutes by delving deeply into each era. By attempting to determine the relation between the parts and the whole of history, he seeks to explain the gradual process of transformation in terms of its causes. There is another type of historian who does not forget the present in his concern with the past, who does not overlook the developments of the future in his concern with what has already come to be, and who asks how much of the present has actually become an intimate part of the present and not just something that has been handed down superficially from the past. A historian of this type will not be content merely to understand the past and the present. Instead, he will look into the future, yearning to make smoother the road that leads to it. . . . For, after all, the historian, too, is a product of his time. With all his dispassionate detachment, with all his clear understanding of the conditions of the past and respect for the products peculiar to an era long since gone, he will not be able to suppress his desire actively to champion the interests of the present day and zealously to advance their goals . . .

This is the point in Judaism where the writer and the rabbi come to a parting of the ways with regard to the methods by which they fulfill their tasks. It seems to me that the writer functions here as the priest of *true* science who reveals the mysteries of the total interrelationships of the ideas of his time. . . . The writer in the field of Jewish theology is now faced with an arduous task which is frequently painful to him personally and is often misunderstood by others, namely, to comprehend the present and its ideas in their total unity and to examine the attitude of Judaism to the present time. He must openly admit and clearly show that Judaism was molded from an eternal and solid core under the most unfavorable circumstances. He must demonstrate that the predominance of outer religious practice and the repression of other spiritual potentials have had an injurious effect upon religion itself, that is, upon the free absorption by the individual of the higher ideals of Judaism. He must point out, too, that the ideas of a better-rounded education now prevailing will have a beneficial effect on the original religious idea of Judaism and guide it to a point of genuine purity. He must candidly confess that, with the inner life which it has taken on in its isolation, Judaism cannot achieve full harmony with the world outside, and that, therefore, Judaism must give up its one-sided features without forgoing its unique character, in order to become a peaceful member in the organism of humanity. It is not enough that the writer should merely avow this conviction; . . . he must also seek to spread it in vivid and effective language if he is to live up to his traditional calling. For therein lies the infinite strength of the spirit, the ever-repeated rejuvenation of mankind, that any overt inconsistency will destroy itself and that, once it is realized that what exists has become obsolete, new creations will come forth, strong and vigorous, and remove the old. Of course, these new creations will come to life only after inner conflict, and the malaise of inconsistency will make itself unpleasantly felt. There will be many who will fight him for a long time; . . . others will simply dismiss him, so that it may well be doubted if the writer has indeed achieved success in his own time. But it is for the very reason that he can achieve his goal only when his conviction has become commonly accepted and deeply felt, that it is impossible to tell immediately whether or not he has succeeded. It may well be that, weary of the struggle, he may close his eyes long before his efforts bear fruit. The fact that, most of the time, he contents himself with pointing out that basic changes are necessary, without, at the same time, suggesting ways and means for achieving innovations and describing the new picture in detail, may be explained by his faith in the collective energy of his public and by his justifiable distrust of his own insight. The community as such is never entirely negative. It creates and establishes from within itself and casts off whatever is no longer of use. . . . The writer may indeed create the impression that he knows nothing except how to find fault and takes pleasure only in destruction. . . . The fact, however, is that he is simply fulfilling his very essential task. From him emanates a reconciling force which stands high above all manner of discord; he sends forth faith in the Divine spirit within and beyond mankind. . . . It is only natural that the impetuous admonisher should be deemed a nuisance.

Must I forever be stirred by doubt when I could very well live in peace and harmony with myself? . . . Must I be constantly reminded of the universal context, of the dominant place of ideas and of the needs of the time, when I would much rather confine my horizon to my own home? . . . I am not conceited enough to believe that I am that ideal writer . . . but I live with the firm conviction that a complete cure of the ills of present-day Judaism can come about only through a fearless exposure of everything that does not befit it and through a clear demonstration of our distorted position.

I am, however, far indeed from failing to appreciate the somewhat more safe and peaceful approach which must be adopted by the rabbi. The writer sees Jewry as a whole, in terms of the differences among its separate segments and their relation to the present as such. The rabbi, on the other hand, has his sights set on his own more immediate sphere of activities, namely, his congregation, its level of education and its social relationships. In this limited sphere discords frequently vanish, either because certain outside influences have not yet forcefully asserted themselves and troubled its pristine innocence, or because many innovations have already taken root so firmly that there is no longer any need for struggle . . .

Furthermore, however strange their outward appearance may be, all religious institutions stem from a solid core. For the rabbi it must always be this core that counts; and if this core manifests itself in a certain form, then that form must be of significance for him, since it constitutes the link with the concept contained therein. He might prefer some sensible reforms, but he makes use of what is already in existence. He knows, too, that some outer support is necessary, that it is easier to abolish a sacred institution than to create one . . . and hence he will always want to preserve the existing institution, giving it the most salutary interpretation possible.

His relationship to his own small sphere of activity is a purely personal one. The writer broadcasts his views outward, into the world at large, so that they may make their own way and exert a lasting influence even through the very resistance which they encounter. Who the writer is or the extent to which he may be trusted is no one's concern; the cause he champions must speak for itself. He will not worry about losing the confidence or the good will of those to whom he addresses himself. He relies on the merit of his cause; and in the struggle which they wage against him, his opponents gradually achieve clarity without even being aware of it themselves. After a fair and honest battle, the opposing sides actually find themselves closer to one another than they could have thought possible. The writer's cause has not suffered from this inimical encounter. His own person remains unaffected, for what he preaches is not his own ego, but solely objective truth.

The rabbi's situation is altogether different. Within his immediate circle, his personality and his views form one single and cohesive unit, and his influence is based primarily on the confidence which both his person and his views inspire. His message must gain effectiveness because it comes from him. Nor does he stand in the large arena where the opposing parties gather to watch their leaders fight the battle. He dwells together with a small group, whose forces he must keep united if good intentions are to become reality. He does not deal with outstanding personalities, but with simple people who, of course, are propelled by the tendencies of the time in which they live, without having control of these matters. He must be careful in dealing with them; he must not confuse them. He is a loyal steward who understands that he cannot remedy every defect he finds. He must allow his actions to be guided by circumstances. He may make an effort to provide bases for certain improvements and to effect certain reforms, but he will defer further action until circumstances change, or else he will leave such steps to his successor in office. . . . As a man of peace he must either seek to avoid conflict altogether, or at least to prevent it from becoming too violent. He has so many beautiful, peaceful and impressive functions to perform, he may be active in so many good causes that have nothing to do with partisan issues, that he must not cut himself off from such opportunities to be a force for the good.

Generally speaking, the difference between these two approaches may be defined as follows: The Jewish writer, bearing in mind the idea with all its consequences, the totality of circumstances with their inevitable results, and the total Jewish community, calls for the dominance of the purely Jewish concepts in their harmony with the concepts of science. He demands that these concepts should rule every expression and ramification of life. He demands, too, that the practical institutions should reflect these concepts in all their clarity, and that no impure admixtures should give religious life the wrong direction and thereby make it impossible for the ideal to penetrate.

The rabbi, in his smaller sphere, uses as a point of departure whatever is at hand, seeking to purify it as much as possible. He stresses the worthwhile aspects of the existing circumstances and makes every effort to develop them to best advantage.

Therefore, although these two, the writer and the rabbi, proceed from two different points of departure, they must have one and the same goal. The former fights what already exists, while the latter makes use of it for good purpose. Yet both of them seek to establish the supremacy of the ideal of Judaism and hence work hand in hand.

It goes without saying, of course, that the position of the practicing rabbi is a most difficult one. If he is convinced that many of the existing institutions are not beneficial, he will find it difficult to preserve them, and, in fact, there are some things which cannot possibly be seen in a favorable light. If, for this reason, he should feel compelled to make changes in such instances, he will have to reckon with opposition from many of the members of his congregation, often in matters that would seem petty. On the other hand, he will see many in his congregation who would be alienated entirely from religious life if he were to seek to lead them back to institutions that date from ancient days. He would have to be blind not to take such people into account. He cannot close his eyes to the obstacles which many rites and customs present to social and professional life and thus also to humane and genuinely religious views, and it is his duty to remove such obstacles. There is no doubt that there is real greatness in self-restraint, in the inhibition of those forces and energies which forever threaten to burst forth from their confinement within the enclosure of petty circumstances, and it is our duty to place the supremacy of such an attitude above our most cherished spiritual longings. It does not take too much greatness to be willing to forgo pleasures and to live in penury. But to pursue one's own ideal boldly, and by continuous efforts to secure a small place for it, and to renounce the rewarding hope of recognition in wider circles of posterity in order to strive with greater certainty in a much narrower sphere takes a good deal of greatness. Indeed, it takes relatively little courage even to pry oneself loose from familiar circumstances and finally to give up temporal prosperity and even life itself for the sake of one's convictions. But to hold back these convictions, without denying them, out of good will and the desire to benefit one's brethren by proceeding slowly and prudently, requires much more fortitude. It requires much more courage to jeopardize one's own inner peace the better to assure the progress of one's fellow men and smilingly to allow constant pinpricks from without to wound one's own deepest emotions and aspirations throughout a lifetime. Ah, this ideal with its pain of blissful transfiguration, how I worship it!

The present-day rabbi, however, can no longer afford to indulge in this ideal. For we have come to a point where this is no longer an ideal. Only in times of utter innocence and naive adherence to tradition with all its advantages and shortcomings may the individual with a keener awareness and higher will-power silence his own bold hopes and, in quiet solitude, turn his exalted view to the future. He may then mingle with those others who do not suspect that there is a stronger spirit hidden beneath that humble frame. We today, however, live in an era of movement and change. Every conceivable subject has come up for re-evaluation. Hence, for the practical man, there is now only the way of moderation, of conciliation and prudent reform. Who would presume to prescribe for him a course of action in the chaotic conditions of the present-day, in view of the conflicting demands of the situation and of the people themselves? A man is fortunate indeed if he is able to retain a clear concept of his position, if he does not allow himself to be led astray in either direction, if he does not turn entirely dishonest, if he does not entirely fail to appreciate the potential inherent even in the prevailing circumstances, if he does not lose sight of his goal and does not lose his firm grounding.

Thus each of these two professions has its own great task, each with its own joys and sorrows. . . . And what of him who, with youthful exuberance, is bold enough to seek to combine the two in his own person! He who, as a writer, takes on the task of fighting the battle against what is cherished, who must first destroy before he can rebuild; and who, at the same time, as a rabbi, must grieve at seeing the goal that dominated his inmost being, the fulfilment of his most cherished wishes, recede into the far distance, and who feels himself to be in a state of inner conflict resulting from inconsistencies in his work and conduct. He should at least not be disdained. He should be credited with being fully aware of the difference between the two approaches, but also with being certain that the two cannot be kept entirely apart in our day and age . . .

To this day, I myself have tried to hold them together without confusing them, and have hoped that each would benefit the other. To this very day I believe that the union I have tried to bring about is not an unnatural one, and I confidently await that sole righteous sentence which the Lord of Truth will pronounce upon me. It is to Him that my life and my work will always be consecrated.

NS, I, PP. 492 FF.; CF. VOL. IV, PP. 321 FF.

on renouncing judaism

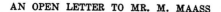

AN OPEN LETTER TO MR. M. MAASS

Breslau, 1858

The "discovery" of my correspondence[1] has prompted you to publish two discourses on the subject of renouncing Judaism. The matter is much too important to be dismissed with the few words that I have said about it. On the contrary, it calls for further elaboration, not only within the community of scholars, but also before the forum of the educated public. . . . I agree with the general trend of your reflections; if the results at which I arrive differ from the conclusions to which you have your hypothetical friends S. and B. come, the decision, in the final analysis, must rest with that segment of the public which is competent to pass judgment . . .

Let us examine the victorious weapons of your friend B. "To renounce ceremonial law," says Mr. B., "would mean, not only to cease to view the talmudic precepts as binding, but also to throw over all the biblical ceremonial and ritual laws—not merely those that have already become obsolete in the course of history, but also the entire code of dietary laws, festival observance, and so forth. Can anyone who subscribes to such wholesale renunciation of Jewish Law still claim to be a Jew?"

"What, after all," he concludes, "will be left of Judaism once ceremonial law is discarded? At best, a *negative* peculiarity consisting in the fact that Judaism does *not* possess the Christian doctrine of the Trinity and other dogmas. But if that were the case, then Judaism would be in accord with the deism of an era that is already closed, which has long since been abandoned because of its abstraction; and all that would be left the modern Jew would be, at most, the sad distinction of being what is known as a *Voltairien arrière.*"[2]

Generally speaking, B. is of the opinion that the laws must

be accepted as infallible and unalterable, for otherwise the whole position held by Judaism would be invalid. No reasons must be sought for this, for "as long as Judaism has been in existence, no justification of the religious duties in themselves, namely, before the judgment seat of reason, has ever been called for . . ."

As for myself, I am speaking here in the name of present-day Judaism as manifested, at least in Germany, in the sum total of its trends and tendencies in both life and scholarship. . . . In that present-day Judaism this is the truth that obtains: The old and modern Orthodox alike, and the Conservatives, too, must join with the adherents of historical progress in admitting that many things in the ceremonial law which appear meaningless nowadays and which even they consider trivial would have been obstinately defended a hundred years ago, and that many things in scholarship and communal life are not immune to doubt but are either deemed openly controversial or considered moot questions to be decided by the future. These are facts which no one who does not purposely close his eyes to them can deny. My own scholarly concepts of Judaism and those of likeminded thinkers are of no concern to us here. I have no desire to make converts. . . . All I seek to do is to show Judaism in its true nature to those who may be on the verge of leaving it because they feel that Judaism as it is at present cannot satisfy them. I want to do this without elaborate scientific proof, but only insofar as religious issues are close to cultivated minds and must be brought even closer to them.

I did not content myself with adducing this argument from our own present day. I wanted, from the very beginning, to deprive those who showed an inclination to desert Judaism of the excuse . . . that Judaism at the present time has strayed away from the basic teaching to which it had actually clung throughout its history. . . . For this reason I noted that "even at the time when the bulk of ceremonial law was held in far higher esteem and was deemed far more binding [*than it is now*], the sages of old nevertheless declared that he was a Jew in the true sense of the word who would merely reject idol worship and would not associate any other power with the One and Only God." . . . Contrary to the assumption of your Mr. B., this thought was not set forth as a refutation of Christianity in order to define the genuine core of Judaism. It may be found in the Babylonian Gemara in which allusions and references to Christianity are extremely rare and insignificant, and where polemics and emphases of differences are not to be found at all. Our sages found it unusual that Mordecai, the cousin of Queen Esther, should be called a Jew or a Judean, for that designation would indicate that he had sprung from the tribe of Judah, although it had been explicitly stated elsewhere that he was a Benjaminite. To answer this question they advance the explanation that anyone who rejects idol worship is called a Jew, and that Hananiah, Mishael and Azariah were called Jews for the same reason. Thus they set forth this verse as a general explanation of the word "Jew" as used in the Bible, with neither a desire to offend others nor with any allusion to Christianity intended. It is in such remarks, made without any ulterior intention, that the most profound secret of Judaism in the days of old is revealed.

I could have cited a good many other striking passages from the writings of our sages in answer to those who feel that, since they no longer consider themselves bound by ceremonial law, they are, in fact, no longer Jews and therefore think that they are justified in leaving the Jewish fold, or even consider it obligatory to do so. . . . One passage, for example, which recurs in several places, implies that in the far-off future for which we all yearn biblical law will no longer have validity. Elsewhere we are told that the Hebrew term *hazir* for "swine" is derived from the Hebrew *hazar* meaning "to return," implying that, at some future date, the swine, now forbidden, will "return" or revert to the status of a "permissible" animal. Of course, I know full well that these sayings . . . refer not to the present but only to the longed-for messianic era. I know, too, that this era, in which God will reign supreme, is not yet upon us. . . . I am also advised by Mr. B. that "racial differences" are still quite powerful factors in this world, so that the promises of universal brotherhood on earth have not yet been fulfilled. . . . Just the same, these passages do express the concept [*of our sages*]of the messianic era, the ideal for which they all longed; in the days of the Messiah, it was felt, the spiritual life of Judaism would be realized in the fullness of its purity and would rise to universally binding supremacy, and this ideal is not the stern rule of ceremonial law but, on the contrary, its complete commutation. Thus the spirit of Judaism victorious is quite a different one; it is the pure faith in God.

Still, much as these and similar statements truly reveal the deeper convictions of Judaism at all times, I will be . . . glad to agree with Mr. B. that [*as he puts it*], "the sages of old merely sought to define of what the genuine core of Judaism is composed, but they certainly never meant to say that the protective shell of ceremonial law is superfluous and might be stripped with impunity from the fruit still hanging from its tree." But what else does this mean but that the actual core of Judaism is indeed the pure faith in God and that whoever firmly cleaves to this basic core is a Jew, after all, that such a person is fully a part of the position held by present-day Judaism as well as Judaism throughout the ages, and that he therefore has no cause to claim that he has outgrown it? And if only he will once again hold fast to this core with joy, if he will nurture and cherish it, then the trunk, the branches, the leafy dome and the fruit—the manifold aspects of the rich, full life of the Jew—will sprout forth of themselves. The totality of actions based on a powerful, vital inner life as well as meaningful ceremonies truly representative of the spirit in noble symbols, will inevitably follow.

However, I would prefer to dispense with allegorical terms. The core is the pure faith in God. At a time when unbelief and superstition, idolatry and nature-worship were rampant everywhere, this core had to be enveloped in a mass of ceremonies, so that the pure spiritual treasure would not be crushed. But now spring has long since come into the life of mankind. All the civilized world has discarded primitive idol worship and the concepts of God and His worship have been refined. Hence, the spirit of Judaism now no longer needs this rough mantle; on the contrary . . . it must shed it in order to sow the seeds of its ideals that they may bear fruit in the total development of mankind.

The opinion of your Mr. B. is as follows: Judaism is and always has been composed of the totality of its ceremonial code. These laws constituted its essence at all times; hence they are binding upon the Jewish people and must remain so forever. If Geiger terms the observance of ceremonial law as "outer works," B. feels, Geiger has derived this terminology from Christian Protestant concepts. The same goes for such expressions as "Judaism has become powerfully *transformed*," or "it has *worked its way up* to a stage of awareness in the course of the *historical process*," or "*fundamental* conviction," and so forth, which are concepts altogether alien to the sphere of Judaism. Judaism is ceremonial law, and shall always be so; should Judaism discard these laws, all that will remain of it will be an *abstract deism*. B. says that "it has no ethical position of its own, and its philosophical and historical viewpoints are highly unsatisfying." This is approximately the burden of the bold assumptions of your Mr. B . . .

Permit me, first of all, to discuss "the expressions that are alien to the religious sphere of Judaism." Is it really true that the term "outer works," as applied to actions which do not take place from full inner consecration but are merely practiced by rote is not Jewish but borrowed from Christian Protestant concepts? What about the splendid saying of Isaiah after he had lashed out at the hollowness of the heart: "thus their reverence for Me is only a *human commandment learned by rote*"? What about the stress which the sages of old placed on proper sentiment or devotion? And what about the fine distinction which Bahya ibn Pakudah, the 11th-century moralist in Spain, made between the "duties of the limbs" and the "duties of the heart" and his lament that ordinary men so often pursue the duties of the limbs while neglecting the duties of the heart, which are more important? What do the cabalists mean when they call actions a "garment," or a "body," but term pious thoughts "the spirit"? What else is this but a distinction between the inner value of sentiment and the outer superficiality of action by rote? . . .

[*According to B.*] the term "fundamental" is supposed to be alien to Judaism. Yet the fact is that all of medieval Jewish lore is replete with such terms as *yesodot* and *ikkarim*, the "*fundamentals* of the Torah," and in everyday Jewish terminology he who completely rejects Judaism is referred to as a *kofer be-ikkar*, "one who denies the very basis and root."

As far as Mr. B. is concerned, all the Jewish works on religious philosophy beginning with Saadia in the 10th century down to the present day just do not exist. But is it not a fact that Maimonides explicitly devoted a large part of the third book of his *Moreh Nebukhim*, his "Guide of the Perplexed," to a justification of the commandments? . . . I admit that the validity of the commandments has not been made dependent on arguments in their favor based on reason; nevertheless, life, even in the days of antiquity, has always accepted the axiom that, once the inner motivation for it was no more, then the Law itself would gradually cease to exist. Thus, for instance, sacrifices did not cease simply because the Temple had been destroyed. Much rather, the physical practice stopped because, spiritually, it had long been superseded by prayer as a more profound expression of worship. Nor did the laws concerning ritual purity fall into disuse solely because the waters of purification could no longer be prepared; they lost their validity because this entire concept of outward purity and atonement had long been replaced in the minds of men by non-symbolic conceptions of ethical purity and purification. Time merely waited for an historical excuse, as it were, in order to destroy in practice what had long been abolished in theory. Then this historical excuse would be given great emphasis so that, in pious self-deception, one would not be forced to admit that such an inner change had taken place. Modern Judaism goes about this work much more candidly and with much greater awareness of what is actually happening within it. When something in Judaism has become spiritually extinct, modern Judaism does not hesitate to admit that fact; it knows that it proceeds with much greater intelligence and clarity when it unequivocally aims at the removal of whatever has become obsolete and when it does not view argument by reason as a secondary factor only but as essential and as the one justification for survival. Is Judaism, for that reason, less Jewish, or less pious today then it was in the past?

I am not willing to subscribe to a complete abolition of all ceremonial law in Judaism; but, even if such a situation were to come to pass, would it really be true that nothing would then be left of Judaism but a form of abstract deism? Judaism acknowledges and has always acknowledged the One holy and living God . . . as the Originator of the laws that govern nature and human life, and as the Creator and Preserver . . . who is revealed in the history of the nations. In all the aspirations of the arts and sciences it is the spirit of God that imbues men with a sense of higher striving. . . . Judaism sees in man the only creature into whom the "spirit of God has been breathed from on high" and who was created "in the image of God." . . . Man has been endowed with two Divine gifts— reason and free will—by means of which he may strive for perfection, "to sanctify himself and to emulate God". . . . It is man alone, as a spirit born out of the spirit of God Himself, who has been granted the privilege of communing, not only with the spirit of God above him, but also with kindred spirits on earth below. Man views himself as an individual member of the human family, and he regards it as his function "to love his neighbor as himself." . . . This, in broad outline, is the essence of the faith of Judaism. . . . Is this really abstract deism, or vestigial Votairianism?

Such a slander of a living and vigorous faith that has

become part of the spirit of history is highly unworthy and will utterly fail to impress any thinking person. As for us, we are entirely satisfied with this content for our faith and feel no need for any such mysteries or concrete dogmas as you may have to offer.

Should present-day Judaism be robbed of its solemn sanctity just because it does not punctiliously adhere to *all* the ceremonial rites of old? Is it not true that, even today, Judaism joyously marks the Passover holiday as the celebration of Israel's entry into the history of the world; that it still solemnly celebrates Shavuot as the feast marking revelation and the glorious beginnings of true faith; that it views the New Year even now, not as an occasion for gay and noisy congratulations, but as a solemn admonition for introspection, and the Day of Atonement as a magnificent solemnization of self-abasement and spiritual purification? Should I really be deprived of my portion in the great history of Judaism, in the splendid spiritual struggles of the prophets, in the heroism of the Maccabees against decadent Hellenism and in Israel's persevering fight against the Roman world conquerors; should I lose my share in the intellectual flowering in Spain, in the Provence and in Italy, and in the great upsurge of the modern era; in short, should I forfeit my portion in the profound spiritual nature of the entire history of Judaism just because I do not entirely share the views of the talmudists and casuists and the philosophies of Ibn Gabirol and Maimonides with regard to ceremonial, and because I do not join Judah Halevi in the pilgrimage to Jerusalem? . . . Just because I do not share the attitudes and the conduct of my ancestors, since I live in an era different from theirs, does this mean that I should not be uplifted by the thought that their names are cited in connection with every event or act of historical significance and that they stand out as the leaders in every such historic endeavor? . . . We are not "chosen from among all the nations," but we do have a vocation in history, to which we have remained true despite all the aberrations of which we may have been guilty and to which we intend to remain true also in the future. As for you who seek to abandon it, who seek to renounce it for the sake of convenience or ambition, for sheer arrogance or under all manner of pretexts, you shall also not escape your historic calling. You ought to remain aware of this historic patent of nobility and be worthy of it, and not think that casting it aside will render you a superior being . . .

Now, Mr. B. continues, the Israelites have every reason even today to court the love and good will of their Christian fellow-citizens. Of course, he admits, this cannot be achieved so quickly, and has not been achieved in other countries either, even where Jews have been given full civic equality. . . . For there is a racial difference between the Jewish and Christian population that is given even greater emphasis by existing religious differences. B. points out that, to this very day, national and tribal differences are still very strong between the German and the Slavic peoples and similar nationality groups, nor is there any sort of amicable understanding between the Catholic and the Protestant elements even in the same localities. But this is nothing compared to the "far greater racial differences that exist between the descendants of the House of Jacob from far-off Asia, on the one hand, and the descendants of Teut and Hermann the Cheruscan who have dwelt within the heart of Europe since times immemorial, on the other—between those proud and at the same time good-natured tall men with blond hair, and the dark-haired, versatile little men with the sharp Asiatic features." According to Mr. B., races so different from one another will confront each other with a certain "instinctive aversion against which every argument of reason will be powerless." "Even the Jew who has been converted," Mr. B. concludes his presentation, "will always remain what he was before, as far as race is concerned, and no amount of baptismal water can turn him into a member of the Germanic group. This difference will be overcome only by his children and grandchildren, in case he should marry a Christian, and only they will be able to merge entirely with the Christian population . . ."

To this I can only reply as follows: If there are social rules which will discriminate even against a man who enjoys respect and popularity, just because he is a Jew, whereas he will be accorded unqualified acceptance once he has undergone baptism —and that he himself will be accorded this acceptance after baptism, and not just his descendants in the second generation, born of Christian wives and hence free from the "instinctive aversion of racial difference"—the inanity of the whole argument is clearly demonstrated.

. . . You, Mr. B., have made a magnificent discovery with your theories of racial differences and "instinctive aversion." Shall I tell you for whom it really is that not only the Jew but every Christian too who is not blinded by prejudice and ambition has "an instinctive aversion?" They all have "an instinctive aversion" for blockheads who, stupid and brazen at the same time, preen themselves before society and impertinently seek to meddle in matters of which they know nothing. But as for the Germans, the Jewish German loves them, not because they are tall and blond-haired (for he does not set store by physical features), but he loves and respects them because he identifies himself with their intellectual development, *since he himself has participated in it*. Yes, indeed, I feel I am a better German than Mr. B. because I do not insult the German spirit with such narrow-minded assumptions. I search for the pride of Germany, not in any descent from Hermann the Cheruscan of whom the Germans have learned only through Roman historians . . . nor in descent from Teut who is not a patriarch at all but an ancient Germanic god, but in the contribution which Germany has made to the history of mankind and in the great spirits which it has produced.

. . . The Jews no longer have a language of their own which they would use in literature or in everyday life. And this does not stem from the era of the leveling efforts of "modern Judaism" with its "abstract deism," but it dates back to quite ancient times, almost to the time of their Second Commonwealth. When they dwelt in Babylonia, the Jews used the Babylonian-Chaldean dialect; when they lived among the Arabs they talked and wrote in Arabic, and when they were in Spain and Portugal their language was Spanish and Portuguese, respectively; in short, wherever the Jews have lived in Europe they have spoken the vernacular of the countries in which they dwelt and have used it in their literature as soon as it had developed into a literary language.

This is no more than natural. The Jews were a nation only for a limited period of time; their vocation has always been religious and never national in character, and hence cosmopolitan even as is the vocation of any other religion. The spiritual and intellectual development of a national entity is expressed in its language, and whoever destroys that language thereby does violence also to the development of the nation as a whole. But the spiritual life of a religious faith, such as that of Judaism and Christianity, stands out above and beyond national life; it is universally human and has no language of its own. The sages of old express this thought most ingeniously when they say that the Ten Commandments of God were graven upon the stone tablets in fiery letters in all the "seventy tongues" of mankind.

In view of the foregoing, there is no difference whatsoever between the Germans and the Jews as regards national features; differences of this kind are far greater between the German Jews and the French Jews than between the Jewish German and the Christian German. No rational human being today will concern himself with the question of whether the Teutons, the Goths, and so forth, actually came to Germany before the Jews who had come there with the legions of ancient Rome. Today there is no German who could trace his ancestry back to a time when there were no Jews in Germany . . .

In general, is not the social antipathy which is said to prevail between Christians and Jews grossly exaggerated? The two were kept apart by mighty legal and religious barriers of which traces are still evident today, all the more so since many an influential faction deliberately strives to bolster such barriers even now. But the healthy instinct of the people has long leveled these confining walls. People of culture and education on both sides are becoming friends to an ever increasing extent, and wherever this is not yet the case it is simply indicative of the fact that, in those quarters, minds and hearts are not as yet truly educated. A type of martyrdom such as this is an easy thing to bear. Any slight by the law, of course, does hurt and every resulting loss is painful. This is the reason why every Jew with a sense of honor must adhere all the more firmly and unswervingly to his ties with Jews and Judaism, unless, of course, he feels obligated by his conscience to renounce Judaism for reasons of inner compulsion, by virtue of a *conviction that Christianity is the one true faith.*

. . . Let me repeat: No Jew to whom the truth and right, honor and conscience are more than empty words may renounce Judaism, unless, of course, he should be convinced in his inmost heart of the divinity of Jesus and of the existence of a Trinity in accordance with the doctrines of the Church. Or should such conversion be nothing else but a means whereby a scientist or scholar may enter his professional career, thus selling his birthright for a mess of pottage and trading truth for a paltry position? Should the man who has already earned the respect of society augment his position of honor by taking a step which, in fact, involves the sacrifice of his integrity? Should fathers and mothers be justified in having their children converted, while they themselves remain Jews, thus avowing that they themselves are not convinced of the truth of Christianity? ... Or should a rich man deem his children too good to continue the long struggle for truth and right, which is nearing its conclusion even now? Should he deem them too good to be upright, honest albeit *untitled* Jews? Should he be allowed to persist in the belief that his children will attain greater honors if they break away from their kind for the sake of outward glitter and glory? Should he really believe that this is the way to assure the happiness and the moral welfare of these children? Things will never come to such a pass in Judaism. That which oppression has not brought about, dissembling speech will certainly not bring to pass; nor will that which fanaticism has failed to achieve be attained by mere faintness of heart.

NS, I, PP. 247 FF.

notes

---◦◦◦---

BIOGRAPHY

1. Both these men came to be Geiger's lifelong friends. *Joseph Naftali Dernburg* (Derembourg) (b. Mayence 1811, d. Bad Ems 1895) was his closest friend, to whom he freely unburdened his heart. A distinguished Orientalist, Dernburg moved to Paris in 1833, where he served as Professor of Hebrew Language and Literature at the *Ecôle Pratique des Hautes Etudes.* He always maintained a keen interest in Jewish issues.

2. *Hermann Hupfeld* (b. Marburg 1796, d. Halle-on-the-Saale 1866) was a pioneer in the field of Protestant theology. One of his outstanding works was his four-volume *Commentary on the Psalms* (1867-71).

3. All these men were leading personalities in the movement known as the "Science of Judaism."

Issac Marcus Jost (b. Bernburg, Anhalt, 1793; d. Frankfort-on-the-Main 1860) was the greatest modern Jewish historian prior to Heinrich Graetz. His works on Jewish history, which were published volume by volume beginning with 1820, aroused lively interest in scholarly circles. Jost was a rational thinker and adherent of the Reform movement. He was one of the first to attempt to draw a clear line of distinction between Jewish religion and nationality, and envisioned Western Jewry as a purely "religious" community.

Salomon Munk (b. Gross-Glogau, Silesia, 1803; d. Paris 1867) was a 19th-century classic Orientalist. His edition of the Arabic version of Maimonides' *Guide to the Perplexed* with French translation and notes is still acknowledged today as one of the outstanding achievements in that field.

Shelomo Yehuda Loeb Rapoport (b. Lwow 1790, d. Prague 1867) skilfully applied the methods of historical criticism to rabbinic literature. The biographical writings which he published in the Hebrew periodical *Bikkurei ha-Ittim* were widely read and admired. He took a conservative stand on practical Jewish religious issues. Geiger's radicalism led to a break between the two men.

4. *Ludwig Philippson* (b. Dessau 1811, d. Bonn 1889) was one of Germany's most outstanding 19th-century Liberal rabbis. More moderate in his views than Geiger, he made his influence felt for decades as editor of the *Allgemeine Zeitung des Judentums* which he had founded in 1837. He was a leading figure at rabbinical conferences and synods in Germany, published a popular German translation of the Bible and was one of the early advocates of a Faculty of Jewish Theology. He was one of the founders of the Hochschule fuer die Wissenschaft des Judentums (Academy for the Science of Judaism).

5. *Hermann Cohen* (b. Coswig, Anhalt, 1842; d. Berlin 1918) was professor at the University of Marburg, Germany. During the last years of his life he taught at the Berlin Hochschule fuer die Wissenschaft des Judentums. One of the most articulate Jewish thinkers, he based his philosophy on his version of neo-Kantian thought, and sought to formulate a synthesis between Germanism and Judaism. In line with this endeavor he demanded that Judaism, and especially its religious and ethical principles, should be taught at a German university, on the same level as any other field of higher studies.

6. *Samson Raphael Hirsch* (b. Hamburg 1808, d. Frankfort-on-the-Main 1888) was the founder of the German Neo-Orthodox movement which sought to combine strict adherence to Jewish Law with modern culture. These views were already advanced in his very earliest writings, the *Nineteen Letters* (published in 1836 under the pseudonym of "Ben Uziel") and *Horeb* or "Essays on Israel's Duties in the Diaspora" (published in 1838). The *Nineteen Letters* made a deep impression on Geiger. *Horeb* is a presentation of the dogma, ethics and ritual symbolism of Rabbinic Judaism. The allegorical bent of these and other works of Hirsch which at times bordered on the peculiar showed the wide gulf that separated this type of Orthodoxy from the sober, non-romantic attitude advocated by Geiger and his adherents. While serving as rabbi in Frankfort, Hirsch successfully fought for the separation of strictly Orthodox congregations from any movement with even the slightest tendency to Liberalization, and thus became the founder of the Secessionist or Separatist movement in German Orthodoxy.

7. The Bundestag, with headquarters in Frankfort, was the representative body of the states that were part of the German Confederation.

8. *Melo Hofnayim*; lit. "a handful" of various previously unpublished writings, consists of two sections, one Hebrew and one German. The anthology includes the famous sarcastic letter of Profiat Duran, a marrano, to his friend David Bonet Bongoron who had become a convert to Christianity (c. 1391), a liturgical hymn by Judah Halevi, responsa by Maimonides and a biography of Joseph Solomon del Medigo. The texts, translations and notes prepared by Geiger were published by Wolf Wilzig (Berlin, 1840). The biography of Del Medigo is reprinted also in the *Nachgelassene Schriften* (Posthumously Published Writings), III, 1-33.

9. *Bettina (Elisabeth) von Arnim* (1785-1859), wife of the romantic poet Achim von Arnim, was a fervent admirer of Goethe.

10. *Hirsch Baer Fassel* (b. Moravia 1802, d. Nagy-Kaniza, Hungary, 1883), scholarly rabbi who also had considerable modern secular learning, was regarded as an exponent of Liberalism in Hungary. In Breslau, however, his conservative views were a counterpoise to Geiger's more radical ideas.

11. *Isaac Noah Mannheimer* (b. Copenhagen 1793, d. Vienna 1865)

was one of the most eloquent preachers in the German synagogue pulpit. Tending to moderate Reform in his views (i.e., he advocated dignified and impressive services but objected to the organ), he was able to preserve the unity of the Jewish religious community of Vienna.

12. *Hirsch Aub* served as rabbi in Munich for almost half a century (until 1876). His cousin, Joseph Aub, was Geiger's friend and colleague in Berlin.

13. *Neue Beitraege zur Geschichte des Streites ueber das Studium der Philosophie in den Jahren 1232-1306* (New Contributions to the History of the Controversy over the Study of Philosophy from 1232-1306). Published in 1844, this work contains:

a)*Milhamot Adonai*, an open letter to the Jews of the Provence by Abraham, the son of Maimonides (published by Heimann Pollak, Hanover, Germany, in 1840);

b) an open letter to the Jews of France with Preface and Epilogue by Rapoport in *Kerem Hemed*, vol. V (Prague, 1841);

c) *Minhat Kenaot*, a collection of documents of Abbamari ben Moshe ben Joseph, with an appendix on the *Guide to the Perplexed* (published by M. L. Bisselechis, Pressburg, 1838: *Wissenschaftliche Zeitschrift*, V, 82-123).

14. *Zur Entwicklungsgeschichte der hebraeischen Sprachkunde, biblische Exegese und hebraeische Dichtkunst unter den arabischen Juden im zehnten, elften und zwoelften Jahrhundert.* First article, "Saadia ben Joseph Gaon," see *Wissenschaftliche Zeitschrift*, V, 261-324.

15. *Bruno Bauer und die Juden*, with reference to his essay entitled "Die Judenfrage" ("The Jewish Problem," *Deutsche Jahrbuecher*, no. 274-282), see *Wissenschaftliche Zeitschrift*, V, 199-234, 325-371. Bauer (1809-1882), philosopher and critic of religion, was as unpopular with conservative Christian elements because of his scurrilous treatment of the Gospels, as he was among the Jews due to his hostile attitude toward Judaism.

16. *Beitraege zur juedischen Literaturgeschichte in vier Abhandlungen ueber die im hebraeischen Teile enthaltenen Stuecke:*

a) "Die nordfranzoesische Exegetenschule im 12. Jahrhundert" (The Northern French School of Exegesis in the 12th Century);

b) "Die Anthropomorphismen in der Haggada und die Rabbinen der arabischen Schule" (Anthropomorphisms in the Haggadah and the Rabbis of the Arabic School);

c) "Die Gutachten des Maimonides" (The Opinions of Maimonides);

d) "Der Mischnah-Kommentar des Maimonides" (Commentary on the Mishna by Maimonides), published in Breslau in 1847.

17. *Ernst Wilhelm Hengstenberg* (1802-1869) was generally acknowledeged as the major theologian of Protestant Orthodoxy.

18. *David Friedlaender* (b. Koenigsberg 1750, d. Berlin 1834). A disciple of Moses Mendelssohn, Friedlaender, a protagonist of radical Reform, led the Jews of Prussia in their early fight for emancipation.

Ludwig Boerne (1786-1837), a countryman of Geiger's, was a Liberal writer, noted journalist and Germany's outstanding political pamphleteer. A convert to Christianity, he was thoroughly hated in reactionary circles.

Berthold Auerbach (1812-1882). A lifelong friend of Geiger, Auerbach, originally a candidate for the rabbinate, chose a literary career instead. His short stories enjoyed wide popularity in Germany.

Gabriel Riesser (1806-1863), a famous lawyer, generally recognized as German Jewry's leader in the fight for political and social equality.

19. *Henriette Herz* (nee de Lemos) (1764-1847) was the wife of Marcus Herz, a Jewish physician and philosopher in Berlin. She was not greatly interested in things Jewish, but played a prominent part in German cultural life. Her drawing room was the gathering place for the wits and sophisticates of the Prussian capital during the Romantic era.

Adolphe Crémieux (1796-1880). An outstanding Jewish statesman in France, Crémieux vigorously and successfully championed the rights of Jews the world over. A liberal member of the French Parliament, he held several Cabinet posts during his political career.

Wilhelm von Humboldt (1767-1838), liberal scholar and Prussian statesman. A friend of the Jews, he was one of the great German spokesmen of broad humanism.

20. *Zacharias Frankel* (1801-1875) first served as rabbi in Dresden and eventually became first dean of the Jewish Theological Seminary in Breslau. He was the chief exponent of the middle-of-the-road "Historical" trend, also known as the "Breslau School" of German Jewry.

Michael Sachs (1808-1864). Rabbi of the strict conservative trend in Berlin. A master in the eloquent use of the German language, as shown in his sermons and his German translation of the prayer book, he combined thorough modern secular training with profound rabbinic erudition.

21. *Isaac Bernays* (1792-1849). Chief Rabbi—or *Hakham*, as he preferred to be called—of the Jewish community of Hamburg. A leader in the fight against the Reform temple in Hamburg, he was greatly respected by Jews of every ideological trend for his rabbinic and secular scholarship. His most outstanding disciple was Samson Raphael Hirsch.

22. *Samuel Holdheim* (1806-1860) was greatly esteemed by Geiger. The most radical rabbi in the German Reform movement, he became the first spiritual leader of the Berlin Reform Congregation, the only religious organization of this trend in Germany.

23. See p. 1.

24. *David Chwolsohn* (b. Vilna 1819, d. St. Petersburg, Russia, 1910). Noted Russian Orientalist. Geiger had helped him secure admission to final examinations at a Breslau *gymnasium* and to the University. After his conversion to Christianity in 1855 he taught at various theological seminaries in Russia, but remained a vigorous advocate of Jewish interests. He is remembered particularly for his fight against the ritual murder charge.

25. *Divan des Castiliers Abu'l Hassan Judah Ha-Levi*, with biography and notes, Breslau, 1851. Revised edition without notes, *Nachgelassene Werke*, III, 97-177.

26. *Leon da Modena, Rabbiner zu Venedig (1571-1648) und seine Stellung zur Kabbalah, zum Talmud und zum Christentum* (Leon da Modena, Rabbi in Venice [1571-1648] and His Attitude to the Cabala, to the Talmud and to Christianity), Breslau, 1856.

27. *Isaac Troki, ein Apologet des Judentums am Ende des 16. Jahrhunderts* (Isaac Troki, Apologist of Judaism at the End of the 16th Century), Breslau, 1853. Reprinted in *Nachgelassene Werke*, III, 178-223.

Juedische Dichtungen der spanischen und italienischen Schule (Jewish Poetry of the Spanish and Italian School), Leipzig, 1856. Reprinted in *Nachgelassene Werke*, III, 224-251.

28. *Isaac Abraham Euchel* (b. Copenhagen 1758, d. Berlin 1804). A disciple of Mendelssohn and competent Hebraist, he was proposed by Kant for a professorship at the University of Koenigsberg but was rejected because of his religion. For a time he was the editor of the Hebrew periodical *Ha-Meassef*. He was the author of the oldest German translation of the Hebrew prayer book, but consistently opposed the use of any language other than Hebrew in the actual synagogue service.

29. *Moritz Steinschneider* (b. Prossnitz, Moravia, 1816; d. Berlin 1907) spent most of his life as an independent scholar in Berlin. One of the foremost authorities on Hebrew and related literature, he conducted research at the most important libraries and contributed to the discovery of hitherto unknown manuscripts. An anthology of his writings was published in Berlin in 1929 with a valuation of his achievements by H. Malter and Alexander Marx.

Leopold Loew (b. Czernahora, Moravia, 1811; d. Szegedin, Hungary, 1876) was one of the earliest rabbis to preach in the Hungarian language. An erudite historian and prolific writer, Loew edited a periodical entitled *Ben Hananiah* (1858-1867).

Theodor Noeldecke (b. Harburg near Hamburg 1836, d. Karlsruhe, Baden, 1930), a noted Christian Orientalist and authority on Islamic studies, was well-versed also in rabbinic and talmudic literature.

30. *Raphael Kirchheim* (b. 1804, d. Frankfort-on-the-Main 1889), bibliophile and publisher of Hebrew manuscripts. Originally Orthodox, his views changed under the influence of Geiger. He sharply criticized the allegorical writings of Hirsch, on the grounds that they lacked scientific objectivity.

31. *Jules (Julius) Oppert* (b. Hamburg 1825, d. Paris 1905). An authority on Indian and Assyrian studies, he was professor at the College de France in Paris.

32. *S. (Simcha) Pinsker* (b. Tarnopol, Galicia, 1801; d. Odessa 1864). Much of his life work was devoted to the clarification of the history and religion of the Karaites.

33. *Eduard (Israel) Kley* (b. Bernstadt, Silesia, 1789; d. Hamburg 1867) served as preacher at the Hamburg Temple until 1840, when he resigned.

34. *Ernest Renan* (b. 1823, d. Paris 1892), French Orientalist and student of religion. His critical writings on the origins of

Christianity, particularly his *Vie de Jesus* (Life of Jesus) which was published in 1863, brought him fame even outside strictly scholarly circles.

Renan's German counterpart was *David Friedrich Strauss* (1808-1874), originally a Protestant theologian, who incurred the violent displeasure of ecclesiastical circles by his writings which were diametrically opposed to traditional religious views. Among his writings were *Das Leben Jesu* (1835-36), which was translated into English by George Eliot in 1846; *Die Christliche Glaubenslehre* (1840-41); *Das Leben Jesu fuer das Deutsche Volk* (1864); *Der alte und der neue Glaube* (1872). These writings, which reflected a grossly unjust attitude to Judaism, made a profound impression on many a German reader.

35. *Heinrich von Treitschke* (1834-1896). A German-nationalist historian and professor in Berlin, he exerted great influence on German university students. His anti-Jewish attitude is most clearly shown in the essays which he published between 1879 and 1880 in his *Preussische Jahrbuecher* (Prussian Year Books). These essays were then collected in an anthology entitled *Ein Wort ueber unser Judentum* (A Word On Our Judaism).

36. *Moritz Lazarus* (b. Filehne, Posen, 1824; d. Merano 1903), Professor of Philosophy in Berlin. Together with Hayim Steinthal, he originated the new science of ethno-psychology. A man of liberal mind, he was frequently able to effect reconciliations between sharply opposing views by the influence of his own conciliatory personality.

37. *Jacob Raphael Kosch* (b. Lissa, Posen, 1803; d. Koenigsberg 1872), physician and progressive member of the Prussian Diet. That the discriminatory "Jewish oath" was abolished was largely due to his tireless efforts.

38. *Edward Lasker* (b. Jarochin, Posen, 1829; d. New York 1884), member of the German Parliament in the days of Bismarck. One of the principal organizers of the powerful National Liberal Party, he showed great strength of character in his fight against Neo-German imperialism. A Prussian law, initiated by him and passed in 1876, made it possible for minority groups within German Jewry to set up independent communal organizations. When he died in New York, the U. S. House of Representatives extended its sympathies to the German Reichstag.

39. *Moritz Veit* (1808-1864), who published some of the writings of Zunz, Zacharias Frankel and Michael Sachs, was also a book-dealer, journalist and poet. A resident of Berlin, he served as member of the Prussian Diet and of the German National Assembly. He was active, too, in the Jewish community of Berlin.

Salomon Neumann (b. Pyritz, Pomerania, 1819; d. Berlin 1908), a physician, played an active part in the improvement of public health in Berlin. An ardent advocate of the advancement of the "Science of Judaism," he was a member of the board of directors of the Hochschule fuer die Wissenschaft des Judentums.

40. *Emil G. Hirsch* (b. Luxembourg 1852, d. Chicago 1923) was a leader in American Reform Judaism. He was the son of Samuel Hirsch (1815-1889), noted Jewish religious philosopher.

Immanuel Loew (1854-1944), Chief Rabbi of Szegedin, Hungary. The son of Leopold Loew, Immanuel, in his capacity of chief rabbi, was a member of the Hungarian House of Lords. He was a noted researcher, particularly in the field of talmudic studies.

LETTERS

To Joseph Naftali Dernburg

1. This letter refers to the so-called "Damascus Incident." In 1840 an accusation of ritual murder leveled against the Jews of Damascus led to a bloody pogrom in that city. Salomon Munk was in the party that traveled to the Orient with Moses Montefiore to plead in behalf of the Jews. Eventually Munk, Adolphe Crémieux and Baron James Rothschild managed to persuade Mehmed Ali, the Egyptian ruler of Damascus, to proclaim an edict condemning accusations of that nature. Due to the conflict between French and other European interests in the Orient, this incident had considerable political repercussions. In the end most of the major powers of Europe, including Russia, supported the Jews in this matter.

For Adolphe Crémieux, see note 19 to Biography.

2. In 1817 a private synagogue with what was then considered a radical Reform ritual was organized in Hamburg. Friends and opponents of this new venture appealed to rabbinical authorities for support. In 1841 the leaders of this movement published a new version of the prayer book and sought to have it distributed in other congregations as well. Though this version was considerably more traditional than that published in 1818, it set off the dispute with renewed force. *Hakham* Isaac Bernays (see note 21 to Biography) then led the opposition to the new temple and its ritual.

3. See note 3 to Biography.

To Various Correspondents

1. H. E. G. Paulus (1761-1851), Professor of Protestant Theology at the University of Heidelberg. Though he entertained liberal views in both politics and religion he did not look with unqualified favor upon either the Jews or their right to full civic equality. At any rate he took issue with Gabriel Riesser's demand for unconditional emancipation.

2. See Biography, p. 4.

3. Salomon Frensdorff (b. Hamburg 1803, d. Hanover 1888). Though strictly traditional in his religious practices, he was inclined

to moderation and far removed from fanaticism. He made many important contributions to Masoretic research.

4. *Sulamith* was a monthly journal which was published in Dessau, Germany, from 1806 to 1833. It was the earliest German periodical of Reform and assimilationist tendency. Geiger's opinion that the journal was at times somewhat superficial in its "enlightened" views was not without justification.

Der Jude, a semi-monthly (1832-1835) was Gabriel Riesser's platform in his fight for the political emancipation of the Jews.

5. See note 6 to Biography.

6. Refers to Geiger's *Wissenschaftliche Zeitschrift fuer juedische Theologie*.

7. We do not know the title of the book to which reference is made here.

8. Jacob Auerbach (1810-1887), an educator, was Geiger's lifelong friend.

9. See note 34 to Biography.

10. This letter has reference to an invitation extended by Geiger to progressive-minded rabbis to meet at Wiesbaden to deliberate on changes in religious practice.

11. Geiger was then in Berlin seeking naturalization by the Prussian government without which he could not have taken the rabbinical position in Breslau.

12. M. A. Stern (1806-1894), a lifelong friend of Geiger, had originally studied for the Rabbinate, then changed to mathematics.

13. *Kerem Hemed* was a Hebrew journal which appeared in Vienna at irregular intervals from 1833 to 1856. Its purpose was to further the cause of "Enlightenment."

14. Max Lilienthal (b. Munich 1815, d. Cincinnati 1882). In 1840, Uvarov, Russia's Minister of Education, charged him with the task of modernizing Jewish education in Russia. Frustrated in his efforts to attain the desired ends, Lilienthal emigrated to the United States in 1845 where he became well known as a journalist and leader in the American Reform movement. This letter has reference to an offer of a position in Russia, made to Geiger by the Russian Minister of Public Instruction. Apparently the Minister had Lilienthal act as intermediary.

15. The *Reformverein* was the Society for Reforms in Judaism. Founded in Berlin in 1845, it was the mother organization of the Reform congregation in that city.

16. Samuel David Luzzatto (b. Trieste 1800, d. Padua 1865). A Jewish philosopher and student of philology, Luzzatto was Italy's outstanding Jewish scholar during the 19th century. He played an active part in the revival of the Hebrew language and himself wrote Hebrew poetry. Geiger carried on a spirited correspondence with him on learned themes. Conservative and tending toward romanticism in his views, Luzzatto had no liking for Geiger's ideas on Reform.

17. Baron Christian Karl Josias von Bunsen (1791-1860), a Prussian diplomat and close friend of Frederick William IV, was an eminent scholar, particularly in the field of theology, and was active in Protestant Church politics. His nine-volume opus, *Voll-*

staendiges Bibelwerk fuer die Gemeinde (Complete Biblical Work for the Congregation) was published in instalments beginning in 1854, with publication completed in 1870 by H. Holtzmann.

18. Bernhard Wechsler (1808-1874), rabbi in Oldenburg, shared Geiger's religious views. Geiger had high regard for his judgment.

19. Orientalist in Leyden, Holland. The letter was dated February 19, 1863.

20. *Lectures on Judaism and its History.* Translated into English by Maurice Mayer, vol. I, 1866. Thalmessinger & Cahn, New York; in two volumes by Charles Newburgh, copyright 1911, Bloch Publishing Co., New York.

21. M. A. Levy (1817-1870) was Geiger's associate and intimate friend. He was an expert on Jewish epigraphics and numismatics, and a student of the language and history of ancient Phoenicia.

22. David Honigmann was a trustee of the Jewish religious community of Breslau. This letter has reference to the Prusso-Austrian War of 1866.

23. See note 29 to Biography.

24. This letter was written during the Franco-Prussian War of 1870-71.

25. Sydow was a liberal Protestant minister.

REMINISCENCES OF DAYS GONE BY

To Leopold Zunz

1. Joseph Johlson (b. Fulda 1777, d. Frankfort 1851), preacher, writer and instructor at the Philanthropin School. He was the author of a book of devotions and began work on a translation of the Bible.

2. Michael Creizenach (b. Mayence 1782, d. Frankfort 1842) also taught at the Philanthropin School. A protagonist of Enlightenment, he openly opposed the Talmud and collaborated with Geiger in the journal published by the latter.

3. Wolf Benjamin Heidenheim (b. Heidenheim 1757, d. Roedelheim nr. Frankfort, 1832), an authority on exegesis and Hebrew grammar, published several critically revised texts, particularly the prayer book, *piyyutim* and other liturgical works. His publishing firm (founded in 1799) did outstanding work in the field of Hebrew literature.

4. Johann Gottfried Herder (1744-1803), Protestant theologian, was a German poet in the classic tradition and a philosopher of history.

Johann Gottfried Eichhorn (1752-1827), Protestant theologian and Orientalist at Goettingen. His critical introduction to the Old Testament and his study on the prophets were significant contributions to biblical scholarship.

5. Zunz's *Zeitschrift fuer die Wissenschaft des Judentums* was first published in 1823 under the sponsorship of the *Verein fuer Kultur und Wissenschaft der Juden* (Society for the Advancement of the Culture and Science of Judaism).

EXCERPTS FROM WORKS

Judaism and its History

1. Elias Levita (b. Bavaria 1469, d. 1549) spent most of his life in Italy where he served as teacher to Christian Hebraists and enjoyed the favor of some of the most highly-placed dignitaries of the Catholic Church. An outstanding grammarian and student of the Masoretic tradition, he proved beyond a doubt that the Hebrew vowels first came into use only in the post-talmudic era.

2. Azariah de Rossi (1514-1578) lived in Italy. His work *Meor Enayim* (Light of the Eyes), written in Mantua during the period from 1573 to 1575, is an anthology of important historical essays which reflects an approach very close to modern scientific scholarship and contains material from both Jewish and Christian sources.

The Original Text and Translations of the Bible

1. *Abot d'Rabbi Nathan* is the tractate *Abot,* in the Mishna, by Rabbi Nathan, an anthology of thoughts on ethics, similar to the Ethics of the Fathers. The tractate, which is found at the end of the Fourth Order of the Babylonian Talmud, also contains a number of historical notes.

2. Simon ben Shetah, the brother of Salome Alexandra, queen of Judea from 76 to 67 B.C.E., was the leader of the Pharisaic party, which rose to power during that period.

3. Simon the Just, or *Shimon ha-Tzaddik,* a high priest, is named in the Ethics of the Fathers (1.2) as one of the last members of the Great Assembly.

4. Mordecai Jaffe (d. 1612), a rabbi in Poland, was the author of the Halakhic treatise entitled *Lebush* (The Garment) which is in many instances at variance with Joseph Caro's *Shulhan Arukh.*

SERMONS AND LEAD ARTICLES

Sermons

1. Though it contained a good many restrictive clauses, in principle the Prussian Edict of 1812 recognized the Jews as citizens of Prussia. In many instances the law was violated both in its letter and its spirit, but it was an improvement in the status of the Jews and gave them a greater sense of their own worth, so that the edict may justly be viewed as marking the beginning of a new era for the Jews of Prussia.

2. King Frederick William III (1797-1840) actually was an ultra-conservative monarch who changed his country's policy on the Jewish problem only after long hesitation and only under the pressure of exigencies that brooked no further delay. When his long reign came to an end, not only the Jews but many of his other subjects hailed the accession of his heir, Frederick William IV, in hopes that the policies of the new sovereign would be more liberal than those of his predecessor.

3. The Battle of Leipzig was recalled as a symbol of freedom by the Germans, and by the Jews who joined in the public feeling. Geiger's words, of course, depict the disappointment of the liberal elements at the reaction which set in immediately after the so-called Wars of Liberation that had been fought against Napoleon I.

Lead Articles from Wissenschaftliche Zeitschrift

1. Geiger's interpretation of Psalm 119.126: *It is time for the Lord to work; they have made void Thy law.*

ON RENOUNCING JUDAISM

1. Cf. correspondence of the same title, published in the same year in Leipzig (see *Nachgelassene Schriften,* vol. I, pp. 230 ff.).

2. A "vestigal Voltairian." Here Geiger refutes the idea that anyone who does not view ceremonial law as binding may assert that he is therefore no longer a Jew.